HISTORY OF SRINAGAR

HISTORY OF SRINAGAR
1846 - 1947

A Study in Socio-cultural Change

MOHAMMAD ISHAQ KHAN
Professor of History
Kashmir University

COSMOS PUBLICATIONS
1999

First Published by Aamir Publications, Srinagar (1978)

History of Srinagar

Printed in India

Second edition published by Cosmos Publications

Computerised and Laserset at Cosmos Computer Centre
Dood Ganga Road, Karan Nagar, Srinagar, Kashmir, 190010.

Printed at: Print Perfect, A-23 Mayapuri, Phase II, New Delhi 110064

Foreword

The study of capital cities and district towns is a healthy development in modern Indian historiography. Works on Amritsar, Lahore, Delhi Lucknow and a few other towns have been published; and now Dr. Mohammad Ishaq Khan has brought out his valuable book *History of Srinagar* (1846-1947), *a study in socio-cultural change*. It is the first work of it kind.

Srinagar, founded by Ashoka, has always remained the capital of Kashmir. In fact, the history of Srinagar is the history of Kashmir. It has been the hub round which has revolved the wheel of Kashmir's social, cultural, economic and political life. However, in the city's history, the last hundred years have been much more significant than any earlier period. Kashmir, in spite of the mountain barriers which surround it, has been exposed to the influences radiating from China, Turkistan, Persia and the subcontinent but the impact of the West, which began to be felt from the middle of the 19th century onwards, has been much more profound and far-reaching. And in Kashmir, owing to historical and political reasons, it is Srinagar which has felt it the most.

Dr. Ishaq has described not only the political history of Srinagar from 1846 to 1947 but also it social, economic and cultural life. He has given what one might call a historical sociology of the city. He has assessed the effects of the western contact on Srinagar's social life and education, marriage and morals, manners and customs, religious beliefs and practices. He has analysed the diversification of economy and changes in trade and industrial patterns, caused, in the first place, by the introduction of the western techniques of production; secondly, by the decline of shawl trade, the mainstay of Srinagar's economy; and lastly by the immigration of Punjabis which also, incidentally, affected the city's racial composition. Dr. Ishaq has described all this objectively, free from any kind of chauvinism, in a language which is simple, lucid and effective. He will not, it is hoped, rest content on his laurels, but will continue with his researches into various aspects of Kashmir's history for which he is in every way amply equipped and qualified.

Mohibbul Hasan
Aligarh
April 13, 1978

PREFACE TO THE SECOND EDITION

In the twenty years since *History of Srinagar* appeared, no indepth research has been conducted by either historians or sociologists into various aspects of socio-cultural change previously described in my book. The publication of this edition has, therefore, given the writer an opportunity to make only a number of small changes in the text and footnotes, and to take account of some suggestions made in innumerable reviews of the first edition of the book.

I would take this opportunity to express my thanks to my reviewers. Among them must be specially mentioned Professor Harbans Mukhia, late Dr. H.K. Naqvi, Professors A.K. Majumdar, Surendar Gopal, S.N. Dhar and late N.N. Raina. My thanks are also due to Mrs. Asha Dhar, Mr. G.N. Ganhar, Mr. Nethar Nath Raina and several others for their reviews of my book published in national newsmagazines.

I am also thankful to the Surveyor General of India for giving me permission to publish two maps of Srinagar which have been included in this edition.

A word of appreciation for Mr. Jalal-ud-din of the Cosmos Publications for his untiring efforts in brining out this edition.

Mohammad Ishaq Khan
Srinagar
August 1999

PREFACE TO THE FIRST EDITION

Srinagar, 'Venice of the East', is the vibrant heart of the beautiful Valley of Kashmir. Great historical events and political upheavals which have taken place here in the years gone by, have left an indelible impress, and have, to a large extent, a direct bearing on its growth and development as the chief city of the Jammu and Kashmir State. Being the hub of political, economic and religious activities of the valley from ancient times, the city of Srinagar has been as much mentioned by visitors as by historians. The eulogies of this ancient city's rivers, lakes, canals, gardens and beautiful handicrafts appear in the chronicles and travelogues. But, unfortunately, no systematic work has so far been done on it.

The transition from the medieval to the modern age is the keynote of Srinagar's history during the Dogra rule in Kashmir (1846-1947). It was during this period that the bases of society of Srinagar underwent a radical change. The present study, therefore, seeks to examine such forces and movements in the political, social, religious, literary and economic life as have produced the Srinagar of today.

It seems important to draw the attention of the readers to the lacuane in the sources. Regrettably, there has so far been no sociological work on Kashmir urban society for a student of history to draw on. Secondly, the Census reports of 1891, 1901, 1911, 1921, 1931, 1941 are incomplete in many respects. For example, there is no statistical data available on rural-urban migration. In addition to the fact that the post-1924 records of the National Archives of India and the Jammu and Kashmir State Archives have not yet been thrown open to the researchers, there also exists the problem of getting at the private papers in possession of some families in Srinagar. For various reasons, they are unwilling to show them to the research scholars. It is, therefore, with considerable diffidence that I write these pages.

I must also crave the indulgence of my readers, for the present work does not include any map of Srinagar. It pains me to note here that although I had prepared two maps of Srinagar, I could not print them for want of permission from the Ministry of Defence. The maps were duly scrutinised by the Survey of India and the same were sent by me to the Defence Ministry for their final approval on Dec. 7, 1977. In spite of the repeated reminders, the Ministry maintained silence.

My grateful thanks are due, first and foremost, to Prof. Mohibbul Hasan, formerly Head of the Deptt. of History of Kashmir University who inspired me to devote myself to the study of Kashmir history, and without whose invaluable guidance and advice, this work could never have seen the light of the day. I owe him a great debt indeed. I am also grateful to Prof. Khaliq Ahmed Nizami, Head of Deptt. of History, Aligarh Muslim University and Prof. Amba Prasad, Professor of History, Delhi University for their valuable suggestions to me in revising my work and preparing it for publication. Thanks are also due to the authorities and the staff of the National Archives of India, New Delhi, the National Library, Calcutta; the Brotherhood House, Delhi; Nehru Memorial Museum Library, New Delhi; Sapru House Library, New Delhi; the Research Library, Srinagar, the Sri Pratap Library, Srinagar; the Jammu University Library, Jammu; the Kashmir University Library, Srinagar; the Jammu and Kashmir Information Library, Srinagar the Jammu and Kashmir Academy of Art, Culture and Languages & the Jammu and Kashmir Sate Archives, for extending me all help and facility at their places. I am also indebted to Mr. John Ray, Principal, Tyndale Biscoe Memorial High School, Srinagar and Mrs. S. Thakur Das of the same school for lending me some rare reports and books. To Prof. Moonis Raza, Chairman, Centre for regional Development, Jawaharlal Nehru University and Dr. S. D. Bisaria, Reader in Sociology, National Council of Educational Research and Training, New Delhi, I owe a deep sense of gratitude for unbounded advice and encouragement. To Prof. T. Y. Jayaraman, Head, Deptt. of English, Kashmir University and Dr. N. H. Kulkarni, Asstt. Director, National Archives of India, I owe more than language can express. I am also thankful to Prof. Bipin Chandra of Jawaharlal Nehru University and Prof. A. C. Bose of Jammu University for their valuable suggestions.

I should be failing in my duty if I do not express my gratitude to Mr. Mohammad Amin (Ibn-Mahjoor) for constant help. Thanks are also due to Dr. S.M. Iqbal, Mr. Fidda Husnain, Mr. Ab. Majid Mattoo. Mr. Gh. Rasool, Mr. Z.L. Jala, Prof. G.L. Labroo, Mr. Malik Mohammad Yusuf, Mr. Mohammad Iqbal Khan, Mr. Autar Krishan Raina, Mr. Kulbushan Warikoo, Mr. Mohammad Amin Rafiqi, Mr. Aslam Mehmud, Mr. Sheikh Owais and Mr. Gawash Lal Koul. My interview with some social and religious reformers of the Dogra period has proved very useful in the completion of this work. Among them I am particularly thankful to Moulvi Ghulam Nabi Mubaraki (*Anjuman-i-Ahl-i-Hadith*) and Mr. Ram Chandrji Abhay (*Arya Samaj*). I am also thankful to the Yuvak

Sabha for allowing me to use the file of the *Martand* in their possession. To Mr. Abdul Rehman Kundoo I am thankful for drawing my attention to Sheikh Mohammad Abdullah's correspondence with Shaikh-ul-Hadith Moulana Anwar Shah. Mr. Vijinder Pal Singh of the Trinity Enterprises, Srinagar and his staff deserve my thanks for getting the book printed neatly and expeditiously.

Last but not the least, I must thank my wife for her cooperation and indulgence in the face of the strain and stress which the writing of this book involved.

Mohammad Ishaq Khan
Srinagar
1978

Abbreviations

A.G.	General Records
J.A.S.B.	Journal of Asiatic Society of Bengal
J. & K.	Jammu & Kashmir
Rajat	*Rajatarangini*
E & R	Ellios and Ross
R & B	Rogers and Beveridge
C.M.S.	Christian Missionary Society
C.E.Z.M.S.	Chruch of England Zenana Missionary Society
E.S.S.I.	Report on the Economic Survey of Silverware Industry
E.S.W.I.	Report on the Economic Survery of Wood-Carving Industry
Valley	*The Valley of Kashmir*

CONTENTS

CHAPTER I

INTRODUCTORY

The importance of cities has been abundantly recognized. "Often condemned as abnormal seed-beds of sin, scepticism, greed, crime, misery, filth, and congestion, cities have also been praised as sources of civilization and progress where innovation, science, education, art and commerce thrive and diffuse to the rural hinterland. In either case, whether in condemnation or in praise, tribute is implicitly paid to the human significance of the city."[1]

Cities can be studied and analysed from any number of standpoints. The present study is primarily concerned with a particular city, Srinagar, from socio-cultural point of view, and to that extent, is limited in its scope.

Society and culture have been described as interchangeable terms. Culture is broadly defined as the sum total of all activities of human life. Some of the activities may be grouped under these heads:

(a) occupational activities (b) social life

(c) educational activities (d) community activities

(e) literary activities

The changes in these spheres have been analysed in an interrelated way in the subsequent chapters.

Social change has characterized all societies. Increase in the size of the group, alteration or diversification of economy, modification of the social structure, new emphasis on religious beliefs and practices, growth of education, new philosophies, change of government, improved means of communication, calamities like floods, famines, fires and epidemics are among the phenomena associated with such changes. Occupations, customs, poetry and almost every other aspect of the society are subject to change.

India was a land of great cities during ancient and medieval times. There were many reasons for the existence of Indian cities. While some cities like Ahmedabad and Madura were emporia of trade and centres of handicraft production, other cities like Benaras and Nalanda were religious and educational centres. Although some towns and cities, for example, Benaras and Patna, have had a long, continuous existence, the sub-continent is marked with the ruins of many others that did not survive into modern times.

The greatest cities of India were the capitals of the empires: Pataliputra, Kanyakubja, Vijayanagar, Delhi and Agra. Travellers have described some of these cities: the splendour of the palaces, temples, and mosques, the cosmopolitan bazars, and squalid conditions in which the common people lived, and above all, the dependence of all on the court.

Srinagar since the dawn of history has remained the capital city of the Kashmir Valley and its growth through different periods of Kashmir history has been very interesting. The city did not owe its importance just to its being a seat of government; it survived several changes of rulers, and it had more than ephemeral reasons for its existence. This *Venice of the East* owed its importance to its compactness and its large population, its organized public opinion and the superior culture of its inhabitants. "Its alliance or opposition almost always proved a decisive factor in determining the fortunes of war".[2] Besides, Srinagar's artizans made the city an emporia of trade. In short, its central, commercial, political and cultural importance explains why the attempts made from time to time to remove the seat of government to some other place proved abortive.

HISTORICAL BACKGROUND

Srinagar has had a chequered history. The name of this city of great antiquity is first found in Kalhana's *Rajatarangini*. According to Kalhana, ancient Kashmir has had a number of capitals. The most important of these ancient cities was Srinagari, which was founded by Asoka in 250 B.C.[3] Srinagari, the city of Sri, an appellation of the goddess Lakshmi, occupied the site of the present village of Pandrethan,[4] about a mile and half east of the *Takht-i-Sulaiman* hill.[5] Pandrethan derives its name from the Sanskrit word *Puranadhisthana*,[6] literally, the old capital.

Srinagari remained the capital of Kashmir till about the middle of the sixth century A.D., when a new city was founded by Pravarasen II near the Hari Parbat hill.[7] This was called Pravarapura, after its founder's name, and extended only along the right bank of the River Jhelum (*Vitasta*).[8] But strangely enough Pravarapura lost its own name and assumed that of the old city of Srinagari. Since both capitals (Srinagari and Pravarapura) were near to each other, the old name remained in common use with the people in preference to the new name. It was the old familiar name of Srinagari which triumphed over the new city of Pravarapura.

Hieun Tsiang, the first Chinese traveller to visit Kashmir in 631 A.D. mentions the two capitals of Kashmir, the old and new.[9] He records that in his time the capital of Kashmir was the new city (Pravarapura) and the old city lay to the south east of it at a distance of ten *li* (2 miles) and to the south of a great mountain.[10] This description seems to agree with the identification of Pravarasena's capital with the present Srinagar, and Asoka's capital with Pandrethan and its surroundings.[11]

In Kalhana's description of Pravarapura[12] one can see a great deal of modern Srinagar. He describes the city as having markets and mansions which reached the clouds, and were mostly built of wood, like the houses of the common people in modern Srinagar.[13] The chronicler goes on to describe 'the streams meeting, pure and lovely, at pleasure-residences and near market-streets'.[14] He evidently refers to the Dal Lake,[15] the River Jhelum,[16] and the numerous canals which intersect the city. From time immemorial the Jhelum and these canals have served as the main thoroughfares for the transport of goods and "all principal bazars are built along their banks".[17] Nor does Kalhana forget to shower praise on the cool water of the *Vitasta*. He has also described the pleasure-hill (Hari Parbat) from which the splendour of all the houses was visible.[18] Besides, there were many splendid temples with which Pravarapura had been adorned by successive kings.[19]

Such is Kalhana's description of ancient Srinagar. His long list of the buildings and sites in the capital of Pravarasen can also be identified in and around the present city of Srinagar and its environs. Sir Aurel Stein was able to identify some of these ancient buildings and localities.[20]

Among the ancient relics the pride of place goes to the embankment which stretches from the Dal Gate along the *Tsunth Kul* canal to the

River Jhelum. Curiously enough, it resembles in shape the bent leg of the legendary *Rakshas*. The following account has been furnished by Kalhana with regard to the foundation of Pravarapura.[21]

It is said that Pravarasen II while in search of a site for his new city was confronted by a demon (*Vetal*) on the other side of the *Mahasarit* (*Tsunth Kul*).[22] The *Rakshas* stretched out his own leg from the other bank, and "thus caused the water of the *Mahasarit* to be parted by an embankment".[23] The courageous king cut off his leg with his dagger (*ksurika*) and crossed over it to the other side which "has since been known as *Ksurikabala*".[24] "The demon then indicated to him the auspicious time and disappeared after telling him to build his town where he would see the measuring line laid down in the morning. This line (*sutra*) of the *Vetala* the king eventually discovered at the village *Saritaka* at which the goddess *Sarika* and the demon *Atta* resided. There he built his city in which the first shrine erected was the famous one of *Siva Pravaresvara*".[25] Whatever the significance of this legend, it cannot be denied that this embankment generally known as *Suth* is undoubtedly of a very early date.[26]

Another ancient relic is the rock on the south of Hari Parbat[27] now smeared with red paint. This was then regarded as an incarnation of the God Ganesha, who in his interest in the new city that was coming up around him, is said to have turned his face towards the east in order to look at it better.[28]

Among other relics of Pravarasen's city are the embankments along the River Jhelum. Constructed of the massive pillars and some blocks these embankments which "used to support the edifices of Pravarasen's city", were further adorned by later kings. Fergusson remarks: "The extent of these ruins and the elaborate carvings which they display testify to the labour and effort which must have gone to the making of the capital and enable one to conceive something of the magnificence which the city must have possessed".[29] Besides, the old Muslim cemetery at the foot of Hari Parbat hillock is also said to contain the remains of Pravarasen's city.[30]

Having thus located some ancient sites of Pravarasen's city, it may then be asked, why was the particular situation of Srinagar chosen and maintained throughout the centuries. The later Hindu rulers are reported to have transferred the capital from one place to another.[31] Lalitaditya[32] founded Parishaspurha.[33] Jayapida laid out the city of Jayapura.[34] Avantivarman founded the city of Avantipura.[35] Samkarapura,[36]

Kaniskapura,[37], Juskapura[38] and Hushkapura[39] were some other ancient capitals of Kashmir. But all these later capitals lost their importance and decayed as is shown by their ruins.[40] It was the capital of Pravarasen alone which has survived various attempts to change it.

It is to be admitted that Pravarasen's choice was impeccable. His well-chosen site for the capital has remained the situation of the capital of Kashmir to the present day. The king must have chosen this site not only for its beauty and strategic importance, but also for its intrinsic value.

First, Srinagar is gifted with great natural advantages. The River Jhelum which winds its way through the thickly populated city, has served as the main artery of communication from times immemorial. The principal bazars of the city are built along the river which "has provided at all seasons the most convenient route for trade and traffic both up and down the valley". Stein has rightly said that "Srinagar enjoys facilities of communications which no other side could offer".[41] Thus economically Srinagar is a distributing centre for the incoming merchandise from the different parts of the Valley. This is still illustrated today by the importance of Srinagar as a chief commercial centre of the Kashmir Valley.

Secondly, Srinagar is the point which commands trade routes to India and Central Asia. "The great trade-route from Central Asia debouches through the Sind Valley at a large distance of only one short march from the capital".[42]

Thirdly, the Dal and Anchar[43] lakes which flank Srinagar with their numerous agricultural products in food supply, fulfil the needs of the city population.

Fourthly. strategically the rivers and the lakes make Srinagar invulnerable. Commenting on the strategical importance of the city of Srinagar in ancient times, Sir Stein remarks:

"The frequent sieges which Srinagar underwent during the last reigns related by Kalhana, give us ample opportunity to appreciate also the military advantages of the position of the city. With the exception of the comparatively narrow neck of high ground in the north, the Srinagar of the right river-bank is guarded on all sides by water. On the south the river forms an impassable line of defence. The east is secured by the Dal and the stream which flows from it. On the west there stretch the broad marshes of the Anchar close to the bank of the Vitasta".

"From the north, it is true, the city can be approached without passing such natural obstacles. But just to the north of the Sarika hill inlets from the two lakes approach each other within a few thousand feet. The narrow passage left here could at all times easily be guarded. It is curious to note that all successful attacks on the city of which the chronicler tells us, were delivered from the north, treachery or the defenders' weakness having opened this passage".[44]

Lastly, Srinagar is centrally situated. The city is equi-distant from the two chief commercial towns of the Valley, Anantnag[45] and Baramulla.[46] Srinagar is almost equi-distant from Jammu, Rawalpindi, Leh and Gilgit.

EXTENSION OF THE LIMITS OF SRINAGAR IN LATER TIMES

It is not correctly known when the extension of the city on the left bank of the *Vitasta* took place. This portion is enclosed by the canal which takes off the river below Sher Garhi and joins it again near Safa Kadal, which was till recently also known as the seventh bridge. The number of ancient relics which is large on the right bank of the river is comparatively small on the left bank of the river. In ancient times the left bank of the *Vitasta* remained of secondary importance, although it was only in the reign of Ananta (A.D. 1028-63) that the royal palace was transferred to it.[47]

Bilhana,[48] the eleventh century chronicler, found Srinagar equally charming. To him, Srinagar was not only the principal city of Kashmir, but excelled in beauty all other cities, even Kuvera's town Lanka and the town of the gods.[49] 'For its coolness in summer and for the beauty of its groves', remarks Bilhana, 'even those who have reached the garden of celestials could not forget it'.[50] It is also significant to note that Bilhana, Ksemendra[51] and Mankha's[52] statements pertaining to the position of Pravarapura also agree with the site occupied by modern Srinagar.[53]

Srinagar in the Sultanate period (1320-1586)

During the 'Muslim rule' (1320-1819) in Kashmir the ancient name of the capital fell into disuse.[54] The city of Srinagar[55] was termed 'Kashmir', the same as country.[56] Accordingly, with the exception of Mirza Haidar, Abul Fazl and Jahangir, almost all Mughal chroniclers call it either *Kashmir or Shahr-i-Kashmir*. Bernier and Desideri who visited Kashmir during the Mughal rule also use the name Kashmir and not Srinagar for this capital. For several centuries Srinagar was thus known, until the advent of the Sikhs in 1819 who restored the old Hindu name, by which it is at present called.[57]

With the appearance of the Muslims, Srinagar underwent a significant change. Though the seat of government changed occasionally, the position of Pravarasen's city, as a whole, remained unaltered. Rinchan, the first Muslim ruler[58] of Kashmir, founded a quarter in Srinagar known as Rinchanpura.[59] It was here that he built the first mosque in Kashmir, known as *Bud Masheed*[60] on the site of the Buddhist temple. Rinchan, who had embraced Islam at the behest of a Muslim saint, Bulbul Shah, also built a public charity kitchen (*Langar Khana*) in the memory of his religious teacher and is still known as Bulbul Lanker.

Alauddin (1344-56) founded Alauddinpura[61] at Srinagar which at present comprises the locality situated between Jama Masjid and Ali Kadal. "The great and wise king", remarks Jonaraja,[62] "made Jayapidapura his capital, and built at Cri Rinchanpura, an edifice named Budhagira". Budhagira of Alauddin is now a *mohalla* near Ali Kadal in Srinagar. "This edifice built by Alauddin was used as a resting place for travellers in his time and thereafter, and appears to have been used by traders from Ladakh and Baltistan". Shihabuddin (1356-74) selected the Hari Parbat for his capital.[63] He was succeeded by Qutbuddin (1374-89) whose reign stands as a landmark in the annals of Islam in Kashmir. Srinagar saw ceaseless religious activity during his reign which engulfed the whole Valley. Sayyid Ali Hamadani[64] who visited Kashmir in Qutbuddin's time,[65] made Srinagar his seat and preached the gospel of Islam at a place in Srinagar which was subsequently known as a Khanqah-i Muàlla. It was at Khanqah-i Muàlla that Sultan Sikandar (1389-1413) built a mosque which in course of time became not only a centre for religious but also for political activities of the Muslim of Kashmir.[66] Qutbuddin is reported to have laid the foundation of Qutbuddinpura[67] on which two *mohallas* of Srinagar, namely, Langarhatta and Pir Haji Muhammad, now stand.

Sultan Sikandar (1389-1413) besides building Khanqah-i Mu lla mosque, erected the Jamà Masjid.[68] Sikandar's son Zain-ul-Abidin[69], popularly known as Budshah, was a man of versatile talents. He built Zainakadal[70] which preserves his memory even up to this day. The king also founded Nau Shahr, near Srinagar, which was, as Dr. Sufi observes, in modern terminology his New Delhi.[71] The Mar canal[72] founded by Budshah in Srinagar was till recently the main artery of communication between the Srinagar city and the villages near the Dal lake. Among other things Budshah built the Khanqah of Sayyid Muhammad Madani.[73] In addition, he built two artificial isles of Rupa-Lank and Sona-Lank[74] to beautify the city. Zain-ul-Abidin is reported to have introduced new industries like that of shawl, carpet, silk, papier mache, paper, wood-carving, *namdah* and *gabha*. The fame of Srinagar rests on these industries. Srinagar thus became an emporium of trade. Besides, he also introduced stone-polishing, stone-cutting, glass-blowing, window-cutting, gold and silver leaf-making and book-binding. No wonder, Mirza Haidar paid glowing tributes to the genius of Zain-ul-Abidin. "In Kashmir one meets", the Mirza observed, "with all those arts and crafts which are, in most cities, uncommon ... In the whole of Mavar-u-Nahar except Samarqand and Bukhara these are nowhere to be met with, while in Kashmir they are abundant. This is all due to Sultan Zain-ul-Abidin".[75]

Sultan Haidar Shah (1470-72) transferred his seat of government from Nau Shahr to Nowhatta, but in Sultan Hasan Shah's reign (1472-84) the capital was shifted to Nau Shahr again.[76]

In 1484, Mir Shams-ud-din Iraqi[77] paid his first visit to Kashmir as the ambassador of Sultan Husain Mirza, the governor of Khurrasan. He had come with a missionary zeal.[78] It should be remembered that from now Shiaism[79] began to gain ground in the Valley.

Mirza Haidar Dughlat (1540-50) found the city of Srinagar thickly populated. In his times there were many lofty buildings constructed of fresh cut pine. According to him, most of these buildings were five storeyed, each storey containing apartments, halls, galaries and towers. The streets were paved with stone. There were only shops of retail dealers-grocers, drapers etc. There were no large bazars, for the wholesale business was done by the traders in their own houses or factories.[80]

Mirza Haidar's short reign was productive of rich cultural activities. Pandit Suka belittles the improvements the Mirza had introduced, particularly in regard to dress and food. The conservative Brahman chronicler criticizes the Kashmiris for imitating the Mughal style of dress and diet which, he says, did them more harm than good.[81] Jahangir, on the other hand, is very appreciative of the cultural excellence acquired by the people of Kashmir under Mirza Haidar. He remarks that during his regime Kashmir had many skilled musicians.[82] Muhammad Azam[83] and Moulvi Hasan[84] praise Mirza Haidar for introducing hot-baths, latticed windows and the apparatus for drying paddy, locally known as *narah lul*.[85]

SRINAGAR UNDER THE MUGHALS

Mirza Haidar's death in 1550 was followed by a civil war in Srinagar which lasted till 1555, when Nasir-ud-din Muhammad Ghazi Shah, the founder of the Chak dynasty, ascended the throne. The Chak rule in Kashmir was marked by internal feuds. This led to the Mughal occupation of Kashmir in 1586. The Mughal emperors entrusted the task of administration to their governors; at the same time, they also visited the Valley. The political history of Kashmir during the Mughal period is centred round the Hari Parbat fort, *Takhat-i-Sulaiman* hill,[86] Nowhatta, Nua Shahr and the area in the vicinity of Jama mosque. The events that occurred in these parts of the city during Akbar's reign were very decisive for Kashmir.

During the earlier period of the Mughal rule in Kashmir, the city became the headquarters of an army of occupation, constantly engaged in war. Though the Chaks were defeated, their leaders did not reconcile themselves to the idea of Mughal rule in Kashmir. The first Mughal Governor of Kashmir, Qasim Khan, had to face stubborn resistance from the Chak troops led by Yaqub Shah Chak and Shams Chak. But they were defeated on the slopes of Koh-i-Sulaiman (Shankaracharya hillock). Once again the Chak freedom fighters made a bold attempt to fight against the Mughals to a finish, but were routed.

Akbar first entered Srinagar on 5 June 1589.[87] During his second visit to the city on 7 October 1592,[88] the Great Mughal enjoyed the saffron blossom at Pampore [89] and celebrated the festival of *dewali*. On this occasion the boats on the Jhelum, the banks of the river and the roofs of the houses in Srinagar were illuminated at the Emperor's command.[90]

Akbar's third visit to Srinagar on 6 June 1597[91] was important. This time he was accompanied by Father Jerome Xavier[92] and Bendict Goez, who are the first known European travellers to visit Kashmir. Father Xavier's description[93] of the famine of 1597 gives an idea of the devastation caused by it. He records that famine forced mothers to expose their children for sale in public places in the city. Most of them were baptized by the visiting Portuguese fathers with the hope that by so doing they would attain salvation and "eternal bliss for souls of the little ones."

To alleviate the sufferings of the famine-stricken population of Kashmir, the emperor is said to have ordered a strongly bastioned stone-wall[94] to be built around the slope of the Hari Parbat hillock in the city. The township within this fort wall was named 'Nagar Nagar.'[95] This fort wall is the only extant monument in Srinagar which is still a living tribute to the genius of Akbar.

Jahangir (1606-1628) became so enamoured of thc Vale of Kashmir as to make it "the place of his favourite abode, and he often declared that he would rather be deprived of every province of his mighty empire than lose Kachemire."[96] His visits to the Valley brought an era of splendour and prosperity to Srinagar. We are told that during his time there were nearly 800 gardens[97] in the neighbourhood of the Dal lake and "the owners, the nobles of the court, were certain to follow the example of their master in making full use of the facilities that Kashmir so readily offers for pleasure-seeking and enjoyment."[98]

The Mughal Governors who followed the example of their masters also laid out innumerable gardens in Srinagar. It is said there were about 700 gardens[99] around the Dal lake on the eve of the establishment of the Afghan rule in 1753. The idea of picnics and excursions by the citizens of Srinagar must have originated in the city during the Mughal times.[100]

Aurangzeb's Governor Islam Khan (1664-65) rebuilt Ali Masjid at Idgah, "a sixteenth century dilapidated structure, and lined its extensive compound with chinar trees."[101] Saif Khan (1665-68) laid out the garden of Saifabad on the banks of the Dal lake. During his second governorship of Kashmir (1669-72) he spanned the Saffa Kadal bridge[102] over the Jhelum in Srinagar in 1670. Fazil Khan (1698-1701) raised the embankment (*bund*) at Haft Chinar,[103] near Hazuri Bagh in the city in order to save it from recurrent floods of the Doodghanga river. The *bund* was lined with the Chinar trees to strengthen it.

But the most historical event of Fazil Khan's governorship in Kashmir was the arrival of the sacred hair *(mui mubarak)*[104] of the Prophet Muhammad in Srinagar in 1669. The holy relic was brought to the city by a rich Kashmiri merchant named Khawaja Nur-ud-Din Ishbari,[105] who had bought it in Bijapur. Ever since its arrival in Srinagar the holy relic has been kept at Hazratbal[106] mosque, which is known as the Second Madina (Madinat-ul-Thani) because of its supreme religious importance in Kashmir. [106a]

Under the Mughals Srinagar was a splendid city by the standards of the time. Father Xavier, Abul Fazl, Francisco Pelsaert, Jahangir, Bernier and Desideri have all described the city as it existed during the Mughal period. Abul Fazl found the capital of Kashmir a very fascinating city.

He remarks: "Srinagar is a great city and has long been peopled. The river Behat (Jhelum) flows through it. Most of the houses are of wood, and some rise up to five storeys. On the roofs they plant tulips and other flowers, and in the spring these rival flower gardens".[107] Jahangir described the practice of planting tulip flowers on roofs of buildings as a peculiarity of the people of Kashmir.[108] Francisco Pelsaert, writing in Emperor Jahangir's time, says: "The city is very extensive and contains many mosques. The houses are built of pine wood, the interstices being filled with clay, and their style is by no means contemptible; they look elegant, and fit for citizens rather than peasants, and they are ventilated with handsome and artistic open-work, instead of windows or glass. They have flat roofs entirely covered with earth, on which the inhabitants often grow onions, or which are covered with grass, so that during the rains the green roofs and groves make the city most beautiful on a distant view".[109]

Francois Bernier, the famous French physician and traveller, visited Srinagar during Aurangzeb's reign. His account of Kashmir's natural beauty and culture of Kashmir is very informative and interesting. He calls the Valley of Kashmir the *Paradise of the Indies*. Bernier describes the city as not less than three quarters of a league in length, and half a league in breadth.[110] During his time there were only two wooden bridges over the Jhelum. Describing the houses in the city, he remarks that although for the most part of wood, the houses were well-built and consisted of two or three storeys. Wood was preferred by the people of the city because of its cheapness, and the facility with which it was brought from the mountains by means of so many small rivers. Most of the houses in the city had also their gardens; and not a few had a canal, on which the owner kept "a pleasure-boat, thus communicating with the lake".[111]

Father Ippolito Desideri[112] and Manoel Freyre[113] arrived in Srinagar on the 13th November, 1714. The latter in a letter from Agra dated 26th April, 1717, dwells on the same points that Desideri[114] had noted—the populous character of Srinagar, its lakes surrounded by pleasant gardens and crowded with boats for pleasure and commerce and the lilies growing on the roofs of the houses. Desideri makes mention of the small and large boats.[115] The latter must have been the *doonga*, the precursor of the modern houseboat. Indeed, Desideri seeing Srinagar at the end of Mughal rule, found it at its best.

SRINAGAR UNDER THE AFGHANS (1753-1819)

In 1753, Kashmir came under the occupation of the Afghans who ruled the Valley from 1753 to 1819. Some of the Afghan governors did much for the beautification of Kashmir's capital. Amir Khan Jawansher (1770-76) reconstructed the Sona lank[116] in the Dal lake and raised a seven storeyed mansion upon it. He rebuilt the Amirakadal bridge,[117] which had been washed away by inundation in 1772. He also laid out Amirabad garden with beautiful pavilions in the Mughal gardens. But the most beautiful building constructed by Jawansher was the fort of Sherghari[118] which is now in ruins.

Another Afghan governor Ata Muhammad Khan Barakzai (1806-13) constructed the massive fort on the top of the Hari Parbat hillock.[119]

George Forster who arrived in Srinagar on 7th May, 1783 during the Afghan rule, like Bernier, calls it Kashmir. Srinagar had evidently grown since Bernier's visit, as Forster says that the city extends about three miles on each side of the Jhelum.[120] While Bernier had noticed only two bridges spanning the river in the city, Forster observes that there were four or five bridges.[121] But the traveller describes the streets of Srinagar as filthy[122] which shows that deterioration had set in under the later Mughals and Afghans.

SIKH RULE (1819-1846)

With the assumption of political power by the Sikhs in Kashmir in 1819, the old Hindu name of the capital of Kashmir was restored.[123] Moorcroft, Hugel, Vigne and Schonberg who visited the Valley during the Sikh rule have left their impressions in their works. It seems that the general lot of the city population did not improve under the Sikh regime. According to Moorcroft, "The general condition of the city of Srinagar is that of the confused mass of ill favoured buildings, forming a complicated labyrinth of narrow and dirty lanes, scarcely broad enough for a single cart to pass, badly paved, and having a small gutter in the centre full of filth, banked up on each side by a border of mire. The houses are in general two or three storeys high: they are built of unburnt bricks and timber, the former serving for little else than to fill up the interstices of the latter, they are not plastered, are badly constructed and are mostly in a neglected and ruinous condition, with broken doors, or no door at all, with shattered lattices, windows stopped up with boards, paper or rags, walls out of the perpendicular and pitched roofs threatening to fall ... The houses of the better classes are commonly detached, and surrounded by a wall and gardens, the latter of which often communicate with a canal, and the whole presents a striking picture of wretchedness and decay".[124]

Moorcroft also describes the several canals in the city which were crossed at various places by stone and wooden bridges. But their general condition during the Sikh rule was that of decay and they were choked with filth.[125]

NOTES:

1. Jack p. Gibbs, *Urban Research Methods*, See foreword by Kingsley Davis, p. XII.
2. R.C Kak, *Ancient Monuments of Kashmir*, p. 2 (1971 ed.).
3. Sir Aurel Stein, *Rajatarangini of Kalhana*, II, pp. 439-41.
4. Pandrethan is situated 3 miles above Srinagar on the road to Jammu. It is famous for an ancient temple of sculptured stone standing in the midst of a tank, surrounded by a grove of willows and *chinars*. For a detailed discussion on the architecture of the temple, see Kak, *op. cit.*, pp-112-116; Anand Koul Bamzai, *Archaeological Remains in Kashmir*, pp. 34-36.
5. Stein, *op. cit.*, pp. 439-441.
6. Ibid.
7. Ibid.
8. *op. cit.*,„ pp. 441-442.
9. Ibid; Sunil Chandra Ray, *The Early History and Culture of Kashmir*, pp. 16-17.
10. Ibid.
11. Ibid; George Buhler, *Detailed Report of a Tour in search of Sanskrit Manuscripts made in Kashmir, Rajputana and Central Asia,* p-17; For Gen. Cunningham's identification, see *J.A.S.B.*, 1848, p. 283. Also see Cunningham, *The Ancient Geography of India*, p. 93 Sqq.
12. Stein, *op. cit.*, II, p. 444.
13. Ibid.
14. Ibid.
15. The Dal Lake which has been sung by Thomas Moore in his 'Lalla Rookh', lies on the northern-eastern side of the city. It is about 5 miles long and two and a half miles broad with an average depth of about 10 feet. The Dal is world unto itself. On its shores and numerous islands are the palaces of the rich and the cottages of the poor. It encompasses rich fields and fruit orchards, magnificent Mughal gardens, extensive sheets of lotus and lily and the long thick lush grass that hides the nests of numerous water birds. The swiftly darting fish of its limpid waters, the floating gardens that grow melons, cucumbers and other vegetables,

the tall poplars and the shady willows and chinars that line its waterways, the rich variety of its aquatic plants are some of its varied attractions.

16. The Jhelum forms the main arterial drainage system for the Valley's mountains, streams, springs and rivers. It is first formed by the meeting of several streams like the Sandran, the Brang, the Arpath and the Lidar which drain the south-eastern portion of the Valley. The meeting takes place in the plain close to Anantnag. The Jhelum is navigable from Khanabal to Khadanyar. In its winding course the Jhelum receives many streams and just before reaching Srinagar, it is joined by a stream which drains the Dal Lake to the east of the city. The surplus waters of the lake flow out towards the Jhelum by a canal which is called *Tsunth Kul*. A large stream called Dudganga, formed by the waters of several streams that drain the south-western mountains, joins the Jhelum on the left bank in Srinagar.
17. Stein, *op. cit.,* II, p-444.
18. Ibid.
19. Ibid.
20. For details, see Ibid., pp. 446-52.
21. Kalhana's story is contained in verses 336-349 of the Third book.
22. *Mahasarit* is the ancient name of a canal in Srinagar. It is popularly known as *Tsunth Kul* and connects the Dal Lake with the River Jhelum.
23. Stein, *op. cit.,* II, p. 442.
24. Ibid.
25. Ibid.
26. This embankment protects the whole of the low-lying portions of the city on the right river-bank as well as the floating gardens and the shores of the Dal which would otherwise be exposed to floods from the River Jhelum. "It is indeed evident", remarks Stein, "that its construction was a necessary condition for the safety of the newly founded city". Ibid., II, -443.
27. "The name of the village *Saritaka* where the demon showed the king the proper site for his city, has long ago disappeared. Its position, however, is sufficiently marked by the mention of the goddess *Sarika*". The latter, who is supposed to be a form of Durga, "has since ancient times been worshipped on the hill which rises to the North of the central part of Srinagar and is still called after her". At present the hill is known as Hari Parbat. "*Har* is the Kashmiri name of the goddess *Sarika* as well as of the *Sarika* bird (*Maina*)". Ibid; Also see Buhler, *op. cit.,* pp. 16 sqq.
28. Stein, *op. cit.,* II, p. 446.
29. James Fergusson, *Kashmir, An Historical Introduction*, p-105.
30. Stein, *op. cit.,* II, p. 447.
31. Ibid., pp. 444-445.
32. He is said to have given orders for the destruction of Srinagar under the

spell of intoxication. Fortunately, the orders were not executed and when the king returned to his senses he anxiously enquired about the fate of Pravarasen's city. See Ibid., I, Book IV, Vs. 310-320.

33. The ancient remains of Lalitaditya's city may be found near the present Shadipur village, about 9 miles in a direct line to the North-West of Srinagar. The king "and his ministers seem to have vied with each other in emblellishing the new city with magnificient edifices which were intended to be worthy alike of the kings glory and the ministers affluence". Kak, *op. cit.*, p. 146.

34. The village of Andarkot is supposed to be the site of Jayapida's capital. See *Rajat* (Stein), Bk. IV, Note 506-511. Andarkot is situated in lat. 34° 13′., long. 74° 42′, on the Sumbal lake about 12 miles North-West of Srinagar.

35. Ibid., I, Book V, Vs. 44-45 Sqq. and note. Avantipur (lat 33° 55′, long. 75° 4′) is situated on the right bank of the Jhelum midway between the city and Anantnag, at a distance of 18 miles from Srinagar.

36. It is named after Shankaravarman who ruled Kashmir from 883 to 902 A.D. Situated on the Baramulla road, it is 17 miles from Srinagar. Two temples built by the king and his queen here, though in ruined condition, are still standing. Shankaravarman was an oppressor of his subjects. It is interesting that the town never rose to importance. As the king's name was considered a word of ill-omen Samkarapura was called only Pattan (city) and to this day it is remembered by this name.

37. It is now the village of Kanispor, 74° 28′ long., 34° 14′ lat; situated between the Jhelum and the road leading from Baramulla to Srinagar. Gen. Cunningham wrongly identifies Kanishka's capital with Kanpur, on the road from Srinagar to Shopian. In reality, however, the name of that place is Khanpur. *Rajat* (Stein), Bk. I, Note 168.

38. A tradition recorded by Gen. Cunningham identifies Juskapura with the modern village of Zukur, North of Srinagar, about four miles from the Hari Parbat hill. *Rajat* (Stein), Bk. I, Note 168.

39. According to Kalhana, the city was founded by Huvishka, the great Kushan king in the second century A.D. The place was identified by Gen. Cunningham (*Ancient Geography*, pp. 99 sqq.) at the modern Ushkur, a village about two miles to the south-east to Baramulla, on the left bank of the River Jhelum, 74° 26′ long. 34° 12′ lat. See also *Rajat* (Stein), Bk. I, Note 168.

40. Stein, *op. cit.,* II, p. 445.

41. Ibid., p. 445.

42. Ibid.

43. The Anchar lake 'is 3.51 miles in length and 2.15 miles in breadth. It covers an area of 7.5465 square miles'. Walter Lawrence, *The Valley of Kashmir*, p. 20 n.

44. Stein, *op. cit.,* II, P. 445.

45. Anantnag (lat. 33° 44′ long. 75° 12′) is also called Islamabad. It is at a distance of 34 miles south-east of Srinagar. The town possesses a large number of springs, which send out numerous streams.
46. It is a town situated on the Jhelum in lat. 34° 12′. long. 84° 23′. 34 miles west of Srinagar. Before 1947 Baramulla was a flourishing trade centre being the easiest of all routes from Kashmir to the Panjab.
47. Stein, *op. cit.*, II, p. 446.
48. His birth place was the present village of (Khunamoh of Kalhana), about 8 miles south-east of Srinagar. He left the Valley early in the regin of king Kalasa (A.D. 1063-89) and after roving hither and thither established himself as the court poet of the Calukya king Tribhuvanamalla Parmadi in the Deccan. In the last canto of his historical poem, the *Vikraman-Kadevacartia*, Bilhana gives us a glowing picture of the beauties of Pravarasen's capital. Although it is panegyrical in character, the "description is laudably exact in its local details". To Prof. Buhler we owe the discovery of Bilhana's chief work.
49. S.C Ray, *op-cit.*, pp. 16-17.
50. Ibid.
51. "His works," observes Stein, "composed in the second and third quarter of the eleventh century, form important landmarks in several fields of Indian literature. Ksemendra seems to have had a genuine interest, rare among Indian scholars, for the realities of his country and the life around him". *op. cit.*, II, p. 375.
52. Mankha was Kalhana's contemporary. His description of Pravarapura is found in the III Canto of his Karya *Srikanthacarita. op. cit.*,.
53. Ray, *op. cit.*, pp. 16-17.
54. Francois Bernier, *Travels in the Mogul Empire*, p. 397.; Federic Drew, The *Jummoo and Kashmir territories*, p. 183; Wakefield, *The Happy Valley*, p. 91.
55. I have come across only a few coins of Akbar's regin which bear the seal of the Srinagar mint. In fact, the name of Srinagar appears on the coins for the first time in the time of the Great Mughal.
56. Bernier, *op. cit.*, p. 397; Drew, *op. cit.*, p. 183; Wakefield, *op. cit.*, p. 91.
57. Drew, *op. cit.*, p. 183; Wakefield, *op. cit.*, p. 91.
58. *Baharistan-i-Shahi*, f.15a.
59. Jonaraja, *Rajat*, III, p. 23.
60. *Baharistan-i-Shahi*, ff. 15a-b; *Indian Antiquary*, July 1908, p-192; Francke, *Antiquities of Indian Tibet*, II, p. 98.
61. Nizam-ud-Din Ahmed, *Tabqat-i-Akbari* (Bib. Ind.) III, p. 428; Jonaraja (tr. Dutt), III, p. 37; *Baharistan-i-Shahi*, f. 18b.
62. *Rajat* (tr. Dutt), p. 37.
63. According to Jonaraja, the king built the town of Sharikapura around the Hari Parbat hillock, *Rajat* (tr. Dutt), p. 42.
Jonaraja names the new town 'Semeru' while in the Persian chronicles

it is described as 'Koh-i-Maran'. The identity of the two names has been shown by Jahangir. *Tuzuk-i-Jahangiri*(R&B)11,p. 150.

64. For the historical role of Mir Sayyid Ali Hamadani, see Ishaq Khan, *Kashmir's Transition to Islam: The role of Muslim Rishis* (Manohar, New Delhi, 1994)

65. Sayyid Ali, *Tarikh-i-Kashmir*, Transcript No. 731 (R.P.D.), p. 4. The transcript is not folioed and therefore I have referred to page numbers.

66. Ever since the beginning of the political movement in Kashmir in 1931 *Khanqah-i-Mualla* has been a political centre. While commenting on the political importance of this place, the special correspondent of *The Tribune* wrote on June 13, 1946: "There is only one trouble spot at present in Kashmir Valley, the Khanka Mohalla of Srinagar where a batch of workers of the National Conference court arrest every evening. Elsewhere complete calm prevails." Also see *The Hindustan Times* May 29, 1946.

67. Sayyid Ali, *op. cit.*, p. 3.

68. Jama Masjid, the largest mosque in Kashmir, has a quadrangle and roughly square in plan, its northern sides being 384' in length. "Its principal features are the four minars, one in the middle of each side. They are covered by a series of pyramidal roofs, which terminate in an open turret crowned by a high pinnacle. All these minars, except that to the west, which contains the pulpit, cover spacious arched entrances which are plain but very imposing." (R.C. Kak, *op. cit.*, p. 86).

69. See Ishaq Khan, Zain-ul-Abidin, *The Struggle*, August, 1969, pp. 27-28.

70. Srivara (Dutt), p. 127; Stein, *Ancient Geography.*, para 98.
For the architecture of the bridge, see G.T. Vigne, *Travels*, p. 237; Moorcroft, *Travels*, II, pp. 121-23; Sir Walter Lawrence, *The Valley of Kashmir*, p. 38. At present, the Jhelum in the city is spanned by over ten bridges.

71. Sufi, *Kashir*, I, p. 161.
The capital city of Budshah extended between Sowra and Hari Parbat. *Rajat* (Stein), BK. III, Note 453-54.

72. Srivara (Dutt), p. 143; Sirvara (text), I 442 and IV, 298.

73. *Baharistan*, f.56a.
For the architecture of the mosque, see W.H. Nicholls, *Muhammadan Architecture of Kashmir* (*Archaeological Survey Report*, 1906-1907, p.162); A J. Arberry, *The Legacy of Persia*,, p.104; See also "Persian Influences in Kashmir during the Sultanate period, 1320-1586," *Islamic Culture*, Hyderabad, January, 1977.

74. Srivara (Dutt), pp. 141-42; *Baharistan*, f.53; Moorcroft, op. cit.,II, pp. 137-39; Stein *Ancient Geography*, para 66.

75. Mirza Haidar, *Tarikh-Rashidi* (E & R), p. 434.

76. Srivara, p. 206.

77. The Shias Chiefly reside at Zadibal in Srinagar, the burial place of Shams-ud-din Iraqi.
78. Mir Shams-ud-din Iraqi introduced the Nurbakshiya doctrines for the first time in Kashmir. Mirza Haidar, *op. cit.*, p. 435; Abul Fazl, *Ain* (Jarret), II, p. 389.
For a detailed discussion on the Nurbakshiya sect, see Mohibbul Hasan, *Kashmir under the Sultans*, pp. 283-88.
80. Mirza Haidar, *op. cit.*, p. 425.
81. Suka, *op. cit.*, p. 380.
82. *Tuzuk-i-Jahangiri*, (R & B), II, p. 148.
83. Mohammad Azam Diddamari, *Tarikh-i-Azam*, p.69.
84. Moulvi Hasan Shah, *Tarikh-i-Hasan* (Persian), II, p.385.
85. For the description of *nara lul*, see Hasan, *op. cit.*, II, p. 385.
86. In ancient times, the hill was called Gopadri. According to Kalhana, the king Gopaditya built a shrine of Jyeshthesavara on the hill. (*Rajat,* I, Verse 341). But the name 'Takhat-i-Sulaiman' seems to be of fairly long standing . Kak (see Kak, *op. cit.*, p. 79) observes that the name is mentioned by Catrou *(General History of the Mughal Empire,* Calcutta edition, p. 196. It was orginally published in 1708), and in a slightly changed from (*Koh-i-Sulaiman*) by Abul Fazl (*Ain*, tr. Jarret, Vol. II, p. 355).
This hill is also named after *Shankaracharya* who is believed to have come to Srinagar in the time of Abhinava Gupta (993-1015 A.D.) and stayed on the hill for some time. (Anand Koul, *Archaeological Remains in Kashmir*, p. 17). However there is no historical evidence to support such belief.
87. Abul Fazl, *Akbarnama* (tr. Beveridge), III, pp. 817, 827, 958.
88. Ibid., p. 956 n.
89. Pampur is situated on the right bank of the Jhelum about 8 miles south-east of Srinagar. Its ancient name was Padmapura. The place is famous for saffron cultivation.
90. Ibid., p. 956 n.
91. Ibid., p. 1084.
92. *Akbar and the Jesuits,* (Broadway Travellers, Payne) Chapter Vii, p. 78; Macalgan, *Jesuit Mission to Akbar*, JASB, 1896, p. 72.
93. Father Xavier has left a long letter which contains his observations on Kashmir. See *Akbar* and *Jesuits*, pp. 74-79.
94. *Akbarnama* III, pp. 1084-85; *Tuzuk-i-Jahangiri,* (R. & B.), II, pp. 139 and 150.
95. *Akbarnama* III, pp. 1084-85.
96. *Bernier, op. cit.*, p. 401.'Kashmir,' remarked Jahangir, 'is a garden of eternal spring or an iron fort to a palace of kings — a delightful flower-bed and a heart-expanding heritage for derivishes.' And he summed up his description with these words, 'If one were to take to praise Kashmir

whole books would have to be written.' *Tuzuk-i-Jahangiri* (R. & B.), II,pp. 143-44.

97. Fergusson, *op. cit., p*-143. For a detailed account of the Mughal gardens, see Stuart, *The Gardens of the Great Moguls,* pp. 153-179. Hasan, *Tarikh* (Persian), I, pp. 281-307; Koul, *Archaeological Remains in Kashmir,* pp. 62-102; Kak, *op. cit.,* pp 93-102.
Among the gardens on the banks of Dal lake, Chashma Shahi, Nishat and Shalamar are the best preserved and most frequented. Among other gardens of Mughal times only remains of the Bagh-i-Nagin and Bagh-i-Naseem exist.
98. Fergusson, *op. cit.,* p. 143.
99. R. K Parimu, *History of Muslim Rule in Kashmir,* pp. 403-04.
100. The people of Srinagar are very fond of excursions. Sir Richard Temple visiting Srinagar in the early part of Ranbir Singh's regin writes: 'On the lake, as on the river, we saw numerous boats plying, full of Kashmiris. These were all pleasure parties, large and small, bound on excursions, which I may here observe, the Kashmiris seem immensely to appreciate." *Journals kept in Hyderabad, Kashmir, Skim and Nepal.* (1859-71), Vol. II, p. 55.
101. Parimu, *op. cit.,* p. 320.
102. Hasan, *op. cit.,* (Moulvi Ibrahim's urdu translation), p. 378.
103. Ibid., p. 384.
104. Azam, *Waqiat-i-Kashmir, p. 156, Hasan, op. cit.,*(Ibrahim's translation), p. 384.
105. Hasan, *op. cit.,* (Ibrahim's translation), p. 384.
106. 'Hazarat' means majesty and 'bal' place. Being the repository of the Prophet's hair Hazratbal has grown into a religious centre of unrivalled importance for the Muslims of Kashmir. The carvings on the walls and the latticed windows of the old mosque of Hazratbal were specimens of exquisite art. But the old building has recently been replaced by a new one.
106a. See for greater details on Hazratbal, Ishaq Khan " The Significance of the dargah of Hazratbal in the Socio-religious and political life of Kashmiri Muslims" in *Muslim Shrines in India*, ed. Christian W. Troll (Oxford, 1989)
107. *Akbarnama* III, pp. 827-28.
108. *Tuzuki-i-Jahangiri* (R & B), (1968 Ed.), II, pp. 144-45.
109. Francisco Pelsaert, *The Remonstrantie*, p. 34.
110. *Bernier, op. cit.,* pp. 397-98.
111. Ibid., p. 398.
112. He calls Srinagar by the name of Kascimir. Fergusson, *op. cit.,* p. 160.
113. Srinagar is called Cazimir by him. *op. cit.,,*, p. 163.
114. He also refers to 'imposing buildings and fine streets, squares and bridges' of the Srinagar city. Ibid. p. 160.

115. Ibid., pp. 160-163.
116. Hasan, *op. cit.,* (Tr. Ibrahim), III, p. 461.
117. Ibid.
118. Ibid.; See also Vol. I, p. 388.
119. Ibid., p. 501.
120. George Forster, *Journey,* II, pp. 397-98.
121. Ibid.; Bernier, *op. cit.,* pp 397-98.
122. Ibid.
123. Drew, *op. cit.,*. p. 183; Wakefield, *op. cit.,* p.91.
124. Moorcroft, *op. cit.,* II, pp. 127-128.
125. Ibid.

Fateh Kadal
The houses shown on this bridge were shops and were cleared away about a century ago.
Courtesy (*Kashmir in Sunlight and Shade*)

A Traditional Pandit lady.

The common task of women in the traditional society was pounding of rice and carrying water from the Jhelum for domestic use.

Milkmen bound for the city

Here are seen typical waterside houses.

Traffic on the Jhelum Valley Road before and after 1890.

CHAPTER II

MODERN SRINAGAR

During the early part of the Dogra rule (1846-90), Srinagar presented a very sad picture.[1] There was an obvious deterioration in the physical appearance of the city. The streets were full of filth.[2] There were only a few public buildings in Srinagar; the principal of them were the *barah-dari*, palace, fort, gun factory, dispensary, school, and the mint; and also some ancient mosques and temples and cemeteries.[3] The narrow streets were dusty and choked with the traffic of pack animals, horses, pariah dogs, donkeys, cows and pedestrians. In the rainy season the streets were extremely muddy owing to the absence of any drainage system. Both the drainage and the water-supply had been grossly neglected.[4]

Srinagar even lacked ordinary sanitary arrangements. The majority of the inhabitants of Srinagar used the public streets or lanes or the court-yards of their own houses as latrines. This had been going on from time immemorial, wrote Major General de Bourbel,[5] who submitted a report on the epidemic of 1888. As a result of the accumulation of filth, soil had become contaminated. Private houses with a few exceptions had no privy, and even those few were seldom cleaned. Dr. Mitra, the able and energetic Chief Medical Officer of Kashmir, in a pamphlet on Medical and Surgical practice in Kashmir, tells the same story regarding the want of sanitary arrangements in Srinagar. "*Barustal gus*, filth at the door, is proverbially admitted to be a mark of affluence. Human ordure is scattered ... all over the town from the roads and houses on the river bank, drains carrying slush, filth and sewage empty into the river, in which the washermen wash unclean clothes, the dyers wash their dyes, and the butchers entrails of animals".[6]

The city of Srinagar started with certain initial advantages.[7] In the first place, the Jhelum provided a regular highway as well as a means of water supply. Besides, the city was so well situated that it became since ancient times the natural capital of Kashmir, the emporium of trade and the seat of culture and industry. But, unfortunately, as the population grew, the defects of the city became apparent. Firstly, Srinagar was subject to floods owing to its low lying position. Secondly, the river which was the main means of transport, became by its pollution from the drains of the houses on its banks, a great source of danger to public health. Thirdly, as the population grew, the city limits expanded. This expansion took place without any systematic town-planning. This resulted in irregular narrow streets,[8] ill-ventilated and ill-planned houses, congestion and defective drainage.

The consequence of all this was that the health and sanitation conditions in the city became unsatisfactory. Not only did the River Jhelum carry filth and drainage, but also the canals[9] inside the city were mostly silted up. Other insanitary evils that existed in Srinagar were over-crowded burial grounds, unclean slaughter houses, want of proper surface drainage, dirty cow houses, slimy tanks, etc.[10] It may also be noted that thousands of pariah dogs, starving donkeys and cows lived on this filth.[11]

Such was Srinagar about a century ago. Dr. Ernest Neve remarks that infection from want of sanitary precautions played a great part then.[12] Contagion was responsible for many of the local diseases which were rampant —such as opthalmia, scalhead and the itch.[13] Srinagar, indeed, was a filthy city.[14] The constant presence in the city of cholera and other infectious diseases was therefore scarcely to be wondered at.[15] Lawrence wrote that 'the centre and nursery of cholera in Kashmir' was 'the foul and squalid capital, Srinagar'.[16] Cholera was the one great scourge of Srinagar, where the accumulated filth of ages afforded a fertile breeding ground for the germs of this terrible disease. A cholera epidemic once it broke out, became very difficult to control, still worse to eradicate; it ran its course month after month ruthlessly decimating the population. In the last century cholera broke out ten times in Kashmir, causing considerable loss of life.[17] Dr. Neve, in his *Kashmir Mission Report* for 1888 wrote:

"The wonder is not that cholera came, but that it never went away; not that it slew 10,000 victims, but that so many escaped its ravages." Again "enough that cholera came and will come again, aye, and again, as long as it is thus prepared for, and invited and feasted by, a city reared on filth, a people born in filth, living in filth and drinking filth".[18]

Dr. A. Neve gives a very gruesome picture of Srinagar of 1888 and 1892 when the city was affected by cholera.

"In 1888 and 1892 Srinagar was a 'city of Dreadful Death'. We are looking from the bows of our mat-roofed boat for the first sight of Srinagar, the so-called Venice of the East. The turbid and lazy stream sweeps against the prow, masses of dirty foam, floating straw, dead bodies of dogs, and all the garbage of a great city ... Upon one bank stands a neat row of wooden huts. This is a cholera hospital. Upon the other bank the blue smoke curling up from a blazing pile gives atmosphere and distance to the rugged mountains. It is a funeral pyre. And as our boat passes in the city, now and again we meet other boats, each with their burden of death. All traffic seems to be suspended. Shops are closed. Now and again, from some neighbouring barge, we hear the wail of mourners, the shrieks of women as in a torture den, echoed away among the houses on the bank".[19]

Lawrence has also narrated the horrors of the epidemic of 1892. As he observes:

"Defoe's plague of London shows how even the strong English character fails in an awful pestilence, and it is not to be wondered at if the less stable orientals become unhinged in a visitation such as that of 1892. All business was stopped, and the only shops which remained open were those of the sellers of white cloth for winding sheets. Men would not lend money, and in the villages the people would sit all day long on the graveyards absolutely silent. In the city the people would go out at dawn to the gardens and parks in the suburbs, returning at night to hear that more of their relatives and friends had perished. The long lines of coffins borne to the graveyards resembled an endless regiment on the march, while on the river a sad procession of boats floated down to the burning-ghats and living passengers in other boats passed by with averted faces. Men telling me how they had lost all the members of their family would break into hysterical laughter and I have never seen such utter despair and helplessness as I saw in 1892". [20]

It was stated by the Chief Medical Officer of Kashmir that 5,781 persons died in Srinagar as a result of cholera.[21]

It is apparent that cholera epidemics[22] and other preventible diseases were frequent visitors to the city. The principal "foyers" of the disease in the city were at Chattabal and Maisuma[23]—the poor quarters of Srinagar.[24] The ignorant, apathetic and often obstructive attitude of the people[25] and their habits and customs[26] were also responsible for the outbreak of cholera in Srinagar.

Apart from cholera, earthquakes, floods, fires and famines were the recurrent visitors to the city.[27] At various times during the second half of the nineteenth century, natural calamities caused scarcity of food[28] which in their turn "contributed largely to the extension and fatality of the disease by driving the people to eat bad grain, raw and rotten vegetables, sour unripe apples, mulberries and other fruits".[29]

The destructive effects of fires were chiefly experienced in Srinagar, where the wooden structures of the houses and their thatched roofs fell an easy prey to the flames.[30] There were no roads in the city along which fire-engines could be brought, and small pitchers of water were of very little effect when the fire broke out.[31] Twice in the reign of Maharaja Ranbir Singh the greater part of Srinagar was ravaged by conflagration,[32] and before his accession the large parts of the city had been burnt down sixteen times.[33] During the time of Maharaja Pratap Singh there broke out a disastrous fire in the city on May 7,1892.[34] The Earl of Dunmore who was in Srinagar on this occasion wrote: "The damage done by the fire is computed at twenty lakhs of rupees and 5000 houses, mosques and temples have been destroyed".[35] It was not, however, until the construction of good roads in the city and introduction of water-works that the people of Srinagar were able to protect themselves against fire accidents to some extent.

Many disastrous floods are reported in the vernacular histories,[36] but the flood of 1893[37] was unprecedented, because it swept away most of the bridges in the city, and damaged houses, besides submerging the lake garden, destroying the melons, cucumbers, vegetable marrows and tomatoes, which form an important part of the citizen's diet in the summer.[38] This drew attention of the Government to the need of preventive works. High embankments were raised and a very large flood canal was constructed which drained the flood water direct from the city to the Wular lake.[39]

Srinagar has suffered terribly from famine.[40] The famine of 1877-79 was a great calamity.[41] It is stated that the population of the city was reduced from 127,400 to 60,000.[42] The unfortunate poor shawl weavers were the chief victims of famine.[43] "Oil cake, rice, chaff, the bark of the elm and yew, and even grass and roots were eagerly devoured by the starving people, who became so much demoralized that each was like a ravenous beast, struggling for his own life".[44] As Ernest Neve observes: "The corpses of those who had perished were left dying or hastily dragged to the nearest well or hole, until these became choked with dead bodies. Dogs wandered about in troops preying upon the unburied carcases.

Pestilence dogged the steps of want and cholera broke out. Everything combined to intensify the disaster".[45]

One of the chief causes of famine was the isolation of the city. Owing to bad communications, grain[46] became difficult to obtain from outside[47] and a failure of crops resulted in prolonged famines.[49] Consequently, the general appearance of the city gave an idea of poverty.[50] The great majority of the people were not adequately 'fed, clothed and housed'.[51] There were very few men of respectable, and none of wealthy appearance.[52]

Figures of house occupancy are in fact available before the first Census of 1891. In 1863 there were 16,529 houses in the city.[53] This number is said to have risen to 20,304 in 1868.[54] The Census of 1891 records that there were 22,448 houses in Srinagar.[55] The increase was owing to the fact that a large number of villagers migrated to the city after the famine of 1877-79 to escape from forced labour.[56] Whereas in 1891 the average number of persons per house was 5, in 1901 it was 7.[57]

It is not, therefore, surprising that the conditions of life were extremely insanitary in Srinagar. Huddled together on both the banks of the river, the houses presented a long line of structures varying in form, height and material. In many, wood predominated;[58] in others stone or brick; the greater portion was, however, a happy combination of both.[59] These houses were generally two or three storeyed high. They were mostly "in a neglected and ruinous condition with broken doors or no doors at all, with shattered lattices, windows stopped up with boards, paper, or rags, walls out of the perpendicular and pitched roofs threatening to fall".[60] The roofs were formed of layers of brickbark covered "with a coating of earth in which seeds dropped by birds or wafted by the wind vegetated. They were constantly overrun with grass and flowers".[61]

The houses were usually "lighted by windows (*pinjara*), formed of trellis work which took the place of glass".[62] Some of the *pinjaras* work was very beautiful. During winter, papers of different colours were pasted over the inside of the trellis work.[63] As late as 1875 glass windows were unknown out of the palaces and the mansions of the wealthy.[64] In 1880 Biscoe found only the Governor's house having glass windows.[65] The houses of better classes were "commonly detached and surrounded by a wall and gardens".[66] They were three or four storeyed high. Every house had a door and flight of steps leading to the water, and here boats were moored.[67] The condition of the gardens was no better than that of the buildings, and "the whole presented a striking picture of wretchedness and decay".[68]

It is apparent that the houses in Srinagar were not exactly built in blocks and lines,[69] but, as pointed out earlier, crowded together in complete disorder. Biscoe writes in 1880: "Many of the houses were off the straight [sic], often leading one against the other, like two drunken friends supporting each other".[70] Lawrence observes: "The city consists of 22,448 houses crowded together in utter confusion on either side of the Jhelum river, which winds through Srinagar with an average width of the eighty yards. The houses occupy a length of about three miles and a breadth of about one and a half miles on either side of the river, but the great part of the city lies on the right bank. The houses vary in size from the large and spacious burnt-brick palaces of the Pandit aristocrat and his 500 retainers, warmed in the winter by *hamamas*, to the doll house of three storeys, and three rooms of wood and sun-dried bricks where the poor shawl-weaver lives his squalid cramped life and shivers in the frosty weather ... Their wooden walls and their thatched roofs make them an easy victim to the fires which sweep at steady intervals through the city".[71]

The history or urban improvement in Srinagar dates back to 1886,[72] when the first Municipality Act was passed. At the beginning, the Srinagar Municipality comprised five official and 11 unofficial members.[73] All members were the nominees of the Government.[74] In 1913 a new Act introducing an elected element in the Constitution of local bodies of Srinagar and Jammu was passed.[75] The Municipality was authorised to elect its Vice-President in 1921.[76] In 1940 the Committee was composed of 18 members, two third of whom were elected and one third nominated.[77] By 1941 the Srinagar Municipality's administrative staff consisted of a paid President, a Secretary, a revenue Officer, a Municipal Health Officer, and a Municipal Engineer. Under these officers was a large staff of executive employees comprising supervising and subordinate services of conservancy, health and engineering. Below them worked a ministerial staff connected with the maintenance of records, the compiling of accounts and other clerical work. The services which were ordinarily under the Municipal management, and not under the control of the Srinagar Municipality, were the city water works and the fire brigade.[78]

As in other cities of India,[79] the problem of urban improvement was complicated in Srinagar. Sanitation was the first care of the Municipality. But it should be borne in mind that progress in this direction was limited. Most of the reforms of the Committee ran counter to the customs, prejudices and ideas of the bulk of the inhabitants of the city.[80] All innovation was met with opposition. The opposition to the structural improvements proposed in 1893 for the reconstruction of the burnt portion of Habba Kadal was so keen that the proposal had to be practically abandoned.[81] Thus writes Sardar Muhammad Hyat Khan: "The people of (Srinagar) are generally opposed to measures which interfere with old customs and prejudices. The people want to stick to their ancestral houses and lands and strongly oppose parting with them even on favourable terms of compensation and land in exchange".[82] Biscoe repeats the same story. The people of Srinagar, writes Biscoe,[83] are very conservative and abhor any change. Their answer to any improvement is always the same — i.e "our fathers and forefathers were always very happy and contented under the existing order of things. So why should not we be satisfied". It is not, therefore, surprising that the Municipal bye-laws were disregarded with impunity.

Like other municipalities of India, the Srinagar Municipality was not popular. The reasons for this are not far to seek. It should be remembered that the Municipality gained unpopularity on account of its exercise of a too minute and vexatious interference with the domestic life of the people and want of knowledge and sympathy with their views. It has already been noted that the task of Municipal improvement became very difficult once it began to interfere with the people's age-long habits. Srinagar was to see the quarrels between the "improvers" and the "conservatives".[84] No wonder, the enthusiasm of the reformers was sneered at by the people.[85]

But things could not go on like this for ever. As education spread and civic sense developed, municipal reforms were welcomed. One could hope for improvement. The long-established apathy of the people to reform was slowly disappearing. They had come to realise the benefits of local self-government, as is evident from their active participation in the municipal elections, which were held from time to time. By 1922 some keen and intelligent citizens had joined the Municipality. They supported the President in their arduous duties of fighting prejudice, age-old customs and dishonesty.[86]

The principal sanitary works carried out by the Srinagar Municipality were the construction and repair of roads and bunds, the improvement of drains in different parts of the city.[87] The construction of many metalled roads[88] marked a great step forward. The Municipality constructed partly at Government expense and partly at its own the Hari Singh High Street. Ganga Nath in his report says: "This locality approximates in point of communication to conditions prevailing in some of the modern Indian cities".[89] The Municipality provided certain amenities such as foot-paths on roads in civil lines, widening of roads, a garden for *pardah* ladies, known as Pratap Park and some other gardens for the general use of the public were also provided for.[90] Such improvements certainly led to an appreciable change in the outlook of the people. By 1220, ladies residing in the vicinity of the Pratap Park could be seen flocking in large numbers to this garden in the evenings.[91] Garden parties became a new feature of entertainment.[92]

Attempts were made to improve the conservancy of the city by erecting stand-pipes, especially in Maisuma. All unripe and over-ripe fruits were destroyed. Gallons of phenyle were distributed and poured down the drains. The dangers of drinking river water and eating unripe fruits were proclaimed by the beat of drums.[93] Thus the Municipality did much to change the traditional mode of life of the people. At the same time, at the instance of the Municipality, the Government constructed a sewer from Sara-i-bala to Chattabal.[94]

Until 1920 the main streets of Srinagar were lit by the shabby-looking dim kerosine oil lamps which were later replaced by electric lamps.[95] This was of immense benefit to public traffic and of much use to the police in the suppression of thefts in the city at night.[96]

One of the most important problems before the Municipality was to relieve the congestion of the city streets, especially on its main roads. In fact, the congestion was the result of political instability which Kashmir witnessed during the 19th century. The Afghan, the Sikh, and the early Dogra rulers neglected the principles of town planning and administration. Houses and shops crept further out, encroaching on the roadways, which became more tortuous and obstructive. No attention appears to have been paid to any regular formation of streets, roads and thoroughfares. Houses were gradually constructed in consonance with the social habits of the people and the political condition of the country, without any control or interference of the city authorities of the time. The forced labour (*begar*) which was resorted to during the early Dogra period led many villagers to migrate to the city.[97] This influx resulted in the construction of houses in a haphazard manner in Srinagar on a very big scale. In consequence, the congestion grew worse.

According to the Census of 1891, Srinagar extended for about two miles along the banks of the river.[98] But in 1911, the city extended more than three miles in a curve, occupying an area of 5,139 acres.[99] In 1941 the density of the city was 18,890 per square mile as against 14,870 of 1891, 15,327 of 1901, 15,735 of 1911, 15,653 of 1921 and 15,779 of 1931. The figures show that the increase in the population of Srinagar was not slow when compared with the expansion of the jurisdiction of the city. It should be remembered that the limits of Srinagar were extended several times. It was Sir W.Lawrence who had fixed the limits of Srinagar in the regular settlement.[100] But after a few decades local conditions changed. In 1915 the suburbs of Buchwara[101] and Zadibal were included within the limits of the Municipality.[102] These extensions were welcomed by the people of the suburbs. It is significant that Zadibal was included in the limits of Srinagar Municipality on the appeal of its inhabitants.[103] In 1920 the proposals for extending the limits to all suburbs around the city were made in order "to remove the anomaly and incongruity of the boundaries which existed".[104] According to the President of the Municipality , the suburbs of Srinagar were "in a primitive insanitary condition. They were simply thorns or microbes in the flesh of Srinagar. Here the disease easily found a foothold and then invaded the city itself".[105] In pursuance of these proposals, the municipal limits were further enlarged during 1921-23 by the addition of (1) the Zunimar tract containing 36 *mohallas* and the villages of (2) Batmalloo (3) Baghi Nand Singh (4) Sonawar (5) Bonamsar (6) Shivpora and (7) Rathpura.[106]

As a result of these extensions, Srinagar expanded rapidly. By 1941 the city extended over an area of about four miles in length and by about two miles in width.[107] In other words, Srinagar extended from Sonawar to Rambagh on the south, to Sowra and Chattabal weir on the north respectively.[108]

After considering the way Srinagar has grown, it is now easy to understand the complexity of urban social values. We have seen that usually, several villages existed on the fringe of the city. As the latter expanded, these villages were sucked in and the villagers lost their land. They took to new occupations such as selling milk, factory-work, domestic-service and tongá driving. One can still find a colony of tonga-drivers at Chattabal. The sucked-in villages presented a striking contrast to the other areas of the city. Socially, the villagers, especially the older people, were rural in their habits and outlook. Their attitude to work, leisure, recreation, ritual etc. was different from that of the people in the other areas. For instance, the educated and the upper class citizens in a fashionable area valued silence and privacy, while the rustics did not mind noise and did not care for privacy. Again, the former were hygiene-conscious, while the latter had no conception of hygiene. In fact, for many years such areas remained socially backward.

It has already been noted how Srinagar grew in area since the beginning of this century. It should, however, be borne in mind that the increase in the area of the city, its growth as a centre of economic, political, administrative and religious activities and the increase in the number of inhabitants are all interdependent. The population might grow as a result of increasing opportunities of employment which also might make it necessary to expand the limits of the city to make room for the increasing population.

Migration is one of the vital processes which alters the size of a population.[109] Excepting natural increase, "it is the only source of change in the population of a particular territory".[110] The most consistent pattern in migratory current is rural-urban drift of population. The term urbanization can imply urban living from the standpoint of either civic amenities (i.e. housing, transport, sanitation, etc.), or 'behaviour pattern'. The first has been described as a town-planners outlook, and the second, that of the historian sociologist. J. Clyde Mitchall defines behaviour pattern as "the process of becoming urban, moving to cities, changing from agriculture to other pursuits common to cities and corresponding changing of behaviour patterns".[111] In a nutshell, it means rural migration to the urban centre and its socio-cultural consequences.

Cities have broader fields of employment as a newer way of life than rural areas. And "these attractions", remarks Barclay, "often coincide with rural distress, which helps to induce people to move".[112]

The earliest reliable information on rural migration to Srinagar can be obtained from Lawrence's *The Valley of Kashmir*. The author refers to the migration of a large number of villagers to the city during the famine of 1877-79, so as to "escape from forced labour and to obtain cheap food".[113] The rural drift is also evident from the fact that, during famines, many villagers were employed on roads by the missionaries.[114]

The rural migration is also attested to by the domestic servant class in Srinagar. They were vital links between the city and the countryside. The Census figures regarding occupations in Srinagar are important in this respect. The city as a magnet for the rural population can be projected here. While in 1911 the domestic service supported 7.1 of the earners,[115] in 1931 it claimed 18% of occupations in the city.[116]

But an increase in the population of Srinagar was natural with the improvements in sanitation, lighting, water works, medical aid and general administration. Further, rapid growth took place because of the introduction of fresh fields of labour like the Silk Industry, the Tourist Industry, the Woollen Industry, the hotels and restaurants, electric installations, the neighbouring quarries for road and metal and the general industrial development that was noticeable in many quarters of the city.[117] In 1901 the Srinagar Silk factory alone employed nearly 7,000 persons.[118] A large number of the workers in the factory came from the suburbs of the city.[119] The rapid growth of population[120] within the municipal limits is shown in the following table:-[121]

Population with variations since 1891

Year	Persons	Variation	Net Variation 1891-1941
1891	1,18,960	—	—
1901	1,22,618	+3,658	—
1911	1,24,240	+1,622	—
1921	1,39,520	+15,280	—
1931	1,73,573	+34,053	—
1941	2,07,787	+34,214	+88,827

The city not only provided employment to the labourers from the villages but also it changed the way of life of the rural people living in its hinterland. With the growth of the tourist industry[122] Srinagar's increased demand for food-stuffs and a work force tied the surrounding areas even more closely to the economy of the city. Its hinterland was pushed further and further away. Nearby villages[123] took to dairying, poultry-keeping and market gardening to supply the urban demand for milk, fruit and vegetables. The villagers made use of the medical, educational and recreational facilities available in the city. More money circulated in the nearby villages, and villagers got increasingly urbanized. In fact, the political and administrative changes that were introduced had an important effect on the urban and the rural social structure.

It is apparent that urbanization on a massive scale had taken place during the period under review. The whole of Kashmir rotated round the city of Srinagar. There had been a continuous and ever-increasing rural response to the urban challenge. Naturally, the city acted as a catalyst for socio-cultural change. Daily contact with diverse elements resulted in gradual transformation. The confirmed urbanite was poles apart from his rustic origin. The presence of a college, schools, hospitals and hotels in Srinagar meant a new kind of existence for the rural immigrants.

Thus, Srinagar did send ripples to distant corners of the valley of Kashmir. A new social mobility led to a new awakening. Like immigration to the city, there was also a reverse migration to the mofussil of professionals-teachers, lawyers and government servants. The outcome of this reciprocal pull between the city and the country, modernization of Kashmir, was well under way at the turn of the 20th century.

THE BRITISH IMPACT

While giving an account of the urbanization of Srinagar during the Dogra rule, the contribution of the British Residency to the city should not be lost sight of.

Kashmir, having been wrested from the Afghans by the Sikhs in 1819, was attached to the Punjab until the British occupation of Lahore in 1846, when it was handed over to the British Government in lieu of indemnity. Instead of retaining Kashmir, the British assigned it by the treaty of Amritsar dated March 16, 1846 to Gulab Singh,[124] the ruler of Jammu, in consideration of the valuable services he had rendered to the British during the Anglo-Sikh war.[125]

Maharaja Gulab Singh and his successor Ranbir Singh regarded Kashmir as their personal property. They banished every thought of reform and reconstruction from their mind. They showed little or no interest in the social uplift of their subjects.[126] But with the accession of Maharaja Pratap Singh in 1885 occurred a big change. His reign saw the establishment of British Residency in Srinagar. The new Maharaja like his predecessor, resisted this encroachment on his power, but ultimately yielded to the British.[127]

The British Resident in Srinagar carried with his title the same power, as that possessed by the British Residents at other courts. The British flag was hoisted at the Residency. All the British officers employed in the State were responsible to him. The Resident took an active part in the administration of the State affairs, and owing to the largely extended nature of his duties, was helped by an Assistant Resident.

During 1885-1910, the Residency with its charming garden was occupied by a succession of British Residents. The better known among them were Colonel Parry Nisbet, Sir David Barr, Sir Adelbert Talbot — whose period of office was marked by striking industrial developments. Sir Louis Dan, subsequently Lieutenant-Governor of the Punjab and Sir Francis Younghusband of Tibetan fame were other Residents. Some of the Residents were more sympathetic to the people than the rulers and were better administrators as well. They certainly proved an asset to the State and the people in general.

The transition from the medieval to the modern age is the keynote of Srinagar's history in the last decade of the 19th century. It ushered in those forces and movements in the political, religious, literary and economic life which have produced Srinagar of today. In the history of this transition, again, the improved transport in the country, as conceived by the Residents, had an important role.

The importance of transport in the development and progress of human civilization is now universally recognized. W. T. Jackman, while writing the history of the development of transport in modern Britain, lays much stress on the relation of transport "to the progress of agriculture, the growth of markets, the advance of industry, thc increase of wealth, and many other economic and social factors ..."[128]

Prior to the establishment of the British Residency in Srinagar, communications in Kashmir were primitive, country boats[129] along the rivers being the only means. The River Jhelum [130] was the main artery of commerce in Kashmir. The bulk of the internal commerce was carried along this natural highway. But there was one great limitation to river traffic. During the winter, when the Jhelum was low, it was less navigable and there was a comparative decline in river traffic. Owing to this it was very difficult to bring the heavy barges past the shoals, and the boatmen had to work hard, "often digging out a channel with their heart-shaped paddles".[131]

Lawrence writes: "There are roads along which ponies and bullocks can pass in fair weather, but roads as understood in other countries do no exist. The main roads at present connect Srinagar with Islamabad, Vernag and Jammu via the Banihal pass (9,200 feet) with Shupiyon, Bhimber and Gujrat in the Punjab via the Pir Panjal pass (11,400 feet) with Gandarbal at the mouth of the Sind Valley, and Ladakh via the Zojila pass (11,300 feet) with Bandipura and Gilgit via the Rajdiangan (11,700 feet) and Burzil (13,500 feet) or Kamri (13,101 feet) passes and with Baramulla, whence a cart road runs down the Jhelum valley to the Punjab".[132]

In good weather these roads were easy for the traveller, but heavy rains and snow rendered them difficult. The weak bridges over the side streams often tumbled during inundations.[133] The usual method of proceeding to Srinagar from Baramulla was by boat and it was twenty hours journey.[134] As such the boatmen of Baramulla and Srinagar were the chief transporters in the Valley.

Such was the condition of roads in the Valley in 1890. There was an absence of roads for wheeled traffic.[135] "Except low trollies resting on wheels, roughly fashioned from the round trunk of trees and used for carrying crops, there was no other kind of wheeled carriage in Kashmir".[136] Even in 1900, there was no road worth the name in Srinagar.[137]

The state of communications in the Valley on the advent of the British may be referred to here to show how far Kashmir lagged behind in this respect. Bad communications with the rest of India hindered the development of the commercial resources of the Valley.[138] Under such conditions the forced labour (*begar*) had to be resorted to for want of wheel traffic roads.[139] This state of affairs was the result of a complete lack of any constructive policy as regards the development of communications in Kashmir which characterized the greater part of the rule of Maharaja Gulab Singh and his successor.

In the Department of public works the British Residency gave prominence to opening up main lines of communications with the rest of India.[140] It was through Col. Nisbet's tact and energy that the Jhelum Valley cart-road was cut along the mountain-sides from Domel to Baramulla. It was a magnificent piece of engineering, the work of the State Engineer, Mr. Alkinson, and carried through by Spedding and Co. contractors.[141] This great work, commenced in the reign of Maharaja Ranbir Singh in 1880, was completed in September, 1890, when Maharaja Pratap Singh was driven through from Baramulla to Kohala on the borders of Jammu and Kashmir State. The Jhelum Valley road connected Srinagar with the rail-head at Rawalpindi.

The object of the British Indian Government in constructing the Jhelum Valley road has been misunderstood by some writers. Relying on Tyndale Biscoe, Bamzai attributes purely imperialistic motives to the British.[142] But humanitarian considerations also seem to be explicit in the correspondence between Col. Nisbet, the then Resident in Srinagar, and W.J. Cunningham, Secretary to the Government of India. Wrote the former: "The Jhelum Valley road will do more to develop the civilization, the trade, and the moral and material improvement of the Valley of Kashmir".[143]

The Jhelum Valley road ran 196 miles. One could travel in one day from Rawalpindi to Srinagar by motor and in about four days by tonga.[144]

It was most commonly used by travellers and was spoken of by competent judges as being one of the finest mountain roads in the world. The volume of trade also passed by this road in bullock carts and *ekkas*. [145]

EFFECTS OF THE JHELUM VALLEY ROAD

It goes without saying that as late as 1890 Srinagar was like a medieval city. Its old institutions still flourished, the ancient crafts were still the basis of its economy, and its imports and exports were carried by the coolies on their backs along the narrow unpaved lanes, flanked by high, wooden houses. But Srinagar could not remain a medieval city for ever. Two decades after 1890 saw the breakdown of its isolation, and on account of the impact of outside forces social and cultural changes came into being.

Firstly, the opening of the Jhelum Valley road[146] helped to diminish the isolation of the city from outside influences. Journeys to Srinagar by the English officers, travellers and missionaries became faster and more frequent.[147] After 1890 the British Indian Government sent to Kashmir several selected officers, both civil and military, to superintend the much-needed reforms in the administration of the country.[148] In half a century Srinagar under the fostering care of the Residents progressed. The habits and customs of generations began to change slowly. Srinagar was in a transitional state,[149] and "reforms of the most radical description" took place. In 1911 visitors returning to the city, after an absence of a few years, found many material improvements—new houses,[150] metalled roads, substantial masonary bridges, solid embankments and electric lights. Such changes at once struck the eye. But they only pointed to still greater reforms. The inauguration of the land settlement and reorganization of the Financial, Public Works, Postal Telegraph and Forest Departments contributed a great deal to the social and material uplift of the city's inhabitants.[151]

Under the able and inspiring guidance of the Residents and the British officers, vigorous measures were taken to prevent the recurrence of epidemics through improved sanitation of Srinagar.[152] In 1890, Col. Nisbet commenced a small project for the supply of pure water in the city.[153] Roads and streets were widened and paved, latrines built and arrangements for scavenging made.[154] Metalled roads with side drains were also constructed in different parts of the city, "with benefit to the passengers and householders as well as to sanitation.[155] The water works were completed under the skilful direction of Sir M. Nethersole. As a result of it, an ample supply of pure water was now available for every part of Srinagar.[156] The necessity for improved sanitation and trustworthy water supply was further recognised in Hari Singh's reign.[157] It was undoubtedly due to the improved sanitation that the cholera epidemics[158] of 1900-1907, 1914, 1919,1925 and 1929 "got so little footing in the city".[159]

Secondly, there was a large influx[160] of the Punjabis[161], 1925 into Srinagar for business or employment[162] — never for pleasure. In consequence, the predominance of the large Srinagar houses was weakened to the advantage of enterprising businessmen, officials, clerks and other new comers. Most of the Punjabi traders settled in the city permanently or semi-permanently. In Maharaja Bazar and Maharaj Gunj, the Punjabi businessmen established their trade monopoly[163] which continued before the advent of militancy in 1989. These bazars were centres for retail and wholesale business and import-export trade. Salt, sugar, tea, tobacco, snuff, seeds, cotton, metals etc. came to these markets mainly from the Punjab.

To other commercial centres of the Valley like Islamabad, Baramulla and Sopur,[164] Srinagar was an important centre of exchange. The Punjabi traders made the city one of the chief marts of the Valley and the centre for the collection and distribution of goods over a large region of Kashmir. The growth of trade[165] led to the mobility of the population. With other transportation facilities domestic trade grew by leaps and bounds, with more men participating in commercial transactions in the growing trade marts. With the extension of trade and commerce new centres of trade slowly came up. Hari Singh High Street,[166] Amira Kadal, and the Residency and the Government Central Market are such examples. New shops and offices necessitated the clearing away of buildings[167] that were less profitable as habitations and the resident population was pushed back farther and farther from the commercial centre. By 1936 Srinagar was transformed beyond recognition. The transformation is recorded by Moulvi Abdul Majid. The traveller divides Srinagar into two parts—old and new. While the former remained medieval, the latter had beautiful 'bungalows', big shops, factories, schools, colleges, hotels, clubs, cinemas, clean and wide metalled roads.[168].

With the growth of the internal market, as has already been noted, rural towns came up as a sort of a link between the metropolitan city of Srinagar and villages. Simultaneously, a rural-urban reciprocity was established and the flowering of a new cultural trend was clearly discernible. The Punjabi settlers' activities in Srinagar played no less a role in influencing the social life of its citizens.[169]

Thirdly, the road brought the threat of competition. Srinagar's artisans were now faced with great outside competition. But while some indigenous handicrafts of Srinagar like the manufacture of high quality paper declined because of competition from the mills of India, other handicrafts like the making of carpets, *namdahs*, *gabhas*, wood-carving etc. revived as a result of the development of road communications.[170]

An important consequence of the improved communications was the growth of the tourist industry.[171] The tourist industry greatly influenced the city economy. When a tourist visited Kashmir his expenses were mainly spread over transport, accommodation and purchase of local products. The benefits of transport industry were distributed among the bus operators who brought the tourists from outside, the local sight-seeing bus operators, boatmen (*hanjis*) and owners of the two-wheeled horse drawn vehicles (*tonga-wallas*). *Tongas*, *shikaras* and houseboats maintained the construction industry both for manufacture and repair work.

Another effect was the establishment of hotels and restaurants in the city. Hotels,[172] houseboats, and restaurants gave direct employment to cooks, bearers and other servants required to man these places. Additional employment was also generated in bakeries, laundaries, entertainment places, retailing trade etc. Considerable additional demand for food stuffs, vegetables, fruits, eggs, meat and milk was created which was met from local products. The visitors also bought local products which supported a large number of cottage and small scale industries engaged in making shawls, carpets, embroidery work, *gabhas*, *lois*, wood-carving, jewellery and papier-maché articles. Thus, the impact of tourism on Kashmir in general and Srinagar in particular was fairly widespread,[173] and the employment[174] created directly or indirectly through it was considerable.

NOTES:

1. Lt. R. G. Taylor, Assistant to the Resident at Lahore, was on deputation to Kashmir in 1847. We learn from him that Srinagar presented a very miserable appearance in 1847. As he records in his diary:

   "The houses made of wood and tumbling in every direction. The streets filthy for want of drainage. I saw the houses of the shawl weavers from the outside, and thought they looked miserable enough ..." He further notes that none of the bazars looked "well-filled and prosperous."

The Pather Masjid was used as a rice granary. *Lahore Political Dairies* 1847-1849, Vol 6, p. 37 (P.G.R.).

2. Sir Richard Temple who visited Srinagar in July 1859 remarks: " I asked (the Maharaja) whether Srinagar city could not be drained and cleaned and to this he answered , that the people did not appreciate conservancy and that they would much prefer to be dirty than to be at the trouble of cleaning the place. Such is always the idea of a native ruler." (*Journals kept in Hyderbabad, Kashmir, Sikhim and Nepal,* vol II p. 94).
3. Wakefield, *Op. cit.* p. 109; John Ince, *The Kashmir Handbook*, p. 128; Temple, *Op. cit.* I, p. 288; *Census,* 1891, p. 7.
4. Col. Harvey's report dated June 22, 1892 regarding insanitary conditions of the Srinagar city. NAI/Foreign,Extl A, sept. 1892, Nos. 102-115, p. 2; See also Major W. R. Edward's letter dt. Sept. 12, 1901 to the Resident in Kashmir. J & K/ G.R. File, No. 32 of 1901.
5. See NAI/Foreign, Extl A Sept, 1892, Nos. 102-115.
6. Cited in above.
7. "But", observes C.G. Bruce, " the temptation to build a city on a river is always a great one, the advantages are so numerous, and it gains in beauty what it loses in health." *Kashmir,* p. 32. W. Lawrence writes that considering the unhealthy surroundings of lakes and swamps of Srinagar and also its low lying position, " it is a matter of regret that some higher and more healthy side was not chosen." *Op. cit.* p. 35. See also Ernest Neve, *Beyond the Pir Panjal*, p. 310.
8. Major W.R. Edward's letter dt. Sept. 12, 1901 to the Resident in Kashmir. J & K (G.R.) File No. 32 of 1901.
9. There are many canals which intersect Srinagar. But the most important of these was till our own times the Nalla Mar, the snake canal. It connected the city with the Anchar lake and the Sindh Valley. The wonderful stone bridges and shady waterway of the canal were extermely beautiful. But, unfortunatly, the canal was full of dirt. The dreadful odour of the canal had become a source of great danger to the health of a great majority of the people of the city whose houses were located on the banks of the canal. This explains why this historical waterway after being filled up with earth is now known as the Nalla Mar road.
10. Harvey's report. NAI/Foreign, Extl A. Sept., 1892. Nos. 102-115, p. 2.
11. Biscoe, *Autobiography* p. 49; See also Bisoce, *Kashmir in Sunlight and Shade,* p. 125. Major General be Bourbel in his report on the epidemic of 1888 writes:

    "It is not too much to say that the inhabitants eat filth, sleep on it, bathe in it and are steeped in it, and surrounded by it on every side." NAI/Foreign, Extl. A. Sept., 1892. Nos. 102-115, p.2

    The deplorable insanitary condition still prevails in some old *mohallas* of the city. The entire drainage sytem in the traditional part of Srinagar is defective. The sweepers empty the night soil pots directy into the drains. During rains the drains overflow—creating indescribable mess and stink.Thus a street in old Srinagar has generally become thriving ground for flies, mosquitoes and other dirty insects.

12. Ernest Neve, *Op. cit.* pp. 275-76.
13. Ibid; NAI/Foreign, Extl. A. Sept., 1892, Nos. 102-115, p.2; Lawrence, Ibid. p. 34. Regarding the diseases of the people of Kashmir, Dr. Ernest Neve remarks : "Their ailments are very various. Some have old-standing indigestion of chronic coughs. Other are suffering from opthalmia or from various parasitic disease. The latter are largely propagated by infected drinking water. And young children are specially liable to suffer. Skin diseases, too, largly due to dirt, abound." *Op. cit.* p.163.
14. "If Srinagar wants anything, it is the cleaning of its streets." *The Amrit Bazar Patrika,* Jan., 30, 1890. See also NAI/Foreign, Sec. E, Dec., 1890, Nos. 232-242; Wakefield, *Op. cit.* p. 92; John Ince, *Op. cit.* p. 128. Since this book was first published in 1978, the Government attempted to make the traditional part of the city more habitable in the light of my criticism of the existing insanitary conditions. Notwithstanding the measures taken for cleaning up the mess by providing suitably located garbage dumps and widening of the drains, much remains to be done.
15. W. D. Mar, *The Romantic East*, p. 161.
16. Lawrence, *Op. cit.* p. 219.
17. Ibid., p. 218; See also copy of a letter No. 690 dt. May 17, 1888 from the Resident in Kashmir to the Council of Kashmir State (MS), NAI/ Foreign, Extl. B., June 1886, Nos. 213/215.
18. Qouted in A.K. Bamzai, *Geography of Jammu and Kashmir,* pp. 44-45.
19. See *Beyond the Pir Panjal,* p. 272; See also Shephered, *Arthur Neve of Kashmir,* pp. 55-56.
20. Lawrence, *Op. cit.* pp. 219-220.
21. Ibid., p. 218.
22. See the *Vakil,* Amritsar, dated August 26, 1901 *(Report on Native Newspaper,* Punjab 1901, p. 537); Mir Saif Ullah, *Tarikh-nama Kashmir*, p. 83.
23. The ancient name of Maisuma was Maksikasvamin. *Rajat* (Stein) Book II, V. No.88 and note. "From the way it is referred to by Kalhana, it appears that it was already partly inhabited in old times." *Ibid.,* IIp. 450. It was not until the close of the last century that the great island of Maisuma began to be chiefly occupied by the houses and camps of European residents and visitors.
24. Report of the Chief Medical Officer of Kashmir, NAI/Foreign and Political Department, Gen. B. April, 1915, Nos. 86-96.
25. Ibid., NAI/Foreign, Extl. B., June 1888. Nos. 213-215.
26. Ibid., Bates, p. 17; See also chapter on Social Life.
27. Lawrence, *Op. cit.* 205 Sqq; *The Punjab Gazette*, Sialkot, June 11, 1892 (*Report on the Native Newspapers*, Punjab 1892, p. 117); *Sirmur Gazette*,

Aug. 1, 1892 (*Ibid.*, 1892, p. 280).

28. Mirza Saif-ud-Din, *Akhbarat,* Vol. I, 1847, f. 31; Vol. III, 1850, ff. 116a, 146a; Vol. V, 1852, ff. 67a, 73b, 95b ; Mir Saif Ullah, *Op. cit.* pp. 89-90 ; Khalil Mirjanpuri, *Tarikh-i-Kashmir,* II, p. 313.
29. NAI/Foreign, Extl. A, Sept., 1892, Nos 102-115; Lawrence, *Op. cit.* pp. 214-215. See also Bates, p. 17.
30. Lawrence, *Op. cit.* p. 204; Pir Hasan, *Tarikh,* I, pp. 476-79.
31. Lawrence, *Op. cit.* p. 204.
32. Ibid., See also Mirjanpuri, *Op. cit.* II, p. 315; Mir Saif Ullah, *Op. cit.* pp. 96-97.
33. Lawrence, *Op. cit.* p. 204.
34. The Earl of Dunmore, *The Pamirs,* I, p. 48.
35. Ibid.
36. *Rajat* (Stein) BK VII. Vs. 1219, 1624; Bk. VIII, Vs. 2449, 2786, 1417, 1422. Pir Hasan, *Op. cit.* I, pp. 473-476.
37. Ghulam Nabi Khanyari, *Wajeez-ut-Tawarikh,* f. 73b; Lawrence, *Op. cit.* p. 209.
38. Lawrence, *Op. cit.* p. 209.
39. Arthur Neve, *The Tourist Guide to Kashmir, Ladakh, Skardo etc.*, p. VII; Norris Dermot, *Kashmir : The Switzerland of India*, p. 8; *Census Report* (J & K), l, p. 13; See also Younghusband, *Kashmir*, p. 164; *Report with regard to the floods in Jammu and Kashmir*, 1928, pp. 7 Sqq; Capt. R.G. Wreford, *Report on State Granaries, Srinagar*, 1927-28, pp. 11 Sqq.
40. Henvy's note on famines, NAI/Foreign, Sec. E, Mar. 1883, No. 86; Foreign, A Pol E, Sept., 1882, Nos. 253-265; Foreign, Sec. E, Mar., 1883, Nos. 83-85; Fanshawes' note on famines, NAI/Foreign Sec. E. Mar., 1883, Nos. 81-82; Col Nisbet's letter to the Secretary to the Government of India, NAI/Foreign, Sec. E. Feb., 1891, Nos. 295-326; See also A.K. Bamzai, *Geography of Jammu and Kashmir State*, p. 40; *Beyond the Pir Panjal*, p.265; Knight, *Where Three Empires Meet,* p. 44; , *Thrity Years in Kashmir*, p. 31; Hasan, *Op. cit.* l, pp. 463-65; Walter Lawrence, *The India We Served*, p. 126. *Sirmur Gazette,* Aug. 15, 1892, (*Report on Native Newspapers,* Punjab, 1892, p. 280).
41. Nearly three-fifths of Kashmir's population was affected by the catastrophe. (*Punjab Adminstration Reports,* 1878-79, pp. 2-3; See also W. Barton, *The Princes of India,* p. 122). The Anglo-Indian as well as the British press largely ascribed it to the maladminstration of the bureaucracy of Kashmir. While some suggested the annexation of the 'the Happy Valley' in the name of humanity, others impressed upon the British Government the need of intervening in the affairs of Kashmir so as to render some immediate relief to the people. (*Civil and Military Gazette,* 5 Sept., 1878, p. 1; *Friend of India*, 17 Sept., 1879). The official reaction to the horrid incident was equally strongly marked as is evident

from the fact that Crankbrook was shocked at the reports of Kashmir misgovernment during the famine (Crankbrook to Lytton, 5 Oct. 1879, Lytton papers, 518/4, No. 81). Also, both Henvy, the Officer On Special Duty in Kashmir, & Lyall, Lytton's Foreign Secretary, urged "immediate and effective intervention." (Lytton to Egerton, Dec. 2, 1879, Lytton Papers/518/4 pp. 1065-76).

42. Lawrence, *op. cit.* p. 213. Younghusband writes that "some suburbs of Srinagar were tenantless, and the city itself was half destroyed." Trade almost came to a standstill. In consequence, "employement was difficult to obtain." *Op. cit.,* pp.162-63; See also Fanshawes' note on famine, NA/ Foreign. Sec. E, Mar. 1883, Nos. 81-82, p.9.
43. Lawrence, *op-cit.,*p. 215; Khalil Mirjanpuri, *op. cit.* II p. 314.
44. *Beyond the Pir Panjal,* p. 265.
45. Ibid., page-19; J&K (G.R) F.No.278/p-16 (1915)
46. The scarcity of grains often resulted in a hullabaloo in the city. *Wajeez-ut-Tawarikh,* ff. 65a, 71a, 73a; See also Mirza Saif-ud-din, *op. cit.* Vol. V, 1852, ff. 67; 73b, 95b, vol.III, 1850, 116a, 146a; Mir Saif Ullah, *op. cit.* pp. 89-90, 98. Many Kashmiris are stated to have arrived in Lahore in January 1848 having been driven from the valley by the high price of grain. *Lahore Political Diaries,* 1847-1848, Vol III (P.G.R.), p. 411. The famine of 1877-79 also forced many starving Kashmiris to migrate to the Punjab. See Administration Reports from Punjab, NAI/Foreign, K.W. Pol. A. Sept. 1879, Nos. 63-69, p. 2; also Durbin, Lahore, May 1, 1892 (*Report on Native Newspapers,* Punjab 1892, 8. 128).
47. Younghusband, *op. cit.* p. 163; Arthur Neve, *Thirty Years in Kashmir,* p. 30.
48. Mirza Saif-ud-din, *op. cit.* Vol. I, 1847, f. 31, Vol V, 1852, f. 1852, f. 73b; Col. Nisbet's letter dated Jan. 1891, Nos. 295-326, p. 16; Fanshawe's note on famine, NAI/Foreign Sec. E, Mar. 1883. Nos. 81-82, p. 13; Bamzai, *Geography,* p. 40.
49. Mirza Saif-ud-din, *op. cit.* Vol. I, 1847, f. 31; *Where Three Empires Meet,* p. 43; Mir Saif Ullah, *op. cit.* pp. 98, 89-90. Revenue Members Note, NAI/Foreign, Extl. A, Aug. 1903, Nos. 94-101, pp. 27-28.

Speaking of 1878, Mr. Wade says : Today I have ridden through a great part of the city, and I saw a large number of persons, especially children and women, whom death certainly has marked for his own very shortly. A half-dozen times I tried to buy and distribute some kulchas—small cakes made of the flour of Indian corn, rice or wheat—and was as often mobbed. Poor children crept from underneath the verandah boards of closed shops, and others from holes and corners that pariah dogs generally occupy, and sourrounded my pony. Parda women, and apparently most respectable men, stopped and begged and struggled for a piece of bread. I found it impossible to keep the people from thronging me or to maintain anything like order. Directly I obtained kulchas, the hungry pressed upon me, the stronger pushing aside the weaker, and all reaching forth their hands, and begging or screaming, they laid hold of my coat. They took bread out of my pockets. Two men with baskets of bread, from whom I attempted to purchase some, were besieged and their bread speedily seized and eaten. After having paid for the bread, I made my escape by riding as fast as I could away from the hungry crowd." (Quoted in *Beyond the Pir Panjal,* pp. 265-66.)

50. NAI/Foreign, pol. July 1863, Nos. 73-75, p. 9; Foreign, DSept. 1882, A Pol.E. Nos. 253-265 A; Extracts from a demi-official letter (Ms.) from Hon'ble Lawrence to Secretary dt. Nov. 1846, NAI/Foreign, Sec. Cons, 26 Dec. 1846, Nos. 1240-41 and K.W.: *Papers relating to Kashmir presented to both Houses of Pariliament, London,* 1890, p. 20; Copy of a note by the Revenue Member, Kashmir State Council, on high prices of Shali in Srinagar, NAI/Foreign, Extl A, 1903, Nos. 94-101. p. 6; Also see *Beyond the Pir Panjal*, p. 31; Bates, *Op. cit.,* p.17; Ganesh Lal, *Siyahat-i-Kashmir,* p. 32.
51. NAI/Foreign, Pul, July 1863, Nos. 73-75. p. 9; See also J & K, File No. 15 of 1846 (P.R). J & K., File No. 138-L (P.R).
52. NAI/Foreign, Pol. July 1863, Nos 73-75. p. 9 .
53. Ibid., p.4.
54. Lawrence, *Op. cit.*, p., p. 225 ; Bates, *Op. cit.,* p.355.
55. Lawrence, *Op. cit.*, p.35; Census, 1891, 1,p.10.
56. Lawrence, *Op. cit.*, p.225. For the system of forced labour in Kashmir, see Ishaq Khan, "Some Aspects of Corvee in Kashmir" (*Research Biannual*, Vol.1, No.11, 1976, pp.58-71), See also Appendix A.
57. *Census*, I, 1891, p.10; See Subsidiary Table III, *Census*, I, 1901, p. 20.
58. *Lahore Political Diaries*, 1847-1849, Vol, VI, p.37.
59. Wakefield, *op. cit.*, pp. 94-95; Drew, *op. cit.*, pp. 183-184; Knight, *Diary of a Pedestrian in Cashmere and Tibet*, p.10; *op. cit.,* p. 353.
60. Bates, *op. cit.,* 353.
61. Ibid; see also Biscoe, *Autobiography*, p.49; *Where Three Empires Meet*, p.36; Petrocokino, *Three Weeks in a Houseboat*, p.21; Younghusband, *op. cit.,* p, 52.
62. Bates, *op. cit.,* p.38; *Beyond the Pir Panjal*, p.241; H.W. Bellew, *Kashmir and Kashgar*, p.62; Younghusband, *op. cit.,* p.53.
63. Ibid.
64. Bellew, *op. cit.,* p.62.
65. Biscoe, *Autobiography*, p.49; *Kashmir in Sunlight and Shade*, p.108.
66. Bates, *op. cit.,* p.38.
67. Schonberg, *op. cit.,* II, p.7.
68. Bates, *op. cit.,* p.38.
69. Temple, *op. cit.,* I, p.288.
70. Biscoe, *Autobiography*, p.49; Prinsep, *Imperial India*, p.212.
71. Lawrence, *op. cit.,* p.35.

72. *Ganga Nath Report*, p.309.
73. Narsingh Das, *Tarikh-i-Dogra Desh*, p.709.
74. Ibid.
75. Ibid; *Ganga Nath Report*, p.309.
76. Narsingh Das, *op. cit.*, p.709.
77. *Annual Administration Report of the Municipalities, Town Areas and Visitors Bureau Departments*, 1940, p.37; *Ibid.*, 1942, p.25.
78. *Ganga Nath Report*, p.309.
79. See, for example, Gillon, *Ahmedabad*, p.25.
80. *Report on Sanitation of the Srinagar City* by Sardar Muhammad Hyat Khan (1893), p.6; NAI/Foreign, Extl. A. Sept. 1892, Nos. 102-115, p.9; Denys, *Our Summer in the Vale of Kashmir*, p.168.
81. *Report on Sanitation of the Srinagar City* (1893), p.6.
82. Ibid.
83. *Kashmir in Sunlight and Shade*, pp.63, 125.
84. Ibid., pp.63-64.
85. "Any real sanitation requires the intelligent cooperation of the people, who as a whole seem as opposed to sanitary reform as to religious changes; they (people of Srinagar)seem as wedded to their primitive dirty habits as to their superstitions ..." Quoted in Denys, *op. cit.*, p.168.
86. *Kashmir in Sunlight and Shade*, p.151.
87. *Ganga Nath Report*, pp.90-91; See also *Annual Administration Reports of the Jammu and Srinagar Municipalities, Town area and Visitors Bureau* (1940-1942).
88. *Annual Administration Report of the Jammu and Srinagar Municipalities, Town Planning and Public Health Deptts.*, 1945, p.4.
89. *Ganga Nath Report*, pp.90-91.
90. Ibid.
91. *P.A. Koul, Report on the Municipal Administration of Srinagar*, 1920-1921, p.7.
92. Ibid.
93. NAI/Foreign and Pol. Genl B. April 1915, Nos. 86-96.
94. *The Tribune*, Oct. 10, 1931; *Ganga Nath Report*, pp.90-91.
95. *Report on the Municipal Administration of Srinagar*, 1920-21, p.7.
96. Ibid.
97. Lawrence, *op. cit.*, p.225.
98. *Census*, 1891, I, p.7.
99. Ibid., 1911, I, p.33.
100. *Report on the Municipal Administration of Srinagar*, 1920-21, p.1.
101. The modern name Buchvor or Buchwara has been derived from Kalhana's Bhuksiravatika. King Gopaditya is said to have removed the Brahmans to this place who had given offence by eating garlic, *Rajat* (Stein), BK. I, Note. 342, 343.
102. J&K (G.R), File No-254/P. 25 of 1915; See also J&K (G.R), File No,

263/p-7 of 1915.

103. J&K (G.R), File No. 263/P.7 of 1915.
104. P. A. Koul, *Report on the Municipal Administration of Srinagar* (1920-21), p.1.
105. Ibid.
106. *Census*, 1931, 1, p.8.
107. *Administration Report of J&K* (16 Oct. 1941 to 12 April, 1943), p.4.
108. *Ganga Nath Report*, p.88.
109. Barclay, *Techniques of Population Analysis*, p.241.
110. Ibid.
111. Breese, *Urbanization in newly Developing Countries* p.3.
112. Barclay, *op. cit.*, p.258.
113. Lawrence, *op. cit.*, p.225.
114. *Vide* Chapter VI, *Christian Missionaries and the Western Impact.*
115. *Census*, 1911. I, p.32.
116. Ibid., 1931, I, pp.224-225.
117. *Census*, 1911, I, p.32.
118. Ibid., 1901, I, p.11.
119. Ibid.
120. It is difficult to form any accurate idea of the population of Srinagar before the census of 1891 in view of conflicting reports. According to one estimate, the population of the city was 81,153 in 1863. NAI/Foreign, Political, July 1863, Nos. 73-73. Lawrence says that in 1868 the population of Srinagar consisted of 1,12,715 persons of whom 24,945 were Hindus and 87,770 Muslims (*op. cit.*, p.225). Writing in the sixties of the last century, Sir Richard Temple estimated the population at 1,32,000 (*op. cit.*, I, p.277). Wakefield and Bates computed the population at 1,50,000 souls (*The Happy Valley*, p.96; *Gazetteer*, p.355). Dr. Elmslie, who stayed in Srinagar for six years as a medical missionary, computed the population at 1,27,400 in 1873 (See Lawrence, *op. cit.*, p.224; Bates, *op. cit.*, pp.29-30).
121. *Census*, 1941, I, p.92.
122. *Techno-Economic Survey of J&K State*, p.236.
123. It was the village of Lussjan, five miles from Srinagar, which supplied a large amount of milk, curds etc. to the city. See the letter of the Residency Surgeon in Kashmir and Superintendent Surgeon, J&K State Hospitals, to the First Asstt. to the Resident in Kashmir, dated Sept.1914, NAI/No. 3239, Foreign and Pol. Genl B, April 1915, Nos. 86-96. Chashmashahi, Pampore, Chattabal, Hazratbal etc. were other suppliers of milk to Srinagar.
124. C.U. Aitchison, *Treaties Engagements and Sanads*, Vol. XII, pp. 21-22; Gulab Singh entered Srinagr on November 9, 1946. See No. 335, Nov. 12, 1846, Vol. IX (P.G.R.); *Wajeez-ul-Tawarikh*, f. 61 b; See also Mir Ullah, *op, cit., pp.* 50-51 and 53.

125. Arthur Brinckman, *Wrongs of Kasmir,* Chapter II, p. 11; *Were Three Empires Meet*, p. 28; Digby *Condemned Unheard.*
126. Despatch to Secret Committee (MS.), NAI/Foreign, 22 Jan. 1848, No. 10; Foreign Sec. 28 Jan. 1848, Nos. 41-42; p. 7; Nibets Letter to the Secretary to the Government of India, dated March 16, 1889-Foreign, Sec, E, April 1889, Nos. 80-98, p. 7; Papers relating to Kashmir affairs, Foreign, Sec. e. Aug. 1989 Nos. 162-203, p.27; Brinckman, *op. cit.,* Chapter I, Temple, *op. cit.,* I, p. 320. Lawrence, *The India We Served,* p. 128; Knight, *Diary*, p. 82; *Torrens Travels in Ladakh Tartary and Kashmir*, p. 301, Schonberg, *op. cit.*, II, p. 8.
127. For details, see *Condemned Unheard*; D. K. Ghose, *Kashmir in Transition.*
128. Jackman, *Development of Transportion in England,* preface p. xxxi.
129. That boats were in old days, just as up to the middle of the present century, the ordinary means of travel in the Valley in shown by the frequent references to river journeys in the chronicles and travelogues.
130. For the importance of the navigable waters of the River Jhelum, see *Rajat* (Setin), II, p. 414.
131. Lawrence, *op. cit.*, p. 383.
132. Ibid., p. 23.
133. Ibid.
134. *Where Three Empires Meet*, p. 20.
135. *Beyond the Pir Panjal,* p. 240; Wakefield, *op. cit.*, p. 92; Eckenstein, *The Karakorams and Kashmir*, p. 236; *Kashmir in Sunlight and Shade*, pp. 64-65.
136. P. N. Bamzai, *History of Kashmir,* p. 636; Lawrence, *op. cit., p. 23.*
137. *Beyond the Pir Panjal, p. 240.*
138. Arthur Neve and Ernest Neve, *The Tourist Guide to Kashmir, Skardoo* etc., p.v.
139. Younghusband, *op. cit.*, p. 159; *Administration Report of J&K Government* (1923-1924), p. 2.
140. W. J. Cunningham's letter to the Resident in Kashmir, dated Feb. 22, 1890. NAI/Foreign, Sec. E, Feb. 1891, Nos. 295-326, p. 24.
141. *Kashmir in Sunlight and Shade,* p. 76; *Where Three Empires Meet,* p. 9.
142. *History of Kashmir,* p. 636.
143. NAI/Foreign, Feb. 1891, Sec. E, 295-326, p. 15. Earlier in 1883, Colonel Oliver St. John, the then Officer on Special Duty in Kashmir, had emphasized the importance of the road in no unambiguous terms:-

    "Indeed if nothing else be done the road alone must make a vast change in Kashmir." St. John to Ripon, 22 July, 1883, Ripon Papers/ Add. MSS. 43613, ff, 74-83.
144. It had two wheels, was drawn by a pair of ponies, had four seats, back to back, and carried "a mountain of luggage piled upon the splash-boards and the roof." Younghusband, *Op. cit.*, p. 42.

145. A. K. Bamzai, *Geography,* p. 27.
146. The Banihal cart road formally opened to traffic in 1923. It also attracted a great deal of trade traffic between the Punjab and Srinagar. *Administration Report of Jammu and Kashmir Government* (1923-1924), p.2
147. *Census*, 1941, p.27.
148. *Where Three Empires Meet,* p. 28.
149. Ibid., p. 42.
150. Under the influence of the British tourists and officials there sprang up many mansions of the English villa type in Srinagar along the 'Bund' and behind it. They were "all in much the same style, built of brick and cross-beams of wood with gable roofs." The Residency itself was described by Sir Francis Younghusband as "a regular English country house." (*op. cit.,* pp. 55-56). The construction of new buildings introduced a new trend in the building art. Consequently, we find a curious synthesis "of the Muslim arch and the English steeped roofs in some of the building of Srinagar."
151. *Beyond the Pir Punjal,* p. 308 See also note on Kashmir affairs, NAI/ Foreign and Pol. deposit-Internal, pros. Oct 1921, Nos, 38, p. 6.
152. Knight writes. "People (of Srinagar) were bathing at all the ghauts. The water of these cannals appears too filthy even to bathe in, and yet the population of this great capital entirely relies on it for drinking purposes. That cholera plays fearful havoc here occassionally is not to be wondered." *Op. cit.,* p.89. In 1888, thousands of people in the city are said to have died of cholera from drinking the water of the Jhelum. Col. Nisbet on water supply, NAI/Foreign, Feb. 1891, Sec. E, 295-326, p.58.
153. Col. Nisbet's letter to the Secretary to the Government of India, dated 29 Jan. 1890, NAI/Foreign, Sec. E, Feb, 1891, Nos. 295-326, p. 58; Bamzai, *Geography,* Shephered, *Arthur Neve of Kashmir,* p. 96.
154. NAI/Foreign, 1892, Extl. A, 102-115, p.4, J&K (G.R.), File No 32, 1901; Bamzai, *Geography*, p.44.
155. Arthur Neve, *The Tourist Guide to Kashmir, Ladakh, Skardo etc.* p. vii.
156. Ibid; See also abbreviated General Synopsis of the Administration of the J&K State for the year 1921, NAI/Foreign and Pol. General, File No. 165-G, Serial Nos. 1-19.
157. *The Tribune,* Jan. 28, 1931.
158. The following table shows that the epidemic of cholera was on the decline;

YEAR	TOTAL NUMBER OF CHOLERA CASES IN SRINAGAR	TOTAL NUMBER OF DEATHS IN SRINAGAR
1910	2,125	959
1914	1,112	600

Vide Report of the Chief Medical Officer in Kashmir (1914), NAI/ Foreign, and Pol. Genl. B, April 1915, Nos. 86-96.

159. Neve, *The Tourist Guide*, p. vii; See also Shephered, *op. cit.*, p.96.

160. Col. Hendersons' letter dt. 4 Nov. 1889 to W.J. Cunningham, NAI/ Foreign Sec. E, Jan. 1981, Nos. 118-20.

Henvy's note on famine, NAI/Foreign, Sec. E, Mar. 1883, No. 86, p.86, p.40; Confidential note on Kashmir Affairs for 1907-08 by Major Francis Younghusband, NAI/Foreign, July 1908. Sec. I, p.51.

161. The Punjabis reside chiefly in Srinagar and still preserve their linguistic and cultural identity, though it is not uncommon to see some of the Punjabis speaking Kashmiri language and wearing Kashmiri dress.

162. Maharaja Ranbir Singh and Maharaja Pratap Singh's chief officers are said to have been the 'Natives of the Punjab'. There was a distinct tendency among them to secure Kashmir not for the Kashmiris but for the Punjabis. While writing about the Punjabi importation into Kashmir Col.P.D.Henderson, C.S.I. in his letter dt. Nov.4,1889 to W.J.Cunningham remarked : "Whenever any officer is selected from Punjab for service in this state, he leaves word with his friends and relatives and calls them over as soon as he joins his new appointment." NAI/Foreign, sec. E. Mar 1883 NO; 86, p 40: Foreign Pol. July 1863, Nos. 73-75, p. 9: Confidential note on Kashmir Affairs for 1907-08 by Major Sir Francis Younghusband, Foreign, Sec. 1 July 1908: p. 51. Foreign Sec. E. Jan, 1891: Nos 119-120.

163. *Census* 1931, I.p. 89; *The Ranbir*. Oct. I, 1929; Jan 18, 1937; Kilam, *History of Kashmiri Pandits*, p. 278; Majid, *Sair-i-Kashmir*, pp. 22-24.

164. Sopur of ancient 'Suyyapura' (Lat. 34° 17' Long 74° 31') founded by Avantivarman's minister Suyya (Stein, *Rajat*, Book, V, 118 n) is a large and flourishing town built on both sides of the Jhelum a few miles below the point where it leaves the Wular lake (Bates, *op. cit.*, pp. 351-52; Stein, *Ancient Geography*, para 128). For description of the town, see Moorcroft, *op. cit.*, II, p. 230; Baron Hugel, *Travels in Kashmir and Punjab*, I, p. 357, Ince, *op. cit.*, p. 220.

165. See *Census*, 1931, I, p.33.

166. *The Ranbir*, April 15, 1935.

167. Ibid.,Feb. 7, 1928.

168. Majid, *op. cit.*, p. 20.

169. It is worthwhile to note that in the *Dusserah* celebrations at Hazuri Bagh in Srinagar, the participation of the Muslims was always significant.

170. Census, 1941, I, p. 24

171. The following table shows the number the number of incomming tourists in the Valley during 1940-1944.

Year	Indian *Tourists*	Foreign *Tourists*	Total
1940	20,831	8,106	28,937
1941	21,161	8,165	39,326
1942	18,005	10,666	18,671
1943	14,525	12,953	27,478
1944	15,101	18,575	33,676
1945	18,407	18,890	37,297

172. It will not be out of place to mention here that the present author's father Ghulam Ahmed Khan and his two uncles Abdul Ahad Khan and Haji Ghulam Mohammad Khan were among the few local pioneers of hotel industry in Srinagar. Before the Partition of the subcontinent they first owned Kashmir Muslim Hotel and later Kashmir Guest House at Lal Chowk in Srinagar. The latter remained a rendezevous of many social and political activists, including some State and Union Ministers of Kashmiri origin, till 1978.

173. See J&K (G.R.), F. No. 139 of 1902.

174. See Lawrence, *op. cit.,* p. 202.

CHAPTER III

INDUSTRIES AND OCCUPATIONS

Kashmir has earned a world-wide reputation for its handicrafts. But this reputation rests chiefly on the city of Srinagar which, from ancient times, has been a centre of trade and industry.

Though we don't have any conclusive evidence regarding the origin of the existing arts and crafts of Srinagar, it appears that the great King Sultan Zain-ul-Abidin revived the industries which had either disappeared or declined, and at the same time introduced new ones.[1] That the famous arts and crafts of Srinagar owe their existence to Sultan Zain-ul-Abidin is evidenced by the glowing tributes which were paid to him by medieval historians of Kashmir,[2] including Mirza Haidar[3] who ruled Kashmir for ten years.

Stone-polishing, stone-cutting, glass blowing, window-cutting, wood-cutting, wood-carving, paper making, gold and silver leaf-making, book-binding, papier-maché, and silk, shawl and carpet weaving were introduced by Zain-ul-Abidin.[4] It is said that these arts and crafts developed and flourished under the fostering care of the Sultan whose patronage attracted master artisans from Samarqand, Bukhara and Persia.[5] According to Srivara, the Sultan provided all amenities of life to these foreign craftsmen and they popularised their arts and crafts among the Kashmiris.[6]

SILVERWARE

The traditional artistic bent of mind of the Kashmiri artisan exhibits itself in diverse forms. The production of silverware is one of them. Silver goods have been prized from time immemorial since they have been in a great demand by the artistocracy. The silverware of Srinagar was renowned for its beauty and form. The gold and silversmiths of Srinagar being very clever at their trade, produced admirable works, great quantities of which found their way to England by 1879.[7] As Wakefield remarks:

"In gold they (smiths) fashion the usual articles of jewellery as seen at home, but it is in the silver articles they display more of what may be termed native taste."[8]

The silverware of Srinagar was so well known abroad that every traveller made a point of carrying back a memento of his visit in the form of one article or another of silver.[9]

Wakefield speaks of trays, goblets, jugs, tea-cups and scent-holders being produced by silversmiths in the seventies of the last century.[10] But by 1938 tea and dinner sets (complete or in parts), coffee-sets, tumblers, boxes, cigar and cigarette cases, toilet cases, mirror and picture frames, combs, flower vases, betel-leaf trays, betel cases, toys for children like houseboats etc. stands for different purposes, Indian and Kashmiri dining sets like *thalies*, *katories*, *samavar*, jugs etc. were also manufactured.[11]

In modern times foreign catalogues of wares were also consulted by silversmiths for manufacturing articles of new designs.[12] In engraving, chinar pattern, Persian pattern, lotus pattern etc. were common designs.[13] But the best silver work which was of the old shawl pattern,[14] began to be replaced by European tea-sets in the second decade of this century.[15] However, in the 'thirties of this century, the silversmiths realised the popularity of the shawl pattern and they responded to the popular demand for it.[16]

By 1921 every silversmith possessed electro-plating apparatus which he employed on white metals.

The following classes of workmen were engaged in the manufacture of silverware .

i) Smiths (*khar*)
ii) Engravers (*naqash*)
iii) Gilders (*zarkob*)
iv) Polishers (*roshangar*)
v) Cleaner (*charkgar*)

Formerly these artisans occupied exclusively selected localities or *mohallas* in the city of Srinagar and some of the *mohallas* were even named after them. Roshangar *mohalla* was for polishers. Hazari Bazar and the *mohalla* of Jama Masjid was occupied by smiths. But by 1938 these artisans seem to have scattered all over the city.[17] The reasons for this change are not far to seek. The increasing tourist traffic[18] to Srinagar must have impressed upon the minds of silver traders the need for establishing shops in other parts of the city.

The statistics regarding the number of workers engaged in silver work are not available before 1938. According to the Report on the Economic Survey of the Silverware Industry, in 1938 the whole industry and trade afforded employment to 290 active workers, 1002 dependents, i.e. 1292 in all. This number excludes clerks, sales agents and those engaged in the transport of silver products. In 1938 the total number of establishments was 66 according to the survey conducted by Dr. Bhan, and out of which the largest number viz., 50 comprised those where the number of workers was less than five.[19]

The workmen comprised people of all ages and skill who worked in different establishments, headed by master workmen (*ustads*). The merchants were the middlemen between the producers and consumers. These big dealers or manufacturers, who financed the silver industry and trade, gave raw material to smiths. After the smiths had finished their job, the silver articles were sent by the merchants to engravers and thence to polishers. The third process of cleaning was done by *charkgars*, 'especially in the case of plain silverware'.[20]

Thus the five classes of workmen namely smiths, engravers, gilders, polishers and cleaners were exploited by the middlemen and their wages were determined by them. A number of workers worked generally together under the direction and supervision of their master who was responsible to the manufacturer for the efficient completion of work. Generally the workshops were run in a rented house, though there were some of the workmen who worked single-headed or sought the help of the members of their families at their own houses. There were a few merchants who got work executed under their own supervision.[21]

The artisans of silverware generally followed hereditary occupations. Dr.Bhan states that silversmiths were originally blacksmiths and gunmakers. "With the decrease in the demand for gunmaking these workmen took to the production of silverware. Engravers and other workers have inherited their art. No new entrant is allowed in the trade from among people not belonging to it. The smiths have a strong prejudice in this respect though engravers may train people belonging to other classes also". Thus there was a kind of "caste system in existence".[22] The standard of living of silversmiths was low. Since the work did not continue uniformly over the whole year, the artisans were reduced to debt on account of unemployment.[23]

It is to be noted that all the classes of artisans were in debt. In fact, the master workmen were more in debt than the ordinary workers. They would borrow from Cooperative Credit Societies, money lenders, firm owners, shopkeepers and relatives. Social and religious ceremonies, illness, litigation, unemployment or less employment, ancestral debt, building or repairing of a house and a change of business connections from one firm owner to another, necessitated the taking of advances.[24] This also accounts for the indebtedness of each class of workers.

There was no labour organization which would take care of the general interests of the trade. The physical health of the engravers in particular was not good.[25] Under such conditions they had no initiative to make any substantial improvement in the quality of their work. Nor did they attempt to introduce new designs.[26]

It is unfortunate that the workers did not get higher wages. It is worthwhile to note that the work of the engravers, though demanding more skill and artistic effort than that of the smiths, did not carry higher wages. In 1938, for example, the smiths and the engravers earned from Rs.25 to Rs.40 per month, while the ordinary workers like gilders, polishers and cleaners earned only Rs.10 to Rs.18 per month.[27] The introduction of polishing machines gave a blow to the polishers.[28] The polishers had inherited this profession from generations in the Roshangar *mohalla* of Srinagar. But they were greatly hit by the introduction of machinery. By 1938 they were living in abject poverty and depended "now on other allied occupations, such as the sharpening of tools (*kharan*)."[29]

It is interesting to note that in spite of the low standard of living, the silverware artisans like other classes of Kashmir workmen enjoyed holidays in *doongas*[30] and gardens. We are told that for this purpose big groups of artisans pooled "together their small contributions."[31]

COPPER WORK

Writing in the nineties of the last century, Lawrence observes: "Perhaps the most effective and certainly the best value for the money is the copper work of Srinagar."[32] The copper-smiths worked with both brass and copper, and used hammer and the chisel. It appears from the study of Lawrence that many of the copper-smiths of his times were once silversmiths.[33] Their designs were very elegant, bold and original. They were ever ready to adopt any new pattern that was offered to them. According to Lawrence, the copper work of Srinagar was admirably adapted for electro-plating. Even during his time some copper-smiths of Srinagar produced a beautiful article especially for electro-plating.[34]

A significant change is discernible in the copper work of Srinagar during the last decade of the 19th century. Owing to the rush of visitors to the Valley a large demand had arisen for beautiful copper trays framed as tables in carved walnut wood. It is stated that because of this demand the carpenter now became "the close ally of the copper-smith."[35]

Srinagar, like most cities, had its quarters for certain classes and trades. The copper-smiths quarters was near the Jama Masjid. We are told by Mr.Biscoe that in the copper bazar one could sometimes pick up some really elegant and quaintly shaped jugs and basins of ancient make. Not only that excellent imitations of some were also on sale in the copper bazar of the city. Tyndale Biscoe speaks of a special kind of jug, which, he says, took the fancy of most visitors.[36]

WOOD WORK

Wood work is said to have been introduced in Kashmir by Sultan Zain-ul-Abidin. It appears that the wood-carving industry flourished during the 'Muslim rule' in Kashmir.[37] The wood work of the 'Muslim period' bears an eloquent proof to the fact that this art received a great stimulus under the Sultans of Kashmir. While all old Hindu buildings of Kashmir are of stone, the mosques of the medieval period are mostly of wood. Some of the important religious places of Srinagar such as Khanqah-i-Mualla and the Makhdum Sahib's shrine are models of the carpenter's craft. A speciality in Kashmir wood work, known as *khatamband*, has been mentioned by Lawrence in these words:

"... beautiful ceilings of perfect designs, cheap and effective, are made by a few carpenters, who with marvellous skill piece together thin slices of pine-wood. The result is a charming ceiling in which the various shades of the pine-slips blend together in perfect harmony."[38]

A good specimen of modern Kashmiri wood work and Kashmiri ceiling may be seen in the Naqshband Sahib's shrine. The *khatamband* ceiling of Srinagar elicited such admiration that a few of them were even introduced into England during the Dogra rule.[39]

The modern type of wood-carving is the legacy of the Dogra rule. Carving was done in different articles of furniture of daily use during this period. Dr. A.Mitra, one of the famous ministers of Maharaja Pratap Singh is reported to have arranged an exhibition of all Kashmir arts and crafts in the Government Museum.[40] This action of the able Minister gave an impetus to the wood-carving industry. Maharaja Pratap Singh presented a wood carved gate and frontage of the Kashmir camp to King George V on the eve of the Coronatian Durbar held at Delhi.[41] The monument of Kashmir art presented to the English king must have served to advertise the wood-carving of Srinagar among the British aristocracy. Besides, the visitors to Kashmir also patronised this art. Further, richer classes, both within the State and outside extended their patronage to wood-carving. As a result of this patronage, the famous Kashmiri artisans of the period like Ustad Sultan Muhammad Buda evolved new designs. According to the Report on the Economic Survey of the Wood-Carving Industry in Kashmir, the name of Ustad Sultan Muhammad Buda will be much remembered. The report says that Buda went out of Kashmir, and when he returned home he opened a workshop of carving. "Messrs Ahmed Khan and Habib Joo were the first among the dealers to purchase his goods. He engaged the services of other workers and paid them adequate remuneration. After some time some of the workers withdrew from his workshop, and set up their own independent concerns."[42]

The wood-carving industry received a fillip during the period under review. According to the Census of 1921, Srinagar possessed about 50 factories of wood-work namely (1) carving, mostly of walnut wood (2) *pinjara* or lattice work, (3) panelling in various designs.[43]

The following are some of the important innovations in designs during this period. These designs were copied from foreign catalogues on articles produced in European countries.[44]

i) German, Egyptian and Swiss designs.
ii) Sculpture, elephants, dogs, horses etc.
iii) Trays like chinar leaf and other leaves.

These important innovations point to a change in the religious outlook of the wood-carvers of Srinagar, all of whom were Muslims. The carving of sculpture, elephants, dogs and horses mark a departure from the teachings of Islam.

A large variety of wood-carving goods manufactured during this period for decorative purposes or as articles of daily use also point to the growing demand, strength and popularity of this industry during the Dogra rule. Carving was done on small tables, writing desks, trays, cigarette boxes, cigar boxes, jewel cases, photo frames, chairs and various other articles.[45] It is no wonder, Swinburne[46] describes the wood-carving industry of Srinagar as quite modern. He was struck by the great excellence and ingenuity of the artisans.

System of Production

The wood-carving work in Srinagar was carried on as a cottage industry. The unit of production was the workshop run by a master-craftsman who supplied raw materials and tools. He maintained "the workshop in a building owned or hired by him." He obtained orders from the middlemen i.e. firms of sellers, and executed them. The firms made cash advances to the workers and sometimes purchased walnut wood and supplied it to them, "the price of the wood being adjusted as an advance in accounts." The craftsman was responsible for the payment of wages to the workers and took "all other risks attendant on his business of production." He was himself "a worker as well as the general supervisor of other's work."[47]

In 1938 there was only one designer in the city and so all the manufacturers depended upon him for the designs. The other workers possessed "varying degrees of skill." The workshop was "the training ground for all apprentices."

It is remarkable to note that some workers in wood-carving industry had begun to invest their own capital in the 'thirties of this century. Indeed, taking to direct sales now was a healthy development of the wood-carving trade as the middlemen's profits were eliminated thereby. However, the limited resources of the workers prevented them from bringing about "an expansion of their business on these lines".[48] Besides, the wood-carving goods were things of luxury and a large variety of articles had to be kept in stock for a considerable time. Capital investment was also large. The manufacturers had to "invest capital in raw materials, tools and implements and unsold goods produced according to their own choice."[49] This also accounts for the inability of the workers to produce goods directly for sale on a large scale.

Workmen

There are no reliable statistics available with regard to the change in the number of workers during the period under review. It appears from the study of the Report on wood-carving (1939) that the number of workers in wood-carving trade was increasing. One of the firms (Messrs Ganemede) gave the following rough figures on the compiler of the Report on wood-carving.[50]

Year	*No. of Workmen*
1910	150
1917	300
1925	400
1930	450
1937	565

As regards the living conditions of the workers in wood-carving industry, it was not satisfactory. Their income was low.[51] The fluctuations in demand according to the seasons and the worker's dependence on the firm-owner accounts for their poverty.[52]

System of Training

There was a sort of caste system prevalent in the workshops of the master workmen—only those belonging to the wood-carvers' class were admitted to the trade. The master craftsman's job was hereditary. However, under exceptional conditions, sometimes persons outside the class could also be admitted to the trade. Children were taken as apprentices.[53]

Reasons for Concentration of Wood-Carving Industry in Srinagar

It is strange that the largest majority of wood-carvers are concentrated in Srinagar city. Walnut wood is supposed to be most suitable for carving. It is not only durable but has also a good natural colour. Although it was available in the villages of Kashmir, the rural inhabitants did not make any attempt to augment their income by adopting wood-carving as a subsidiary business. But the reasons are not far to seek for the inability of the rural population to take to this profession.

a) There were no facilities for marketing carved-wood products in the villages. But Srinagar provided such facilities for the disposal of carved-wood products. Lawrence points out that a great impetus was given to the wood-carving industry by the builders of houseboats.[54] Besides, the artisans, industrialists and dealers managed to sell the products to the tourists and visitors by sales conducted in big commercial concerns or through hawkers in the hotels and in the houseboats. With the passage of time, factories and well organized commercial concerns exported carved-wood articles to foreign countries.

b) Secondly, the non-availability of ancillary raw materials, for example, sand paper, screws, colours, varnish, nails and furniture polish etc. in the rural areas also accounts for the concentration of the wood-carving industry in Srinagar.

c) Thirdly, "No attempt has ever been made so far by the State Government to popularise the craft in rural areas by granting incentives and other concessions".[55]

PAPIER MACHE

This craft was introduced in Srinagar by Zain-ul-Abidin who imported experts from Persia which is mostly inhabited by the Shia community. Owing to this, the industry has ever since been confined to the Shias who earnestly and whole-heartedly pursue this art because its production is very profitable. The local Shia artisans were unwilling to teach the technique and the know-how of the industry to non-Shias.[56] The Shias did not even establish an institution for the training of new artisans. This contributed in no small measure to hinder the expansion of the papier maché industry. Thus the handicraft became hereditary and passed on from father to the son. "Even now the latter (son) starts taking practical lessons from his father just when he is hardly of the age of ten years. By the time he attains majority, he acquires high proficiency about the technique of the designs from his own imagination and without any guidance".[57]

Although papier maché has now been in existence in Srinagar for the last over 500 years or more, this handicraft has not taken root in other parts of the State. The reasons for this are not far to seek.

The raw material required by the artisans could mostly be had in Srinagar only. The city provided an easy market for the finished products because of being a hub of tourists. "An equally important reason is that the artizan" was "generally a worker in a well established factory" or produced "goods at his home against orders given to him by the proprietors of large commercial concerns". In other parts of the State, this facility was not available.

During the third quarter of the last century, the papier maché of

Srinagar found a ready market in Kabul, France and various other foreign countries.[58] The French shawl agents gave an impetus to this industry.[59] It is stated that shawls were sent to France in papier mache boxes, which separately fetched high prices.[60]

The papier maché work or lacquered work was also known as *kar-i-qalamdani*, as the best specimens of the old work were the pen boxes (*qalamdan*).[61] It was in the 'eighties of the last century that a variety of articles such as tables, tea-poys, trays, screens, picture frames and candle sticks were made to suit the changing tastes of the aristocracy of Srinagar.[62]

The papier maché artisans also showed their skill in sketching and designing on the roofs of the rooms, walls and palanquins.[63] The richer classes of the city called in the *naqash* for the decoration of their ceilings and walls. Even now some of the old houses, palaces and shrines in Srinagar bear eloquent testimony to the skill of the *naqash*. But during the later period of the Dogra rule the demand for lacquered work for the decoration of ceiling decreased on account of European impact on Kashmiri architecture.

The beginning of this century marked the decline of papier maché craft in Srinagar. Pen cases were no longer in demand[64] because of the inroads of machine-made cheap Indian products. There was also a shortage of the pulp of paper from which papier maché articles were made. Besides, on account of World War I which caused a great deal of distress among the artisans; a large number of papier maché workers were rendered unemployed.[65]

The papier maché industry would have certainly died during the later period of Dogra rule but for the interest and zeal shown by the traders like Suffering Moses and Asia Craft on the Bund, Sadiq Ali and Bros. in Fateh Kadal, and Messrs Jaffar Ali in Hasanabad in popularising this handicraft in European centuries. [66]They introduced new articles like wall-lamp, wall plate, lamp stand, wall flower vases, table flower vases powdered boxes, dressing sets for women, cigarette cases, ash trays etc.[6

Towards the end of the Dogra rule the papier maché industry supported over 400 workmen[68] as against the number of 150 workmen in 1916.[69]

GABHA

According to Prof. Barker, the *gabha* rug industry "is one almost peculiar to Kashmir."[70] *Gabhas* are made of old woollen blankets in a variety of forms and designs. The types are (i) applique or *dal guldar* (ii) embroidery (iii) combined applique and embroidery and (iv) printed.

The *gabha* work was initially localised at Islamabad, whereas printed *gabhas* were a speciality of Baramulla.[71] It was, however, owing to the growth of the tourist industry that in the 'thirties of this century some *gabha* manufacturers established their workshops in Srinagar.[72] This created employment opportunities for some of the city inhabitants. At the beginning the Srinagar *gabha* industry was confined to a few printed *gabha* workers, but later in 1938 there were 63 workers employed in the manufacture of *gabha*.[73] Of these 52 artisans were engaged in applique and embroidery work.[74]

The *gabha* industry created a new class of tradesmen in the city, called *zachagarus*.[75] They would go from place to place for the collection of old blankets and sell them to *gabha* manufacturers. Srinagar being the chief religious centre of the Valley, the *zachagarus* found it convenient to carry on their business here. Even now the transactions are effected by this class not only at religious fairs in Srinagar but in the homes of the city inhabitants. They move from house to house with *kangries*,[76] trinkets for women, dried fish, baskets etc. and get old garments, woollen and cotton, in exchange of their goods.

NAMDAH

There was in Srinagar a most interesting 'carpet-rug' industry, based upon milling up or felting partly woven fabrics, and then figuring them with embroideries in a most ingenious manner. Some beautiful patterns for floor coverings were placed on the market by this means, and were in evidence throughout the Valley, especially in houseboats. These *namdahs*, as they were locally called, were very warm, if used, as bed-mattresses, and made excellent coverings. They were embroidered in numerous designs.

Till the first quarter of the 20th century the artisans of Srinagar engaged themselves in the manufacture of julie-felts only which were made exclusively of pashmina wool. *Namdahs* were then imported from Yarqand.[77] The *namdah* was mostly imported unembroidered, though that of an inferior kind was felted at Srinagar also.

The plain *namdah* then underwent a set of processes-dyeing, designing, embroidering, washing and finally balling-before it was ready for export.

It was in 1918 that the manufacture of *namdah* was "taken up for the first time at Nawab-bazar, Srinagar, by a well-known firm named Khawaja Garib Shah Ahad Bhat after its proprietors."[78] Subsequently two well organized commercial establishments, Achemby Trading Corporation and Modern Felt Co., came into being. These two factories exported *namdahs* to foreign countries and to some states in India.[79]

Owing to the closure of the Leh Road during World War II,[80] the *namdahs* came to be manufactured in great quantity by the artisans on the scale of a cottage industry.[81] The demand for *namdah* in foreign countries, especially in the United States, increased enormously during World War II.[82] As a result, many people who had no knowledge of the technique of the industry started the production of "namdah-rugs". This led to the deterioration in quality and most of the orders received from abroad were cancelled.[83] The Achemby Trading Corporation and Modern Felt Co., however, maintained their quality and standards and by 1947 were transacting business worth Rs.25 lakhs a month.[84]

SHAWL

Kashmir is said to have enjoyed a world-wide reputation for its beautiful shawls from the earliest times. During the Mughal times Kashmiri shawl had become so famous that it was thought worthy of being minutely described by Abul Fazl [85] and Bernier. As Bernier observes: "But what may be considered peculiar to Kachemire and the staple commodity, that which particularly promotes the trade of the country and fills it with wealth, is the prodigious quantity of shawls which they manufacture, and which gives occupation even to the little children." [86] With the advent of Afghan rule in the Valley in 1753, the shawl industry received a further impetus. It was during this period that Kashmiri shawls were in demand in Iran, Afghanistan, Turkistan and Russia. George Forster wrote in 1783: "In Kashmir are seen merchants and commercial agents of most of the principal cities of Northern India, also of Tartary, Persia and Turkey who, at the same time, advance their fortunes and enjoy the pleasure of the fine climate and country over which are profusely spread the various beauties of nature."[87] The State derived about four lakhs of rupees annually from shawls during the governorship of Sardar Azim Khan.[88] The shawl trade seems to have been in a flourishing condition during the Sikh rule in Kashmir.[89] It was during this period that Kashmir shawls found a ready market in Europe.[90]

The condition of the shawl weavers, however, was very bad in the time of the Sikhs. Whether the weavers, worked or not, they had to pay tax to the Government. The owner of a factory (*karkhanadar*) "made it a point to shift the incidence of taxation on to the shoulders of the weavers". The practice of enticing away an operative was penalised by the Sikhs at the instance of the *karkhanadars*. The workmen were thus under the thumb of the factory owners. They were coerced to work hard and were reduced to the position of bondmen. The result was that some shawl weavers chopped off their fingers in order to avoid being forced to weave for the Sikh rulers by their employers.[91]

Schonberg, visiting Srinagar in the early 'forties of the last century, remarks that the daily wages of each weaver were four annas, of which he paid to the Sikh governor of Kashmir.[92] The traveller further adds that the family of the weaver lived in abject poverty. This is why the children were set to work almost as soon as they were able to work. "The son, at five years of age, enters on the business of weaving and his wages are proportionate to his baby exertions. As he advances in growth and skill, his pay is raised subject to the usual taxation; and thus another human being enters on a career of wretchedness and rears children, who in turn, become heirs to his misery". The traveller goes on to say, "As one object of this system is never to allow the workman ready money the Government provides clothes, fuel, and other household necessaries, charging as usual, a hundred per cent profit. This is managed very skilfully, and so arranged that the poor artizan is always in debt, and I will add, that the shawl weavers seem to be the most unfortunate."[93]

Kashmir shawls were of two kinds, loom and hand-made.[94] In the hand-work shawl system the workman was known as *sada baf*. He made the plain pashmine from the spun pashm in his own house which he bought himself directly in the bazar. Upon this plain pashmine the coloured threads were afterwards worked with needles by a workman called *rafugar*[95]. The *sada bafs* were under the complete control of the department of *Daghshawl*[96]. They had to register themselves with this office and they could not leave the Valley or give up their employment.[97] Sometimes the *sada bafs* employed an agent for the purpose of selling pashmine to the merchants and others. But no pashmine could be sold by them without the *Daghshawli* stamps.[98]

In the loom system a *karkhanadar* employed a number of workmen known as *shawl bafs* in his *karkhana*. This number ranged from 20 or 30 to 300.[99] He bought the spun thread from the dealer in pashm and got it dyed of different colours before it was distributed among the workmen.

Robert Thorp says that there were about 100 *karkhanadars* in Kashmir[100] in the 'sixties of the last century. The *shawl bafs* were put under the complete control of the master workman (*ustad*). There was usually one *ustad* over every 25 or 30 *shawl bafs*.[101] At the end of each month, the *ustad* took to the *karkhanadar* "an account of the work performed in that time by each of the man under him" and drew so much pay for each which was regulated by the amount of the work done.[102] Usually the sum realised by the *shawl bafs* from the *karkhanadar* was from three to five *chilkee*[103] rupees a month. This was inclusive of the amount deducted by the Government for *shali*, which was sold to the *shawl bafs*. Robert Thorp laments that such a paltry sum was not enough to support the family of a *shawl baf* "with any approach to comfort even in so fertile a country as Cashmere."[104]

Rice was the staple produce of the Valley. Maharaja Gulab Singh (1846-1858) and his son Maharaja Ranbir Singh (1858-1885) had the monopoly of the sale of rice in the Valley.[105] According to one estimate, 12,35,358 *kharwars* (about 25,00,000 maunds) were yearly stored in Ranbir Singh's time and about 4 lakhs of *kharwar* were sold to the shawl weavers of Srinagar city at the fixed rate of Rs.2/- per *kharwar*.[106] Robert Thorp gives the following description of the manner in which the *shali* was sold to the *shawl bafs*.

"On the arrival of the grain in Srinagar, a large number is set aside for the *shawl bafs* and portions of it are from time to time made over to the *darogha* for them. When that official receives an order for so much *shali* from the Governor he takes his accounts, and writes orders for each of the *karkhanadars* entitling them to receive so much rice, according to the number of men in their employ, from certain specified boats. The *karkhanadar*, on receipt of the order sends for the boat or boats named, and distributes the rice to his *shawl bafs* keeping an account of the amount delivered to each, to be deducted from his monthly wages, the *karkhanadar* being himself charged with the total cost of the rice in his account with the *darogha*."[107] (Italics mine).

As we shall see later, this system of collecting *shali* in large granaries in the city and selling it by retail through Government officials led to many abuses.

It has already been noted that the lot of the shawl weavers was not good during Sikh regime. However, with the accession of Maharaja Gulab Singh in 1846, conditions for the artisans of the shawl industry began to go from bad to worse.[108] The imposed annual tax levied by the Maharaja on each shawl weaver was Rs.47.8.[109] The rapacious[110] Maharaja in order to ensure a constant income from this source even promulgated a regulation forbidding any weaver—"whether half blind or otherwise incapacitated"—to relinquish his operative without finding a substitute.[111] Mr. John Irwin very significantly remarks, that this was a condition which was almost impossible to fulfil. "On top of this", writes he, "an *ad valorem* duty of 25 per cent was charged on each shawl, and its assessment and collection was formed out to a corrupt body of officials, whose own illegal exactions were said to have amounted to a further 25 per cent of the value."[112]

The shawl weavers continued to remain steeped in poverty in Maharaja Ranbir Singh's reign. Andrew Wilson and Sir Richard Temple visited Srinagar during this period. They have given a graphic picture of the social condition of the weavers. Andrew Wilson wrote that the shawl weavers got miserable wages.[113] According to him, the weavers were almost like slaves, for they could neither leave Kashmir nor change their employment.[114] Temple writes that the shawl weavers formed "a numerous and withal a miserable class, badly paid, badly nourished and badly housed and, therefore, physically and morally wretched".[115] Dr. Elmslie, a medical missionary in Kashmir, who had closely studied the weavers remarked that "they were the most miserable portion of the population, both physically and morally. Crowded together in small and badly ventilated workshops, earning a mere pittance, and insufficiently nourished, they suffered from chest infection, rheumatism, and scrofula. When a woman wished her neighbour ill, she said: "may you get a shawlmaker for a husband".[116]

If on the one hand, the shawl weavers had developed a somewhat fatalistic outlook owing to oppression, exploitation and misery, on the other, they had occasionally tended to manifest a spirit of revolt against intolerable conditions. Earlier in 1847, they resorted to strike[117] and demanded the reduction of the various kinds of taxes, such as *baj*, *nazarana* etc.[118] They also demanded that the wages[119] of the labour be fixed and urged the Government to establish a rule of law in respect of this industry and codify it.[120] On June 12, 1847, they struck work and about 4,000 of them fled the Valley.[121] Gulab Singh was annoyed and "he told them that their complaints would be enquired into if they returned to work".[122] The false assurances of the Maharaja had the desired effect and in consequence the agitation died down.

There was restlessness among the shawl weavers in Ranbir Singh's time too. In order to redress the grievances of the weavers, the Maharaja allowed the remission of two and half company's *annas* in the price of each *kharwar* of *shali* sold by the Government to them.[123] "*Shallee*" should, therefore," remarks Robert Throp, "have been sold to the *shawl baf*, at the rate of 17 annas per *kharvar*, but the *darogha* of the *Dagshali*, named Raj Kak[124] through whom the Government *Shallee* was sold to the *shawl bafs*, ordered that they should pay 18 annas per *kharvar*, intending to make half an anna on each *kharvar* for himself".[125]

Faced with such tyranny, exploitation and oppression, the *shawl bafs* petitioned Dewan Kripa Ram, the Governor-designate of Kashmir, at Pampore. "The answer they received from him was that he would listen to their complaints when he reached Srinagar. When that event took place", writes Robert Thorp, "he was again waited upon by the *shawl bafs*, but they only obtained an answer that he would attend to them in a few days".[126]

Having failed to get their grievances redressed, the shawl weavers assembled at Zaldagar in the city to consider their wrongs and grievances, and proceeded in a body to the residence of the Governor where they intended again presenting him with a petition.[127] They made a wooden bier, placed a cloth over it, carried it to and fro in procession, exclaiming Raj Kak is 'dead, who will give him a grave?' This they did out of 'bitter and despairing mood'.[128] The corrupt *darogha,* however, made best of the opportunity. He told the Governor that the processionists intended to attack his house and kill him.[129] On hearing this the Governor was enraged and he immediately sent a company of soldiers to disperse the peaceful processionists. The consequence was that many shawl weavers were killed and a numberless were injured[130] in the stampede following the ruthless demonstration of force by the soldiers. The leaders of the working class movement, namely, Sheikh Rasool (Rasul Sheikh), Abli Pala, Qudda Lala and Sona Shah were taken into custody where they were beaten with a strap.[131] While Sheikh Rasool and Abli Pala died on account of the inhuman crimes perpetrated on them,[132] the other two leaders were put in the Bahu fort at Jammu. Besides, a good number of men taking part in the procession were arrested. Most of them died in prison because of cold and starvation.[133]

When the Maharaja was apprised of the prevailing discontent among the shawl weavers, he remitted Rs.11 from the tax of Rs.49 in 1868.[134] But this belated measure of the Maharaja did not save the industry from disaster. The shawl trade received a fatal blow from the impoverishment caused by the Franco-German War in 1870.[135] Lawrence was told by an eye-witness of 'the excitement and interest' with which the *shawl bafs* "watched the fate of France in that struggle — bursting into tears and loud lamentations when the news of Germany's victories reached them".[136] It was a great calamity for the shawl weavers that on account of the heavy war indemnity, the French had no spare cash for the Kashmir shawls.[137] The ruin of manufacturers and merchants was temporarily averted by the Maharaja who made large purchases to the value of several lakhs of rupees.[138] But this was a mere drop in the ocean.

Neither man nor nature took kindly to the poor shawl weavers. In 1878 and 1879 famine stalked the land.[139] A good number of shawl weavers left for Lahore, Amritsar and Ludhiana.[140] Lawrence writes that "in the city the unfortunate shawl weavers were the chief victims of the famine."[141] They are said to have 'died like flies'. "Most of the survivors, having hands so refined and delicately adjusted to the technique of shawl weaving that they were useless for most other occupations, subsequently died in destitution".[142]

It now dawned upon Ranbir Singh that the once flourishing industry was dead and so he abolished the poll tax, "for the simple reason that in a time of so deep and widespread misery the weavers could not pay."[143] But in place of the poll tax and other imposts on shawl weaving, the export duty on shawl was retained and by 1882 it had been raised to 25 per cent *ad valorem*.[144]

Causes of the decline of the Shawl Industry

Several causes directly operated in impoverishing the shawl industry. To begin with, the State enjoyed virtual monopoly over it. In order to ensure a regular and abundant supply of fabrics, the *Daghshawl* often became a source oppression in the hands of its officers. Armed with the authority of the rulers, the officials of the shawl department subjected the poor weaver to a great deal of tyranny, which, in turn, often led to the extensive migration of the shawl weavers to the Punjab. But even deserting their own families did not assuage the troubles of the shawl weavers. This was so because their escape was made difficult by the high mountain passes which were guarded.[145] And even if they succeeded in managing their escape, the members of their families were not left in peace. No sooner did the weaver give up his employment, than the *karkhanadar* informed the *darogha* in order that his tax may be decreased.[146] The *darogha* then sent a sepoy to the house of the fugitive. It is said that his wife, or mother or father, or 'probably all of them', were brought before the *Daghshawl*.

They were fined a rupee or two; or suffered a few day's imprisonment at the hands of the authorities, whose cruelty and injustice has extorted "from them in some cases, their almost only means".[147] Evidently, shawl was the 'sport'[148] of the corrupt officials of the *Daghshawl*; hence their misconduct paved the way for the ruin of shawl weaving.

Secondly, the taxation policy of Gulab Singh and his successor tolled the death-knell of the shawl trade. Tax was imposed on wool as it entered Kashmir.[149] Besides paying taxes for every workman the *karkhanadar* employed, he was also subjected to impositions "at various stages of the process according to the value of the fabric."[150] And not the least, the merchant was taxed before he could export the goods. The enhancement of the export duty on the shawls already referred to must have certainly discouraged the intending purchaser. This is attested to by the fact that at London sale, while £2,500 worth of Amritsar shawls were sold, none out of the £4,000 worth of Kashmir shawls that were presented was sold.[151]

The European intrusion into the economics of Srinagar towards the close of the last century must have also made the revival of the shawl trade and industry well-nigh impossible. Their coming to Srinagar gave an impetus to the investment of capital in the carpet industry.

Lastly, no effort was made by the Government to protect the industry by the introduction of improved methods.

It is then evident that the shawl trade was doomed mainly on account of the negligence of the rulers of Kashmir.[152] Now it is necessary to discuss the effect of the decline of the shawl industry on the workers.

When it flourished, the shawl industry had provided sustenance to the bulk of the city's population. During the reigns of Maharaja Gulab Singh and Maharaja Ranbir Singh, there were 30,000 to 40,000 shawl weavers in Srinagar.[153] But the Census of 1891 records that there were 5,148 shawl weavers. And as, Lawrence states, of these some 800 to 900 were employed in the manufacture of carpets.[154] The Census of 1901 registered 5,037 shawl weavers in Srinagar.[155] The level to which the shawl trade of Srinagar had declined may be judged from the fact that only 148 persons were found working at it when an Industrial enumeration was held in 1911.[156]

The decline in shawl trade naturally forced the shawl weavers to change their occupations. Lawrence in his letter, dated Dec. 2, 1889, to Col. Nisbet said: "Since the decline of this industry some of these men have taken to agriculture and some have found employment in village looms".[157] Though a good number of weavers were driven to other occupations, such as carpet weaving,[158] sawing[159] and boating,[160] yet there was still a large number who remained unemployed.[161] Social customs also aggravated their miseries. The *burqa*-clad women of the shawl weavers of the city could not help their husbands, for the social inhibitions forbade them to do any work. Moreover, the fine-fingered weavers were not wholly fit for manual work.[162] Their "hands were too soft and knees too weak to cope up with the rough work of husbandry".[163] It was also due to this reason that they could not improve their lot `by carrying on working on the roads'.[164] Even those who took to agriculture did not improve themselves to be fair farm labourers.[165] Thus they preferred "their old, sedentary, unhealthy life to farm work", and sat at the village looms "from early morning to night with only a short respite for food, on wages of 1˘ annas *per diem*".[166] So 'bad' and 'hopeless' was their condition that in May and June, they subsisted "chiefly on mulberries and unripe apples".[167] It is not to be wondered at, therefore, that many of the skilled artisans of the once renowned industry of Srinagar were reduced to destitution.[168]

It should be remembered that the allied industries of shawl like fringe weaving (*hashia bafi*) and embroidery (*yarmodozi* and *jalakdozi*) correspondingly declined with shawl manufacture.[169] The Census of 1911 records only 23 fringe weavers in the city. As regards the embroiders, their number fell to 134 in 1911.[170] In fact, the decline in the shawl trade was bound to affect the embroider. This is evident from the fact that from the finest embroidery work on shawls, this close ally of the once reputed industry, gradually descended to needlework on silks, woolen and cotton textiles, and to hook work on coarser stuff and *namdahs*.[171]

It is, however, interesting to note that the embroiders fulfilled the demand for various goods required in English and Westernized households. For instance, other articles embroidered by them were curtains, table clothes, mantle borders, tea-cosies, tray covers etc.[172]

CARPET

The carpet industry is said to have flourished for a long time after Sultan Zain-ul-Abidin's reign. 'But in course of time it decayed and died'. It was in the reign of Emperor Jahangir that the industry showed signs of revival owing to the effort of Akhund Rahnuma.[173]

However, the industry received a fresh impetus when Europeans entered the field of manufacture.[174] In 1876, Mons. H. Danvergue[175] established a factory in Srinagar. Other Europeans who contributed to the growth of carpet trade in Srinagar were Messrs Mitchall and Co. and Mr. C.M. Hadow.[176] The contribution of C.M. Hadow to the carpet trade[177] was great. He sent Kashmir carpets for being exhibited in the big Chicago world fair of 1890.[178]

The industry 'prospered and flourished' until '1930, when the world depression had an adverse effect on it'.[179] Consequently, there was not much demand for Kashmir carpets from Europe and America.[180] However, by 1935 the industry again showed signs of recovery.[181] The annual State subsidy granted to manufacturers in 1932 was extended from time to time, alike in the interest of the carpet industry and also of local labour, so as to preserve this famous industry. Even during World War II high class carpets were manufactured in Srinagar and exported to Europe and America.[182]

Workmen in Carpet Factory

The carpet industry was one of the immense value to the inhabitants of the city.[183] It is difficult to say anything about the exact number of workers engaged in the industry before 1921. It is certain that the industry afforded employment to a large number of men ever since the Europeans began to take interest in this trade. Lawrence says that the industry gave employment to a considerable number of the shawl weavers, and many of whom were employed in embroidering felts or *namdahs*.[184] Marion Doughty speaks of 1901. "The wool used is grown locally, the industry is one of great benefit to the inhabitants for not only are large numbers of men and boys employed on the actual work but women and children prepare and wind the wool."[185] According to the Census Report of 1921, the six woolen carpet factories of Srinagar gave employment to 1,342 men. Women were not employed in the carpet factories,[186] but a fairly good number of them were engaged in the spinning of wool[187] for the factories in their homes under the direction of head weavers deputed by the Companies. This work was done on contract rates.[188]

In 1930 there were six big factories and 100 individual workers.[189] In factories alone 725 looms were at work which employed 3,625 weavers.[190] Besides, the number of dyers, designers, *talim* writers, factory staff and other subsidiary workers engaged in spinning and twisting if taken into account, will show that four to five thousand workers depended on this occupation.[191] According to Dr. Bhan, if the dependents of these workers were to be added, it will increase the number four times.[192] Thus, directly or indirectly about 12% of the population of Srinagar earned its livelihood from the carpet industry.[193]

Accurate statistics are not available on the wages of the carpet weavers. Wages fluctuated from time to time and from factory to factory. The weavers of carpets are said to have been paid low wages in 1900.[194] The Census Report of 1921 records 'an all round rise in the rates of wages on account of the heavy rise in prices'. It is stated that in 1921 the earnings of adult male weavers varied from 4 annas to 12 annas a day.[195] The wages were paid by piece system. The factory owners paid the wages to the *ustad*, who distributed them among his *shagirds*.[196] The work was carried on generally for eight hours. Holidays were granted on religious festivals.[197]

System of Production

The carpet industry was both in the hands of an independent worker and the factory owner. The former was 'isolated, poor, ignorant and conservative,' who had 'neither the resources nor the knowledge to take advantage of the improvements effected by the bigger manufacturers'. He was 'both the producer and the seller'. The capital invested by him was small and so was his turnover.[198] There was 'no question of competition between the large scale manufacturer and the petty isolated worker,' as the latter produced 'an inferior variety for the local consumers only'.[199] But the factories also began to manufacture cheap varieties of carpets owing to the production of machine carpets. "The growing demand for cheaper varieties coupled with extensive use of aniline dyes, succeeded in ousting the old artistic variety, and the cool harmony of colour was replaced by magenta."[200]

WOOL

Before 1927, beyond the boundaries of the Punjab, very little was known in India of the hand-spinning and hand-weaving woolen industry of Srinagar,[201] and much less than Rs.10,000 worth of purely hand spun Kashmir products were exported.[202] Credit goes to the All India Spinners Association which opened its branch in Srinagar in July 1928 and thus brought about the revival of hand-spinning and hand-weaving not only in Srinagar but also in other parts of the Valley. The Srinagar Woolen Mills made great progress subsequently.[203] The average daily labour employed in it exceeded 1,000 towards the end of the Dogra rule.[204]

By 1946, the Srinagar Woolen Mills was known all over India for its excellent art-manufactures, and the demand for its products could hardly be met, although production increased continuously.[205] The goods produced were *lois*, *pattus*, tweeds, flannels, rugs, blankets and some pashmine fabrics also.

SILK

The mention of silk stuff is made for the first time in Zain-ul-Abidin's reign.[206] Mirza Haidar Dughlat writes: "Among the wonders of Kashmir are the quantities of mulberry trees cultivated for their leaves from which silk is obtained."[207] Jahangir states that Kashmir imported silkworm eggs from Gilgit and Tibet.[208] During the Sikh rule William Moorcroft wrote in 1824 that the silk produced was "insufficient for domestic consumption."[209] But Vigne[210] writing in 1835, remarked that 'a considerable quantity of silk was produced' and that the same was taken over by Colonel Mehan Singh, the then Sikh Governor. It is further stated that the Governor used to pay the producers of silk in rice. Two thirds of the total output is said to have been exported to the Punjab in Mehan Singh's time. Another traveller, Munshi Ganeshi Lal, writing his *Tuhfa-i-Kashmir* in 1846 records that the Government gained a revenue of about £2,000 a year from this industry.[211]

But it appears from the accounts of the pre-Dogra period that the silk industry was not organised as a commercial enterprise because its demand was not as large as that of the shawl industry. Mr. N.G. Mukerji, an expert on sericulture under the Government of Bengal wrote:

"Before 1868 the silk industry of Kashmir had existed in the unorganized, crude state in which it had probably existed for centuries..."[212]

It was in 1869 that Maharaja Ranbir Singh organized sericulture on a very large and expensive scale.[213] 'No expense was spared,[214] and 127 fine rearing-houses[215] were built in all parts of the Valley. Reeling appliances and machinery were imported from Europe, and a large department was formed for the purpose of developing a business in silk'. But, in spite of this, the silk enterprise languished owing to the absence of real skilled supervision and disease in silkworms.[216] It was with the accession of Maharaja Pratap Singh in 1885 that a new chapter opened in the history of silk industry. In 1897, "an expert was employed and the state started sericulture on approved European principles with Italian reeling machinery. All attempts to raise local seed were abandoned, and seed was imported annually on a large scale." As a result of this encouragement, the industry spread all over the Valley.[217] Later in 1907, a factory with large filature containing over 300 basins for reeling cocoons was established in Srinagar. This brought the State a large revenue, and gave employment not only to the rural population who were engaged in silkworm rearing, but also to the urban population. The Census of 1901 found no less than seven thousand inhabitants of Srinagar working in the factory.[218] It is significant that the Kashmiri Pandits also generally overcame their former aversion to manual as well as menial work.[219] By 1901 they were found busy performing several duties in connection with the manufacture of silk.[220] The great expansion of this industry since 1901 will be clear from the following figures.[221]

	1901	1911
Cocoon-rearers	6,000	35,000
Cocoon reared (in maunds)	13,000	40,000
Outturn of all kinds of silk and waste (in Lbs.)	60,000	2,80,000
Average daily attendance at Srinagar factory	900	3,700

The silk factory of Srinagar was the only factory of its kind which employed a considerable number of children of an age below fourteen. The interest and pleasure with which the Kashmiri boy was seen plying his trade of drawing silk tissues from the cocoon was quite amusing.[222] In 1903 little boys of 7 and 8 made 2 annas a day in the filature and 4 annas a day were "paid to the older and better reelers."[223] Men did not care to work at these wages, as they could earn higher rates outside.[224] Besides, the work was tedious and required good eyes and quick hands. This accounts for a large number of children and women in the silk factory.

Of the women employed in the Srinagar silk factory over 2/3rd were 'low class' Muslims. The rates of wages were the same for men and women of similar kinds of work and equal output. But the men being generally more efficient in certain branches of silk work, were "allowed a slightly higher rate of wages ranging between 2 annas and 8 annas per day in Srinagar ... according to the nature of work entrusted to each operative". The children were, however, "generally given a comparatively easier and simpler work", and their wages were "therefore, also comparatively low".[225]

PAPER

Paper making has also been a speciality of the capital city of Kashmir.

In medieval times it was much valued in India for manuscripts, and "was used by all who wished to impart dignity to their correspondence". The practice of making rag paper is said to have been introduced in Kashmir by Muslim immigrants from Persia and Samarqand between the fourteenth and fifteenth centuries. Zain-ul-Abidin patronized and established it is Nau Shahr, his official residence. The paper workers thus got settled in Nau Shahr where there were till recently some families engaged in this industry. The popularity of Kashmir paper was clearly indicated by Sheikh Yaqub Sarfi's letter to Abdul Qadir Badauni.

"If you should have any need of Kashmir paper for rough notes and drafts, I hope that you will inform me of the fact, so that I may send you from Kashmir the rough copy of my commentaries, the writing on which can be washed from the paper so completely that no trace of the ink will remain as you yourself have seen."[226]

Even during the second half of the 19th century Kashmir paper was in great demand for making manuscript copies. It is said that in India it was generally used for 'polite correspondence'. It was distinguished by "its fine gloss and polish, its evenness and freedom from flaws, also by its white wax-like colour and appearance."[227] Bates observes: "The durability of the paper produced in Kashmir is remarkable, contrasting favourably in this respect with much that is made in Europe, where the practice of mixing certain chemical substances with the pulp is said to have caused a great deterioration in the quality."[228] Sir W. Lawrence used the paper to a large extent, because he found it durable and in many ways excellent.[229] Little wonder, "of the specimens exhibited in the Lahore Exhibition of 1864, it was recorded that this beautiful paper, the best of all native manufactures can be purchased everywhere."[230]

No exact figures are available regarding the number of the workmen employed in this industry. In about 1873 there were about 32 paper factories in the suburb of Nau Shahr and about 12 men were employed in each factory.[231] In the 'eighties of the last century, Lawrence found some 36 families in Nau Shahr engaged in paper-making.[232] Before Pratap Singh's accession, paper was a Government monopoly.[233] It is said that the greater part of the paper made in the factories of Srinagar was appropriated by the State. What remained was sold to the merchants and was either retained for home consumption or exported. The Government made payments to the contractors partly in cash and partly in grain.[234]

With the inroads of cheaper machine-made products in the beginning of this century, the Srinagar papeı industry undoubtedly began to decline.[235] In 1931 the mills produced paper at about half the price of Kashmir hand-made paper. Besides, the non-availability of the right sort of raw material was also responsible for the decline of this art. Since the beginning of this century hemp fibre had been rising in price and the poor paper-makers of Srinagar often had to use old gunny bags.[236] By 1931 such paper as bond paper and other superior paper made of rags of good quality has disappeared in the bazars of Srinagar. The paper now chiefly manufactured was *kalam dori* which contained no hemp fibre. The resulting paper was very poor and could not stand competition either in quality or price. But the strong and durable Kashmir paper made out of the rice pulp continued to find some market among the money-leading public, who made *bahis* or *sahis* (account ledgers) of this paper.[237] Some of it was also used in the vernacular correspondence of the outlying State offices where the cost of transporting foreign paper made the local article cheaper.[238] Even *Qurans* were still written on paper made from hemp fibre. In spite of this, the once renowned manufacture of Srinagar could not save itself from the onslaughts of machine. It goes without saying that a good number of the *khushnavis* (men of beautiful pen-manship) were hit by the invasion of painting "just as the Indian paper mills destroyed the once famous hand made foolscap of Kashmir."[239]

LEATHER

There was a large trade in leather followed in the city towards the end of the last century.[240] Hides were prepared in the villages by the *Watals*[241] and were then brought to Srinagar, where they underwent a refining process. The leather work of Srinagar was very superior, owing to a better method of tanning.[242] It should, however, be borne in mind that there was "all round decline" of the leather works when the machine-made cheap Indian products made their appearance in the city.[243]

Among the other artisans of Srinagar may be mentioned carpenters,[244] blacksmiths, gunsmiths, furriers and lapidiaries.

Towards the close of the last century the carpenter carried 'rude and primitive tools' in his leathern apron.[245] He could execute any work which his clients required with his half adze (*tur*, and chisel (*turats*).

A significant change in these articles made by the carpenter is visible during the period under review. The advent of Europeans in Kashmir conferred a great boon on him. Previously, he prepared mostly agricultural implements, boxes, doors, windows, big boxes to store paddy etc. But now he started making chairs, tables, modern cots, almirahs, easy-chairs, sofa-sets, tea-stools, benches, dressing tables and mirror stands. The carpenter of Srinagar showed an obvious tendency towards learning new techniques. As compared to the other classes of workers, there came a change in his mode of life. The reasons for this social change are not far to seek. Owing to the new style of living, houses began to be furnished by the latest designs in furniture. The result was that the carpenter took to the making of modern furniture which he found very lucrative.

A remarkable change is also noticeable in the implements used by the carpenters. With the advent of the Europeans in Srinagar, carpentry improved very much since the carpenter learnt to use more civilised tools than a few primitive implements which till the last decade of the 19th century formed his stock in trade.

Allied with the carpenter were the axemen and sawyers. It appears that previously the Kashmiri carpenters did their work with axes and adzes. They were introduced to the saw[246] towards the close of the last century. By 1890 the sawing industry afforded employment to many of the city's inhabitants. It is interesting to note even the "fine-fingered" shawl-weavers of the city were taken to sawing.[247]

The blacksmiths were found in most bazars of Srinagar. Some of them possessed extraordinary skill. They cheifly produced agricultural instruments and requirements for domestic consumption such as padlocks and shovels. It is noteworthly that by the end of the last century they had started manufacturing excellent surgical instruments which were then used in the Srinagar Hospital.[248] But it cannot be denied that with the import of cheap foreign-made articles the position of the blacksmiths steadily began to deteriorate and their activities were now generally confined to petty repairs.

There were about thirty or more shops belonging to the blacksmiths and gunmakers in the city in 1873. The latter manufactured rifles for the Maharaja's troops. But the number of weapons produced was apparently not great. In 1873, each shop in which four or five workmen were employed, produced one or two rifles a month. The Government supplied the material and paid for the labour of manufacture at the rate of thirty *chilkee* rupees for each rifle.[240] According to Bates, Srinagar produced a good quality of sporting weapons, guns and rifles.[250] Swords were largely made in Srinagar and were much valued at Jammu.[251] Lawrence says that the well-known gunsmiths, Amira and Usmana, could turn out "good guns and rifles", and replaced "parts of weapons in so clever a manner" that it was difficult "to detect the difference between the Kashmiri and English workmanship".[252]

Regarding the furriers, they chiefly depended for their livelihood on the business given to them by sportsmen, who sent in skins to be cured. During Partap Singh's reign, the law promulgated for the protection of game, under which the sale of skins and horns was prohibited, affected the business of the furriers.[253]

The lapidiaries of Srinagar possessed great skill.[254] They are said "to have produced specimens of their skill and taste superior to any in Europe".[255] In 1921, they numbered 1,100 in Srinagar alone".[256]

HOUSEBOAT

The boat-building[257] industry only concerns the people of the city. According to Mr. Biscoe, "The Kashmiris have their own special way of building boats, and very clever they are at their art. I have always been interested in boats and boat-building, but I had never come across boats built as in Kashmir".[258]

It was in the last quarter of the 19th century that the boat-building industry began to develop on account of the increasing rush of British civil and military servants, travellers, artists and sportsmen. All the visitors to the Valley would come across numerous boatmen (*Hanjis*) at Baramulla. These *Hanjis* were the owners of *doongas* and each was eager for his own boat to be hired by a visitor. In the second half of the last century usually the *doongas* were 50 to 60 feet in length and 6 to 9 feet wide at the centre, "walled and roofed with reed matting, the roof being of several layers of matting and the matting of the walls arranged so that it could be rolled up to form a sort of the window opening divided by wooden partitions to form three small rooms; with a long, pointed deck both fore and aft, and with much storage space throughout under the removeable floor boards."[259] The passenger lived in the front part of the *doonga*. The crew of the *doonga* comprised the boat-owner, his family and sometimes an extra hand. During winter, when the passenger traffic was at a standstill, the *doongas* were used for transporting grain.[260]

In the beginning, visitors brought alongwith them all their own paraphernalia and servants. In those days the *doonga* was for the visitors 'not much more than a good serviceable tent on the move.' But gradually the versatile *Hanji*[261] realised the importance of his boat. The business-wise boatman now began to care much for his guests. With the passage of time, he supplied more and more comforts such as a bath tub, wicker and canvas chairs, wicker tea tables, and crockery, while the traveller continued to bring his own camp bed, silverware, linen, cooking utensils and comforts. "The *doonga* then developed from a small craft into a relatively spacious boat 85 feet long and 8 or 9 feet wide (at its centre); from three tiny to five good size rooms; from reed mat roof and walls to shingled room and sturdy wood plank walls. The *doonga's* function as mobile living quarters for visiting foreigners changed in emphasis with the innovation of the modern type of houseboat."[262]

It is apparent that the "birth" of the houseboat was natural. But political factors also helped in its growth and further expansion. Under the orders of the State Government no European could possess land or build houses in Kashmir.[263] Naturally houseboats became the houses for those who wished to stay in the Valley. It was thus the Europeans who were responsible for giving a great fillip to this newly-born industry. Mr. M.T. Kennard is said to be the first Englishman who built a houseboat in Srinagar about 1888.[264]

With the growth of tourist traffic the boat-building industry flourished[265] and Biscoe remarks that one of the chief features of the Jhelum in the city was the increasing number of houseboats, inhabited chiefly by Europeans.[266] The houseboat industry reached a new height during World War II 'when thousands of military personnel from all over South East Asia spent their furloughs in Srinagar'.[267]

As the building of houseboats proved to be a profitable business, it created a distinctly new boatmen community in Srinagar. Many merchants and others began to buy houseboats to cater to the tourists in competition with the boatmen owners. The greater impetus given to the building of houseboats therefore impaired the profits of the *doonga* men as the visitors now preferred to live in houseboats. The *doonga* lost its importance. It was now served as 'cook boat' attached to a houseboat. The *doonga Hanji* was further hit by the opening of the cart road as it seriously affected the passenger traffic of the boat.[268]

One good effect of the industry was the revival of the wood-carving art. The houseboat owners employed a number of wood-carves[269] for the ceilings which were (and are) invariably of the Kashmir *khatamband* type.

OTHER OCCUPATIONS

In Srinagar the practice of medicine was "usually a hereditary profession". Writing about the practice of *hikmat* in the city, Bates remarks: "The son succeeds the father in his practice. The medical knowledge possessed has been derived from a scanty acquaintance with the Greek system of medicine, or of a few nostrums that are handed down from sire to son."[270] The people of Kashmir had 'considerable confidence' in these *hakims*. With the popularity of allopathic treatment in Srinagar these *hakims* lost much of their influence over their patients.

There was also a class of men and women who eked out their existence by applying leeches. Before the advent of medical missionaries in Srinagar, it was a very popular treatment for almost every disease, so much so, that it was reported in the epedimic of 1872 the Maharaja "sent orders to Kashmir that the *hakims* were not to bleed for cholera as they had been in the habit of doing."[271] The practice of applying leeches ceased to exist, thanks to the propaganda of medical missionaries.

Among other traders[272] may be mentioned grocers,[273] who were mainly Kashmiri Hindus of *bohar*[274] caste. Besides, there were bakers, vegetable sellers, fruit sellers, tobacconists, dyers, tailors,[275] masons,[276] washermen, butchers, milkmen,[277] rope-makers and shoe-makers. In the first half of this century, a new class of traders like chemists and druggists and *tongawallas* came into being. The latter weakened the financial predominance of the river transporters. With the growth of the tourist industry another class of traders known as *shikara hanjis* emerged.

There were many people who were engaged in domestic service and "vague occupation". In 1931 domestic service supported 18% of the earners in Srinagar.[278]

Land and river were the next important source of living for a good number of the city's inhabitants. The *hanjis* were also the cultivators who owned floating gardens[279] on the Dal Lake which is rich in agricultural products. Cultivation was alone done in those parts of the city which once formed the suburbs of the city. Fishing in the waters of the Jhelum and the Dal formed yet another occupation of a class called *gaud hanz*.

GENERAL REMARKS

Statistics regarding the occupation of the people of Srinagar reveal that about 43% of earners in the city were supported by industry.[280] Since all the industrial concerns of Kashmir were located in the city, transport and trade claimed a good percentage of occupations. For instance, in 1931, transport supported 4% of the earners.[281] In respect of trade which claimed 8% of the earners, the city occupied a prominent position, being the emporium for the entire province of Kashmir.[282] The city supplied to the villages salt, sugar, tea and tobacco, and a small amount of cotton piece goods.[283] But the greater part of the European and Indian piece goods imported from India was consumed in Srinagar.[284] The main article of the village produce brought to the city was *shali*.[285]

But it sounds strange that from the point of view of the urban population, there were a few indigenous traders in Srinagar.[286] While some traders sold and exported handicraft goods, others were engaged in minor trades. The *wanis* of the city, who formed an important trading community in the old economy, carried on trade in salt, oil, spices, snuff, sugar and tea. They had also in their stock a few rolls of European or Indian cotton piece goods.[287]

It should be borne in mind that the *wanis* allowed the export trade to pass entirely into the hands of the Punjabis[288] when the latter settled in Srinagar for business purpose towards the close of the last century. This was because the former lacked both in enterprise and in capital. That is why unlike the enterprising the resourceful Punjabi traders, the *wanis* did not "engage in large trade operations".[289]

The reason for this absence of enterprise among the citizens of Srinagar will be found in the system of administration. During the reigns of Maharaja Gulab Singh and Maharaja Ranbir Singh, the "development of local trade was greatly hampered by the system under which the State itself monopolised all trade."[290] For example, rice trade was practically in the hands of the Government. In consequence, "the system of holding enormous stocks of unhusked rice and of selling it to the urban population by the State at cheap rates[291] prevented the growth of indigenous grain merchants."[292] Silk, Saffron, violets, various kinds of forest products, hemp, tobbacco, waternuts and paper were at different times also monopolised by the State.[293] Apart from this, the Government subjected various other trades to rigorous impositions.[294] it is enough to remark here that it was the policy of Gulab Singh and his successor to make every product of the Valley a State monolopy.[295] Even prostitutes were taxed[296] and in the words of Lawrence, everything save air and water was under taxation.[297] This policy of the Dogra rulers not only killed the initiative and enterprise of many trading families of Srinagar,[298] but, very often, it gave birth to social unrest in the city.[299]

It was with the accession of Maharaja Pratap Singh that various economic changes began to take place. His reign saw the abolition of many vexatious taxes on trade.[300] There was also a marked improvement in the means of communication and transport. These two factors encouraged many outsiders to carry on trade in Srinagar. Within a very short time, the enterprising Punjabis opened business in various parts of the city.[301] They imported manufactured cotton and piece goods, brass, copper, and iron, salt, sugar, tea, tobacco, and an increasing amount of petroleum.[302] They exported to the Punjab non-intoxicating drugs, fibres, fruits, hides and skins, *ghi*, linseed, rape-seed and *jingli*, wool, raw and manufactured.[303] Thus emerged a new class of traders in Srinagar which weakened the financial predominance of the old trading community of the city.

In the old economic life of the city, almost every occupation was hereditary, the knowledge and skill being passed on from father to son. The growth and development of some industries like that of silk, carpet and wood led to occupational mobility. It has already been noted that in the silk factory all sorts of people including some Pandits[304] and shawl-weavers worked, though a greater majority of the workers were the so-called 'low-born' Muslims. The carpet industry was also responsible in breaking the spell of the hereditary nature of occupation, for it gave employment to about 800 to 900 shawl-weavers.

Another important factor leading to occupational changes was the decline of certain indigenous arts. It should be remembered that paper, leather and copper works of Srinagar deteriorated partly owing to lack of patronage and partly due to a change in people's tastes. Even the judicial member of the State Council admitted in 1902, that the local consumers preferred machine made goods to hand-made articles. He also pointed out that skilled workmen were giving up their ancestral profession and taking to other trades and professionals.[305]

The growth of modern education in Srinagar threw open not only many avenues of getting a living but also made necessary certain adjustments on the part of the old ways of getting a living. Clerical and the teaching professions give rise to a new class of people: the salaried professions.

We have already referred to the condition of the artisans and their dependence on the middlemen. It is well to remember that the latter were to the *karkhanas* what the *banias* were in the rural economy of India.[306] In fact, no artisan in the city would work unless he got an advance for food from the middleman[307] who generally controlled the sale of the finished article. Owing to the absence of better organization and credit facilities, the middleman played a very important role in most of these *karkhanas*. It is true that the local banks financed some of the privately owned *karkhanas* but the number of such industrial concerns was very small.[308] Cooperative sale and purchase were yet in their infancy. All this resulted in a good deal of sweated labour in most of the small *karkhanas*.[309]

Thus a major portion of the population of Srinagar comprised those of borrowers and debtors.[310] The workmen in debt were the serfs of the middlemen. They had to pay a good deal of their earnings to their creditors. In many cases heavy debts were inherited and were passed on from father to son. The artisans are said to have sold even their clothes so as to provide themselves with means of subsistence in very distressing circumstances.[311]

The workmen generally suffered from lack of education. There was 'also a great want of mutual confidence and cooperation among the artizans.'[312] The traders had 'no recognized methods of advertising their goods and pushing on the sale of their ware.'[313] They were more or less agents for the exchange of goods, living on the profit they made in the process.[314] There seems to have been no trade guilds. The result was that the *karkhanas* generally ran into debt and the workmen usually found it difficult to make both ends meet.[315]

There was, practically speaking, no 'factory labour'[316] in Srinagar except in the silk factory. With the progress of this industry, however, industrial labour and its problems began to grow in prominence. In the twenties of this century, the labour problem in Srinagar assumed new proportions when the conditions in the Silk factory worsened. Gradually the workers became conscious of their rights and raised their voice against exploitation. They had no medical facilities. There was no adequate arrangement for the education of their children. They got less wages considering the amount of labour they put in. So they demanded reasonable wages and formed labour associations. The Srinagar Silk factory became a centre of attraction when demonstrations[317] took place in it in the third decade of this century. The strike petered out but heralded a new age—the age of trade unionism and socialism, which reflected the social tension[318] inherent in the emerging industrial system.

NOTES:

1. Mohibbul Hassan, *Kashmir under the Sultans,* p. 92.
2. Srivara (Dutt),p. 151.
3. *op. cit.,* p. 434.
4. Ibid..
5. Srivara (Dutt), p. 151.
6. Ibid.
7. Wakefield. *op. cit.,* p. 149.
8. Ibid.
9. *Census,* 1921, I, pp. 183-184.
10. Wakefield, *op. cit.,* pp. 149-50.
11. *E. S. S. I.,*p 1.
12. Ibid., p. 3.
13. Ibid.
14. Wakefield. *op. cit.,* pp. 149-50.
15. *Census,* 1921, I, pp. 183-184.
16. *E. S. S. I.,* p.3.
17. Ibid., p. 12.
18. *Techno Economic Survey of Jammu and Kashmir State,* p. 236.
19. *E. S. S. I.,* p. 12.
20. Ibid., p.7.
21. Ibid.
22. Ibid., p. 15.
23. Ibid.
24. Ibid.., p. 16.
25. Ibid.
26. Ibid.., p.5.
27. Ibid.., pp. 13-14.
28. Ibid.., p.5.
29. Ibid.., p.4.
30. The *doonga* is one of the most common boats in Kashmir.
31. *E. S. S. I.,*p. 15.
32. Lawrence, *op. cit.,* p. 378; See also Major General De Bourbels' report, NAI/Foreign, Feb. 1890, Extl. P. A. Nos. 293-314.
33. Lawrence, *op. cit.,* p. 378.
34. Ibid.
35. Ibid.; *Imperial Gazetteer,* p. 21.
36. *Kashmir in Sunlight and Shade,,* p. 133.
37. For a detailed discussion on wooden architecture in Kashmir, see Mohibbul Hasan, *op. cit.,* pp. 266-71.
38. Lawrence, *op. cit.,* p. 379.
39. Ibid.; *Imperial Gazetteer,* p. 121.
40. *E. S. W. I.,*
41. Ibid.

42. Ibid., pp. 1-2.
43. *Census,* 1921, I, p. 183.
44. *E. S. W. I.,* p. 6.
45. Ibid., p. 19; *Administration Report of the J & K State,* 16 Oct. 1941 to 12 April, 1943, p. 118; J & K (G. R.) F. No. 278/p-16 (1915): See also Younghusband, *op. cit.,* pp. 214-15.
46. *The Holiday in the Happy Valley,* p. 76.
47. *E. S. W. I.,* p. 7.
48. Ibid., p. 8.
49. Ibid., pp. 8-9.
50. Ibid., p. 14.
51. Ibid., p. 15.
52. Ibid., p. 14.
53. Ibid., p. 15.
54. Lawrence,*op. cit.,* p. 379.
55. *Census,* 1961, Vol. VI, J&K, Part VII-A(1) Handicraft Tables (Urban), p.xii.
56. In 1916 there was only one sunni family pursuing the art of papier mache in Srinagar. *East and West,* XV, July, December, 1916, p. 659.
57. *Census,* 1961, Vol. VI, J&K, Part VII- A(1), Handicraft Tables (Urban), p.viii.
58. *East and West,* XV, July, December, 1916, p. 660.
59. Ibid..
60. Ibid.; *Census,* 1921, 1, p. 183.
61. *East and West,* XV, July, December, 1916, p. 661.
62. Ibid.; p. 660; *Census,* 1921, 1,p. 183; See also Younghusband, *op. cit.,* p.214.
63. Lawrence, *op. cit.,* p.378; *East and West,* XV, July, December, 1916, p.660.
64. *East and West* XV, July, December, 1916, p. 661.
65. J&K (G.R.),F. No. 278/p. 16, 1915.
66. Hamdani, *Shian-i-Kashmir,* p. 303.
67. Ibid., p. 308.
68. *Administration Report of the J&K State,*Oct. 16, 1941 to April 12, 1943, pp. 117-118.
69. *East and West,* XV, July-December, 1916, p. 659.
70. Barker, *A Report on the Cottage Textile Industries of Kashmir,* p. 76.
71. Bhan, *Report on the Economic Survey of Gubba Manufacture in Kashmir,* p. 3.
72. Ibid.
73. Ibid., p. 21.
74. Ibid.
75. Ibid., p.4.
76. *Vide* Chapter IV, social Life.

77. Lawrence, *op. cit.*, p. 377. Heaps of *namdahs* brought to Srinagar were unloaded at Yarqand Serai, near Safa Kadal Srinagar. It was here that the State charged the necessary duties on import.
78. *Census of India,* 1961, Vol. V!, J&K part VII-A(1), Handicraft Tables (Urban), p, xiv.
79. Ibid.
80. Kaul, *Kashmir Economics*, pp. 104-145.
81. *Census of India.* 1961, Vol. VI, J&K Part VII-A(1), Handicraft Tables (Urban) p. xiv.
82. *Kashmir Economics*, pp. 104-5; Sinha, *Kashmir Playground of Asia,* p.82.
83. *Census of India,* 1961, Vol. VI, J&K Part III-A(1) Handicraft tables (Urban), p.xiv.
84. Ibid.
85. *Ain* (tr. Blochman), 1873, Vol. I, p. 98.
86. *Travels,* pp. 402-403.
87. *Journery*, p. 22.
88. *Census,* 1921, I, p. 180.
89. *Wajeez-ut-Tawarikh* (Ms.), fl, 93.
90. For how shawl became fashionable in the West, see G.M.D. Sufi, *op. cit.*, II, pp. 565-567. The introduction of shawl is said to have created a 'furor' in the toilet of fashionable French ladies. The 'furor' lasted for many years and the French Government "levied, at one time, a uniform and high duty (110 fr) on the piece, whatever its value." Notwithstanding this, the consumption increased largely . *Kashmir and its Shawls* (anonymous). pp. 21-22.
91. *Wajeez-ut-Tawarikh* (MS.), fl.93; See also *Lahore Political Diaries*, 1847-49, Vol. VI, p. 48.
92. Baron Schonberg, *op. cit.*, II, p.103.
93. Ibid.
94. Dugsal, *Letters from India and Kashmir,* p.205; *Cashmere Misgovernment (Kashmir Papers*, pp. 62 and 71).
95. Bates, *op. cit.*, p. 54; *Cashmere Misgovernment, (Kashmir Papers,* p. 71).
96. Since the times of the Afghans the shawl trade had been under the control of a department called *Daghshawl*, which was responsible for the supervision of raw material, settlement of disputes among manufacturers and the affixing of State seal on finished products. The department collected a poll-tax on weavers and an impost on manufactured shawls. See Ganesh Lal, *Siyahat-i-Kashmir*, p. 33; Pir Hassan, *op. cit.*, I, pp. 360-65; *Cashmere Misgovernment (Kashmir Papers*, pp. 63-64); Bates, *op. cit.*, pp. 54, 101.
97. *Cashmere Misgovernment (Kashmir Papers,* p. 71).
98. Ibid.

99. Ibid., p. 62; Bates, *op. cit.*, p.53.
100. Ibid.
101. Bates, *op. cit.*, p. 53.
102. *Cashmere Misgovernment (Kashmir Papers,* p. 63).
103. A *Chilkee* rupee worth eight to ten annas (of the British rupee) was introduced by Maharaja Ranbir Singh. See Duke, *Handbook*, p. 45; Drew, *op. cit.*, p. 566.
104. *Cashmere Misgovernment (Kashmir Papers,* p. 63); Bates, *op. cit.*, p. 53.
105. NAI/Foreign, Pol, July 1863, Nos. 73-75, pp. 5-6.
106. Ibid., p.6.
107. *Cashmere Misgovernment* (typed copy), p.19.
108. John Irwin, *The Kashmir Shawl,* p.9.
109. Ibid.; *Cashmere Misgovernment (Kashmir Papers,* p. 63).
110. Hassan, *op. cit.*,(Ibrahim's tr.), III, p. 572; *Lahore Political Diaries*, 1847-1849, Vol. VI, p. 40; Younghuband, *op. cit.*, p.155.
111. John Irwin, *op. cit.*, p. 9; *Cashmere Misgovernment (Kashmir Papers,* p. 67).
112. *Op. cit.*, p. 9; See also Bates, *op. cit.*, p. 254; Wakefield, *op. cit.*, p. 145; Temple, *op. cit.*, I, p. 299; NAI/Foreign, Pol July 1863, Nos. 73-75; Foreign, Sec. March 31, 1848, Nos. 66-70 (Ms.). Dewan Kishan Lal writes that in 1848 the stamp duty on shawls amounted to Rs.90,0000 i.e. Rs. 5,06,250 (British). Thus shawl was a considerable source of revenue of the State. NAI/Foreign, Sec, March 31, 1846, Nos. 66-70 (MS.).
113. *The Abode of Snow,* p.398.
114. Ibid.; See also Prinsep, *op. cit.*, p. 213; *Kashmir in Sunlight and Shade,* p. 115.
115. Temple *op. cit.*, I, p. 276.
116. See Bates, *op. cit.*, p. 33; The shawl weavers were contemptously called *Khandawaos* by the *Khojas* of Srinagar.
117. *Lahore Political Diaries,* 1847-49, Vol VI, p. 48.
118. K.M. Pannikar, *The Founding of the Kashmir State*, p.199.
119. Again in 1853, the workers of shawl industry expressed their resentment against the *karkhanadars* over the question of wages. There broke out some riots in the city. See Mirza Saif-ud-Din, *op. cit.*, 1853, Vol. VI, ff. 9a, 10b.
120. K.M. Pannikar, *op. cit.*, p. 139.
121. Ibid.
122. It is true that Gulab Singh enquired into the grievances of the shawl weavers in an open *Durbar* and announced new regulations for the shawl department. But there seems to be not even scintilla of truth in Dr. Pannikar's statement that as a result of these regulations "the workmen became free" or that the "shagird was no longer a serf." *op. cit.*, p. 139.

The learned historian fails to note that the new rules remained on paper only. In sober fact, the shawl weavers were bound to work for the same master and they were forbidden to give up their operative. Owing to this, they were in terrible plight and earned only 4° *dumri* as their wages. See Pir Hasan, *op. cit.,* I, p. 364.

123. *Cashmere Misgovernment* (typed copy). p. 18.
124. Pandit Raj Kak Dhar was considered to be the 'cleverest' officer in Kashmir. He had amassed huge wealth and was very cruel. NAI/Foreign and Pol. July 1863, Nos. 73-75, p.9; Lt. Col. Taylor described him as "an accomplished intriguer, smooth-speeched and deceitful." *Lahore Political Diaries,* Vi, p.64.
125. *Cashmere Misgovernment* (typed copy), p. 18.
126. Ibid.; See also Mir Saif Ullah, *op. cit.,* pp. 100-101, Pir Hasan, *op. cit.,* (Ibrahim's tr.), III, p. 577.
127. Ibid.., Mir Saif Ullah, *op. cit.,* p. 101; Khalil Mirjanpuri, *op. cit.,* II, p. 310.
128. *Cashmere Misgovernment* (typed copy), p. 19.
129. Ibid.; Pir Hasan, *op. cit.,* (Ibrahim's tr). III, p. 577.
130. Ibid.; Mir Saif Ullah, *op. cit.,* p. 101; See also Khalil Mirjanpuri, *op. cit.,* II, p. 310.
131. Mir Saif Ullah, *op. cit.,* p. 101; See also Khalil Mirjanpuri, *op. cit.,* II, 311.
132. J&K/ File No. 306 of 1865, p. 57.
133. J&K/ File No. 313-E of 1865.
134. John Irwin, *op. cit.,* p.9.
135. NAI/Foreign sec E, March 1883, Nos.86; Bates, *op. cit.,* p. 59; *Kashmir in Sunlight and Shade,* pp. 115-116.
136. Lawrence *op. cit.,* p. 375; See also *Kashmir in Sunlight and Shade,* p. 115.
137. *Kashmir in Sunlight and Shade,* pp. 115-116.
138. Bates, *op. cit.,* p. 59; See also Prinsep, *op. cit.,* p. 213.
139. *Punjab Administration Reports* 1878-79, pp.2-3.
140. The Census of 1921 (p. 181) refers to the decendants of the emigrant shawl weavers in the Punjab.
141. Lawrence, *op. cit.,* pp. 215 and 375; See also Pir Ḥasan, *op. cit.,* I, p. 365; NAI/Foreign, Sec. E, March 1883, No. 86.
142. Quoted by John Irwin, *op. cit.,* p.18.
143. NAI/Foreign, Sec. E. March 1883, Nos. 86, p. 15.
144. Ibid.
145. *Cashmere Misgoverment (Kashmir Papers* p. 68). A good many people of Kashmir are said to have attempted to escape to the Punjab during the famine of 1878-79, "but at the barriers troops were stationed to prevent the migration of the people, and harrowing tales are told of the fathers of families getting past the barrier by bribing the guardians of

the passes, while the wives and children were left to die in Kashmir." Lawrence, *op. cit.,* p.215. The system, under which no person could leave the valley of Kashmir without permission, was known as *Rahdari.*

146. *Cashmere Misgovernment* (typed copy), p. 23.
147. Ibid., p. 24.
148. Temple, *op. cit.,* I, p. 300; For the malpractices of the officials of the *Daghshawl,* see also NAI/Foreign, Sec. march 1848, Nos. 60-70; Bates, *op. cit.,* p. 54; *Cashmere Misgovernment* (typed copy), p. 25.
149. NAI/Foreign, Sec E, March 1883, No. 86, p. 15.
150. Ibid.
151. Ibid.
152. Some writers seem to believe that after the Franco-German war the fabrics of shawl were expelled from the French and American markets owing to the change of fashion (Wakefield, *op. cit.,* p. 142; NAI/Foreign, Pol. A, feb. 1877, Nos. 146-149; Foreign, Genl B, Feb. 1879, Nos. 93-100; John Irwin, *op. cit.,* p. 36).
153. NAI/Foreign, Sec E, March 1883, No. 86; See also *Census,* I, 1921, p.181.
154. Lawrence, *op. cit.,* p. 375; Marion Doughty, *A Foot Through the Kashmir Valley,* p. 158.
155. *Census,* 1921, I, p. 181.
156. Ibid., 1911, I, p. 232.
157. NAI/Foreign, feb, 1891, Sec. E, Nos. 295-326; See also Lawrence, *op. cit.,* p. 375.
158. *Imperial Gazetteer,* p. 120; Lawrence. *op. cit.,* p. 377; Marion Doughty, *op. cit.,* p. 158; Dermot Norris, *op. cit.,* pp. 38-39. Those of the shawl weavers who did not take to the carpet weaving were found engaged in weaving *alwand* or plain pashmine, or *jamawars* and *butadars* for the Persian market. There was 'no export to Europe.' Lawrence, *op. cit.,* p. 377.
159. Lawrence, *op. cit.,* p. 372.
160. Ibid., p. 377.
161. Lawrence writes that the carpet industry was "too small to employ all the poor wretches whose ill-paid toil once made Kashmir art renowned throught the world." *op. cit.,* p. 316.
162. Thus wrote Mr. E.G. Colvin: "There is a large class, such as the shawl weavers, who are wholly unfit for manaul labour and whose women-kind are `Parda-nishin'. They were formerly in comfortable circumstances but owing to the decay of their trade have now fallen into poverty. It is alleged that neither they nor their families will, under any circumstances, come to a relief work ..." NAI/Foreign, May 14, 1903, No. 2611, p. 3.
163. Lawrence, *op. cit.,* p. 316.
164. Ibid.; See also NAI/Foreign, May 14, 1903, No. 2611.

165. Lawrence, *op. cit.,* p. 316.
166. Ibid.
167. Ibid.
168. Khalil Mirjanpuri, *op. cit.,* p. 314.
169. *Census,* 1911, I, p. 232.
170. Ibid.
171. Sufi, *op. cit.,* II, p. 269.
172. *Census*, 1911, I, p. 228; See also J&K (G.R.), F. No. 278/-P-16 (1915).
173. Sufi, *op. cit.,* p. 571.
174. Bhan, *Report on Carpet Indusrty*, P. 1; Norris Dermot, *op. cit.,* p. 39; Lawrence, *op. cit.*, p. 377; *Census*, 1921, I. P. 180.
175. *Report on Carpet Industry*, p. 1; *Census*, 1921, 1, p. 180.
176. NAI/Foreign Intl. A, March 1896, Nos. 9-37; Swinburne, *A Holiday in the Happy Valley*, p. 75.
177. Major General De Bourbel in his report of 1890 says: "The trade in shawls with Europe has fallen off, but that in carpet is rising." NAI/ Foreign, Extl. A, Feb. 1890, Nos. 293-314, p. 565.
178. *Report on Carpet Industry*, pp. 1-2
179. Ibid., p. 2.
180. Barker, *Report on the Cottage Textile Industries of Kashmir,* p. 75.
181. *Report on Carpet Industry*, pp. 1-2.
182. See *Administration Reports of J&K State* (1933-1944).
183. The *Census Report* of 1921 shows the carpet industry as next in importance to sericulture (Census, 1921, I, p. 179); in 1931 Prof. Barker of the University of Leeds found the hand-made carpet Industry of Srinagar the single largest industry in the State (*op. cit.,* o. 75); See also Marion Doughty, *op. cit.,* pp. 155-156.
184. Lawrence, *op. cit.,* p. 377.
185. *Op. cit.,* pp. 155-56.
186. Foreign, Intl. A, March 1896, Nos. 9-37.
187. Marion Doughty, *op. cit.,* pp. 155-56.
188. Foreign, Intl. A, March 1896, Nos. 9-37.
189. *Report on Carpet Industry*, p. 18.
190. Ibid.
191. Ibid..
192. Ibid.
193. Barker, *op. cit.,* p. 75.
194. Marion Doughty, *op. cit.,* pp. 157-58.
195. *Census*, 1921, I, p. 180.
196. Ibid., *Report on Carpet Industry*, p. 19.
197. *Report on Carpet Industry*, p. 19; See also resident's letter to the Secretary to the Government of India. NAI/Foreign, Intl. A, March 1996, Nos. 9-37.
198. *Report on Carpet Industry* p. 8.

199. Ibid.
200. *Census*, 1921. I, p. 180; Sinha, *Kashmir, Playground of Asia,* p. 79.
201. *The Tribune,* Jan. 17, 1931.
202. Ibid.
203. Barker, *op. cit.,* p. 41.
204. *Administration Report of the J & K State* (1941-43), p. 115.
205. Sinha, *Kashmir, Playground of Asia,* p. 76.
206. Mirza Haidar, *op. cit.,* (E & R), p. 434.
207. Ibid., p. 425.
208. *Op. cit.,* II, p. 146.
209. *Op. cit.,* II, p. 155.
210. Quoted in Dr. Sufis' *Kashir* (New Ed.) II, pp. 574-75.
211. Ibid., p. 575.
212. Lawrence, *op. cit.,* 367.
213. Ibid., *Imperial Gazetteer*, p. 64; See also Foreign, Pol. A. K.W. Sept. 1879, Nos. 63-69, p.2.
214. According to Andrew Wilson, the Maharaja set apart £ 30,000 for the development of silk industry, *op. cit.,* p. 365.
215. For detailed description of silk worm rearing and silk production, see Kripa Ram, *Gulzar-i-Kashmir*, pp. 493-503.
216. Lawrence, *op. cit.,* pp. 367-68.
217. Ibid., *Imperial Gazetteer*, p. 64.
218. *Census,* 1901, I, p. 11.
219. Ibid., See also Andrew Wilson, *op. cit.,* pp. 364-65.
220. *Census,* 1901, I, p. II.
221. Ibid., 1911, I, p. 65.
22. Ibid., p. 232.
223. NAI/Foreign, Extl. A, Aug. 1903, Nos. 94-101.
224. Ibid.
225. *Census,* 1921, I, p. 179.
226. *Muntakhab-ul-Tawarikh* (text), II, p. 144.
227. Bates, *op. cit.,* p. 66.
228. Ibid., p. 68; See also Temple, *op. cit.,* I, p. 300.
229. Lawrence, *op. cit.,* p. 380.
230. Bates, *op. cit.,* p. 66.
231. Ibid.
232. Lawrence, *op. cit.,* p. 380.
233. Bates, *op. cit.,* p. 66; *Kashmir Handbook,*. p. 23; Pratap Singh is said to have removed this 'restrictive monopoly.' J.C. Bose, *Cashmere and its Prince,* p. 18.
234. Bates, *op. cit.,* p. 68.
235. *Census,* 1931, I, p. 225; See also Ibid., 1911. I, pp. 223-29.
236. Lawrence, *op. cit.,* p. 380.
237. *The Ranbir,* August 11, 1941.

238. *Census*, 1911, I, p. 239.
239. Lawrence, *op. cit.*, p. 380.
240. Ibid., p. 379; *Imperial Gazetter*, p. 122.
241. The *watals* have been called the "gipsies of Kashmir." They are quite a different race with customs of their own. The chief occupation is the manufacture of leather. They also perform the duties of scavengers. Drew, *op. cit.*, pp. 181-82; Lawrence, *op. cit.*, p. 314; *Imperial Gazetteer*, p.38; *Beyond the Pir Panjal*, p. 84.
242. Bates, *op. cit.*, p. 66.
243. *Cenus*, 1911, I, pp. 238-239.
244. Mirza Saif-ud-Din, *op. cit.*, 1854, Vol. vii, ff. 50 ab; For Mr. C. Tickell's note on carpentry in Kashmir, see Lawrence, *op. cit.*, p. 371.
245. Lawrence, *op. cit.*, pp. 371-73.
246. Mr. Biscoe states that when he first came to Kashmir in 1891 was practically unknown to the makers of boats (*Kashmir in Sunlight and Shade*, p. 169). But by 1905 the sawmills had been established in Srinagar and were the Maharaja's monopoly. See Knight, *Where Three Empires Meet*, p. 45.
247. Lawrence, *op. cit.*, p. 372.
248. Ibid., p. 372; Younghusband, *op. cit.*, p. 217.
249. Bates, *op. cit.*, p. 69.
250. In the last quarter of the 19th century, many arms of Kashmir manufacture were smuggled into Hazara. See Bates, *op. cit.*, p. 69; NAI/Foreign, Sec E, March 1890, Nos. 25-26, K.W. No. 2.
251. Bates, *op. cit.*, p. 69.
252. Lawrence, *op. cit.*, p. 373; See also Younghusband, *op. cit.*, p. 271; Torrens, *op. cit.*, pp. 260-61.
253. Lawrence, *op. cit.*, p. 373; *Imperial Gazetteer*, p. 122.
254. Bates, *op. cit.*, p. 69; Knight, Diary, p. 96.
255. Bates, *op. cit.*, p. 69.
256. *Census*. 1921, I, p. 184.
257. "In Kashmir," writes Abul Fazl, "A model of ship was made which was much admired." *Ain* (Blochman), p. 290.
258. *Kashmir in Sunlight and Shade*, p. 169; Sir Francis Younghusband remarks that among the "industries of Kashmir must be mentioned boat-building, which is indeed one of the most important in the country" (*op. cit.*, p. 217); See also *Census*, 1901, I, p. 11.
259. *Cultural Forum*, Vol. xii, Nos. 3-4, April, July 1970, p. 92.
260. Lawrence, *op. cit.*, p. 381.
261. The *doonga Hanji*, like all other classes, was a tax payer.
262. *Cultural Forum* Vol. xii, Nos.3-4, April, July 1970, p. 92.
263. *Kashmir in Sunlight and Shade*, p. 178.
264. Ibid.; Younghusband, *op. cit.*, p. 44.
265. In 1920 the construction of double and tripple storeyed houseboats was

prohibited by the Maharaja on grounds of public safety. See J & K (G.R.), F. No. 377, Xl-2 (1919).

266. *Kashmir in Sunlight and Shade,* p. 178.
267. *Cultural Forum* Vol. xii, Nos.3-4, April, July 1970, p. 95.
268. But there are still some *doongas* available for hire for transport of cargo.
269. Lawrence, *op. cit.,* p. 379.
270. Bates, *op. cit.,* p. 17.
271. Ibid.
272. See *Diwan Kishan Lal's Account of Cashmere,* NAI/Foreign, March 31, 1848, secret, Nos. 66-70.
273. They do not seem to have been in comfortable circumstances in the reign of Maharaja Gulab Singh. Mirza Saif-ud-din, *op. cit.,* Vol. IV, f. 9b.
274. The *Bohars* of Srinagar intermarry among themselves and do not enjoy caste fellowship with the Kashmiri Pandits. Although they have been almost assimilated into Pandit culture, intermarriage and inter-dining are as yet the exception rather than the rule.
275. Even the tailors were in chains. On one occasion they were brought before Wazeer Panoo who asked them to pay tax on the spot. As the tailors lived from hand to mouth, they could not statisfy the greed of the Governor. They, however, told the Governor that the taxation policy of the Government might force them to give up their profession. Mirza Saif-ud-din, *op. cit.,* Vol. IV, f. 11a.
276. Ibid., 1854, Vol. VII, ff. 50. ab.
277. Ibid., f.75 a.
278. Vide Chapter, II, *p. 32.*
279. Floating gardens (Kashmir *radh*) of the Dal lake are full of interest and of great importance to the people of Srinagar. They are made of long strips of the lake reed, with a breadth of about six feet. 'These strips can be towed from place to place and are moored at the four corners by poles driven into the lake bed. When the *radh* is sufficiently strong to bear the weight of a man heaps of weed and mud are extracted from the lake by poles, and these heaps are formed into cones and placed at intervals on the *radh.*' Each cone can accommodate two seedlings of the melons or tomatoes, or four seedings of water melons or cucumbers. There is a rich soil, ample moisture, and the summer sun of Kashmir which help to produce vegetables in abundance and of excellent quality.
280. *Census*, 1931, I, pp. 224-25.
281. Ibid.
282. Ibid.
283. Lawrence, *op. cit.,* p. 397.
284. Ibid., p. 393.
285. Ibid., 397.
286. Ibid., pp. 390, 392.

287. Ibid., pp. 387, 395.
288. Ibid., p. 387.
289. Ibid., 387, 390.
290. Ibid.
291. *Papers relating to Kashmir,* London, 1890, p. 52; See also Khan Bahadur Ghulam Ahmad Khan, *Note on High Prices of Shali,* 1903, p. 4.
292. Lawrence, *op. cit.,* p. 390; Trade in grain started in Srinagar after the abolition of the State granaries in about 1900. A good number of *doonga hanjis,* who had no work in winter, began borrowing money on high rates of interest, and took to trade in *shali.* They brought *shali* in their boats, and sold it at the various *ghauts* of the city. The grain-dealers advanced money to zamindars before the commencement of the harvest season, and thus secured *shali* at cheap rates. It was in this manner that a large proportion of the produce was "purchased by grain-dealers for sale and by well-to-do persons for their own requirements for the year." (See Revenue Members' note. Appendix A.P. 22, NAI/Foreign Extl, A. August 1903, Nos. 94-101, p. 22). As there were no large grain-dealers, these boatmen made large profits "on account of a small capital outlay by restricting the import than to reap a lower rate of profit on a large capital outlay." Indeed, the grain-dealers had not the "capital for an extensive trade." The Resident, therefore, suggested that other men with capital be "induced to enter the trade and produce competition." (See Resident's letter on scarcity and high prices in Srinagar, NAI/Foreign, extl. A, Aug. 1903, Nos. 94-101, p.1). It should, however, be noted that private trade in grain came to an end when the Food Control Department came into existence in 1918. The State Government adopted the old system of collecting *shali* and distributing it to the city population at a nominal profit. J & K (G.R.), F.No. 245/Sh-184 of 1921.
293. Lawrence, *op. cit.,* p. 417; For how tobacco was bought and sold by the Government, *see Diaries of P. Sandvys Melvill, (Lahore Political Diaries,* VI, p. 197).
294. "The right to legalize marriages was formed out, and it is stated that the office of grave digger was also taxed." Lawrence, *op. cit.,* p. 417; See also Prinsep, *op. cit.,* p. 214; Temple *op. cit.,* I, p. 302; Torrens, *op. cit.,* p. 301. In 1863, the tax levied on vegetables grown on floating islands on the Dal Lake, and also a tax on goods taken in boats over the lake yielded Rupees 31,000. NAI/Foreign Br, Pol, July 1863, Nos. 73-75, p. 5; Robert Thorp writes: "Some children and others were shown to me suffering from different diseases.....their food, is only rice, and the coarse vegetables they produce in their lake gardens, and the only fuel they can procure is dried horse dung ! And these people pay taxes". *op. cit.,* (typed copy), chapter, IV, p. 34; Taxes were forcibly collected from poor people of the city by Wazeer Panoo in Gulab Singh's reign. See Mirza Saif-ud-din, *op. cit.,* Vol. IV, ff, 11a and 12b, 14a, 31a.

295. Lawrence, *op. cit.*, p. 417.

296. Younghusband, *op. cit.*, p. 161; Bates, *op. cit.*, p. 101. All prostitutes were supposed to pay tax to the Government. They were principally of the *Watal* or lower caste and were registered with the State. They were sold at a tender age by their parents to brothel-keepers for Rs. 200 or Rs. 100 per child. The sale was recognized and recorded on stamped paper. They estimated number of prostitutes acquired in this way in the seventies of the last century was 250 or 300 for Srinagar alone. They were divided into three classes according to their "gratifications" and taxed:

1st class.........	Company's Rs. 40 per annum.
2nd class.........	Comapny's Rs. 20 per annum.
3rd class.........	Company's Rs. 10 per annum.

NAI/Foreign deptt. Sec. E, Mar 1883, No. 86. See also Arthur Brinckman, *op. cit.*, (typed copy), p. 16.

297. Lawrence, *op. cit.*, p. 417; See also *The India We Served*, p. 134; Arthur Brinckman, *op. cit.*, (typed copy), Chapter II, p. 13; Bates, *op. cit.*, p. 101.

298. "That everything is in the hands of the rajah, so that there is no chance for private enterprise—no encouragement to genius; in fact, to be in appearance in possession of money is a crime, unless much of it it goes to the rajah." Arthur Brinckman, *op. cit.*, (typed copy), Chapter II, p. 13; Bates observes: "The people of Kashmir have doubtless a strong natural bias to commerce; but this has been crushed by their unfortunate political circumstances." *op. cit.*, p.71; See also Henvy's Note on famine, NAI/Foreign Sec. E, March 1883, Nos. 83-85.

299. Mirza Saif-ud-din, *op. cit.*, Vol. IV, ff. 9a, 10b, 11a and 12b ; Vol. vii, 1854, ff, 61ab. Mirza Saif-ud-din's *Akhbarat* bear testimony to the fact that there was always an undercurrent of opposition among the shawl weavers owing to heavy taxation.

300. Lawrence, *op. cit.*, p. 373.

301. Ibid., pp. 373, 387.

302. Ibid., P. 387; Younghusband, *op. cit.*, pp. 219-20; *Beyond the Pir Panjal*, p. 44.

303. Lawrence, *op. cit.*, p. 387; See also *Beyond the Pir Panjal*, p. 44.

304. In his letter Col. Nisbet, dated dec. 2, 1889, Mr. Lawrence writes about the Pandits of Srinagar.

"... there are large number of needy Pandits, who are casting about for a means of livelihood. Some have started small shops. Others work as tailors, and a few have actually worked as coolies on the road." NAI/Foreign, Sec. E, Feb. 1891, Nos. 295-326, p. 28; Early in the seventies of the last century, Mr. Wakefield found the Pandits working as tailors and cloth sellers, *op. cit.*, pp. 101-102.

305 J&K(Genl), File No. 184-M-17, 1902.

306. *Census*, 1941, p. 25.

307. Lawrence, *op. cit.*, p. 374.

308. *Census*, 1941, p. 25.

309. Ibid., *Ganga Nath Report*, p. 93; Lawrence, *op. cit.*, pp. 374; See also *The Ranbir*, August 4, 1941.

310. J&K(G.R.), File No. 278-p-16(1915); *Census*, 1941, p. 32.

311. J&K(G.R.), File No. 278/-p-16 (1915); An artisan of Srinagar is reported to have committed suicide owing to extreme poverty and hunger. See *The Ranbir*, dec. 8, 1941; *The Khalid,* Dec. 2, 1941; Dec. 27. 1941.

312. *Census*, 1921, I, p. 184; Lawrence, *op. cit.*, p. 374.

313. *Census*, I, 1931, p. 213.

314. Ibid., *The Ranbir*, Aug. 4, 1941.

315. *The Ranbir,* Aug. 4, 1941; Lawrence, *op. cit.*, p. 396.

316. See the letter of the Vice-President, Kashmir State Council, to the Resident in Kashmir, NAI/Foreign, Intl. A, March, 1896, Nos. 9-37; also a letter dated 23rd Sept. 1894, from Messers Hadow and Co. to the Governor of Kashmir, NAI/Foreign, March 1896, Intl. A, Nos. 9-37, p. 3.

317. As the workers in the Silk factory had grown sick of the extortions demanded from them by the officials, they began to show signs of unrest. The situation became critical when on July 20, 1924, twenty five of the twenty seven labour leaders were arrested on the charge of fomenting trouble in the factory. This was followed by a general strike of the workers including a number of children. "They assumed a defiant and threatening attitude and refused to work and to carry out the orders of the Director and his subordinates. The labourers went so far as to appoint their own officers from among their ranks." In order to secure the release of the prisoners a big crowd numbering about 2000 assembled opposite to the Shergarhi Police Station and attempted to enter it by force. "The mob insisted on an immediate release of the accused. On this being refused, they declined to leave the place." However, the strike was finally put down by the Maharaja's cavalrymen and infantry. See NAI/Foreign Pol. File No. 19(2) of 1924, Nos. 1-4; See also *The Ranbir,* Sept. 2, 1924.

318. *The Ranbir*, July 16, 1945.

CHAPTER IV

SOCIAL LIFE

Society showed little tendency to change in Srinagar until the beginning of the present century, when changes began to take place owing to the developed means of communication and transport. Although a majority of the people were conservative, there were a few who were ready to challenge the old traditions and customs.

Before the dawn of the modern era, the Kashmiri had little knowledge of the outside world. The city and its petty concerns were his only subjects of conservation. In winter or the rainy season he listened to folk-tales and the occasional recital of the religious book or ballad. But hard as his lot was, he was quite content if he would escape the great evils of famine, floods, fires and epidemics.

The joint family system remained in vogue everywhere in Srinagar and was regarded as an idex of harmonious relations among the members of the family. Such families were believed to be well behaved and relatively more cultured. But this would not necessarily justify the inference that the joint families in Srinagar existed only due to these considerations. The fact that the inhabitants were not economically well-off and new couple could not afford to maintain a separate kitchen was no less responsible for the joint family system.

HOUSEHOLD GOODS

Changes in household goods were visible only in the apartments of the wealthy merchants and the Westernized section of the population. Their houses were furnished after the European fashion. Elegant chandeliers, pier glasses, couches, chests of drawers, writing desks, chairs, sofas, tables, table lamps, etc. found their way into the rooms of the rich people. But as regards the great majority of the population, their household goods consisted of wooden boxes for keeping clothes and the mat (*wagu*)[1] made in the villages. In the villages and the city the people slept on mats and straw, bedsteads being unknown.[2] A cotton-spinning wheel (*yander*), a wooden pestle and mortar for husking rice (*qanz*),[3] a few earthen vessels for cooking,[4] and earthen jars for storing grain were the utensils found in an average household of a Kashmiri.[5] Earthen or copper utensils were used by different households according to the economic condition of each. *Samavar*[6] (kettle) and *degchi* (cauldron) were used for the preparation of tea and cooking of rice. Generally vegetables were prepared in an earthen vessel called *leig*. It was believed that vegetables could be cooked well only in earthen pots and not in copper utensils.

The *kangar*[7] which forms so important a part of the Kashmiris life continued to be used during winter. The *kangar* or *kangri*, a portable vessel, generally consists of two parts: the inner earthenware bowl of a quaint shape called *kundal*, in which the fire is placed, and its encasement of wicker-work, sometimes simple, sometimes pretty and ornamented with rings and colours. A little wooden or silver spoon (*tsalan*), tied to the handle, completes this oriental brazier. The *kangri* can also consist of only an earthen vessel. It is called a *manan*.[8]

The best *kangries* are made in Chrar, where Sheikh Nur-ud-din Wali is entombed. Anantnag, Shahabad and Sopur are also famed for good *kangries*.

There are numerous sayings about the *kangri* and not a few folk-songs celebrate the virtues of the 'Snow Queen'.

Kami sana kundalay nivi myani kangar,
Kya kara chas tsalaan,
Kapay viviham kopuy kadhas,
kya kara chas tsalaan

"O: which wretch of a woman has stolen my kangar?
What can I do: I bear the loss:
Could I catch that wretch, I would tear the hair out of her head.
What can I do; I bear the loss".

Kashmiri's love and adoration for *kangri* may be known by the following couplet:

"O kangri: O kangri: You are dear to me like a Houri and Fairy;

When I take you under my arm, you drive away pain from my heart".[9]

Every Kashmiri, wherever he goes, whenever seen, asleep or awake, at work or at play, sitting down or walking, carries *kangri* with him. When he sits, he places his charcoal (*tapan tsini*) stove beneath his cloak, which he then frills round him on every side, and basks in its warmth amid the acrid fumes of burning charcoal. Sometimes he falls asleep unexpectedly and serious burns are frequently caused in this way, while cancer,[10] which is believed to be induced by the hot *kangri* being always pressed against the same part of the body, is not uncommon.[11] During the Dogra rule, many houses were reported to have been destroyed by fire every year in Srinagar and in villages owing to the careless use of the *kangri*.[12] Many patients were treated at hospitals for epithelioma, a kind of cancer caused by *kangar* burns.[13]

So closely knit into the life of the Kashmiri has the *kangar* become that it even now has its place among social customs. The Muslims generally presented *kangries* to the *mullahs* and to their newly married daughters. On *Makar Sankranti*[14] day, which falls in the cold month of January, Pandits give *kangries* in alms in the name of their departed ancestors.

DRESS

The dress of the common people in Srinagar, both male and female, commonly consists of a long loose wrapper (*pheran*)[15] and trousers. *Pheran* covers the body and the arms and falls below the calf of the leg. In winter, the people of Kashmir put on *pherans* generally made of woollen cloth so as to keep themselves warm. The sleeves of the *pheran* are folded, so that they do not cause any obstruction at the time of work. The Muslim women use *pheran* of a slightly shorter size than those worn by men. The former are also brocaded near the collar in gold, silk or cotton, depending upon the status of the family. The *pheran* consists of two garments of equal size. The inner garment called *pochh* is invariably made of *khadar* or cotton cloth. The outer one is comparatively expensive, the cloth used being *chhint*, rayon silk, poplin, tweed or Kashmira, etc. The voluminous *pheran* is most suitable for users of the *kangar*, because when they sit down and place the fire pot between their legs "it forms a most excellent tent"

It was in the 'thirties of this century that Pandit Kashyap Bandhu, a great social reformer, crusaded against the use of *pheran* because it was considered to be 'effeminate'.[17] The change of outlook was the result of education and the opening up of the Valley to the outside world. As a result of Kashyap Bandhu's efforts, the *pheran* disappeared among many Pandit families.[18] Though some educated Kashmiri Pandits[19] and some upper class literate Muslim families have discarded the wearing of the *pheran*, among the great mass of the population this article of dress is in use even today.

During winter when journeys were undertaken on foot, men wrapped their legs with two pieces of coarse woollen cloth called *pataw*[20] measuring about four yards in length and six inches in width. This practice died fast when the necessity of undertaking long journeys on foot ceased to exist due to the availability of vehicular transport. Also the new generation of educated people regarded this as a clumsy apparel.

Another change which was visible in the form of dress was the use of the hat[21] and fur caps which gradually supplanted the turban (*dastar*).[22] The fur caps were worn only by well-to-do people who could afford to pay exorbitant prices for them. The English dress was more in evidence among the educated classes.[23]

The usual headdress of little girls was skull caps. After marriage, however, a Muslim girl would have, as her headgear a thicker turban-like red cap (*qasaba*) "studded with innumerable pins and over it a spare of country cloth (*pooch*) to act, in the case of necessity, as a veil which also usually covered the whole back".[24] The Pandit women's headgear was known as *taranga*.[25] It was a white round turban which was skilfully set. Contact with the Punjabi Hindu and Muslim women, however, brought about many changes in the mode of dress of the Kashmiri women. Not only *qasaba* and *taranga* disappeared with the advent of the *dupatta* but also *shalwar*, *churi dar pyjama*, and the frock were preferred because they permitted greater activity.[26] The *saree* was coming into vogue amongst the females of the upper class Pandits.[27] In fact, Kashyap Bandhu did a lot to popularise *saree*.[28] What further contributed to the popularisation of saree was the return home of several Pandit families to Srinagar during the reign of Maharaja Ranbir Singh.[29] They had migrated to India during the Afghan regime.[30] But during their absence from Kashmir "which extended over a period of more than a century, they had changed beyond recognition".[31] Their dress, and their language was not Kashmiri though they had stuck to the old customs with dogged tenacity.[32] Kilam writes that Dewan Badri Nath was first to appear on the scene. He was appointed as the governor of Kashmir in 1877. "With him came a number of outside Kashmiri Pandits". But, observes Kilam, "they maintained a certain amount of aloofness from the local Kashmiri Pandits though inter-marriage was practised to some extent and common customs were followed".[33] This social intercourse must have certainly brought about changes in the dress of those Kashmiri Pandits who came into contact with them.

One common dress of the Pandit women was *lungi*. This was a long piece of cotton cloth, and worn round the waist[34] over the *pheran*. It is said that a Panditani never left her home without this girdle.[35] This article of dress did not find favour with those who discarded the *pheran*.

The women generally adorned themselves with elegant earrings, nose rings, anklets and bracelets.[36] Their mode of dressing the hair was 'peculiar'. As Major Bates writes:

"It is drawn to the back of the head and finely braided; the braids are then gathered together, and being mixed with coarse woollen thread, they are worked into a very long plait, which is terminated by a thick tassel (*gandapan*) which reaches down to the loins".[37]

This complicated practice known as "*wankapan*" slowly disappeared with the increasing education among girls. Formerly the girls used to apply raw butter to their hair, but they developed a hatred for this practice when they began to use cosmetics.

Until the first quarter of this century the Kashmiri Pandits disliked the use of leather owing to religious prejudices. This is why they wore wooden clogs (*kharavas*) instead of leather shoes.[38] On the contrary, the Muslims used the leather shoes in addtion to the wooden clogs. On marriage days, with other finery, they put on shoes of horse or mule skin, which, for such great occasions, were ornamented with silk-work.[39] But the use of *kharavas* gradually began to be discarded by the literate Pandits.

The ordinary veil worn by the Kashmiri women was called *burqa*.[40] It consisted of a long piece of cotton cloth thrown over the head and allowed to hang down the back. Its use was confined to the Muslims alone. However, the working class Muslim women like *hanjis* and *watals* did not wear the *burqa*.[41]

It is significant that in the 'twenties of this century, the *pardah* system began to decline[42] among the families influenced by Moulvi Abdullah of the Ahmediya sect.[43] The national movement started in 1931 also led to a great change in the outlook of Muslims. Women leaders like Begum

Abdullah and Begum Zenab were the first to discard the *pardah*.[44] Even those who did not part with the *pardah* were not immune to outside influences. Fashionable *burqas*[45] made of silk were worn as a challenge to the crusade against the *pardah* system. It was not an unusual sight to see a well-to-do, educated husband attired in the latest western fashion with a fashionable *burqa*-clad wife by his side.[46] Thus imperceptibly changes were taking place in dress and old habits.

FOOD HABITS

The food habits of the common people changed little during this period. The staple food of the inhabitants was rice, but wheat, barley, maize, and several other grains were also eaten.[47] Vegetables, such as cabbages, turnips, radishes, lettuces, spinach, cucumbers and many other varieties were also very plentiful and were exclusively used.[48] The leaves of the dandelion, plantain, and several other plants were made into soup, and the catkins of the walnut were employed as food, seasoned with a little salt, mustard and walnut oil.[49] The stem of the lotus, when boiled and flavoured, was also eaten. It 'is called *nadru* and is of a pale straw colour, cylindrical, about ten inches long and 1° inch in diameter'. It was 'considered to be highly nutritious'.[50] In winter both Hindus and Muslims consumed a large number of turnips (*gogij*) in large quantities.[51] Dried fruit (*hokh phal*) and dried vegetables formed an important article of diet in Srinagar during winter.[52] It was always eaten at lunch time.[53] Clarified butter (*ghee*) was not much eaten, as the Kashmiri found that it irritated his throat.[54] Salt was also a principal article of food as the people liked their food very salty.[55] There were two kinds of salt. The better quality came from the Punjab, and was liked by the people but salt of an inferior quality was brought from Ladakh.[56]

Fish was also eaten. The flesh of sheep and goats was eaten by the Muslims and the Hindus alike.[57] Hindus would not touch poultry or eggs,[58] garlic and onion,[59] but they would eat wild fowl and the eggs of the lake birds.[60] A curious fact that was brought to the notice of Sir Walter Lawrence was that Hindus in Kashmir insisted on having any birds they ate made *halal*[61] in *Mussalman* fashion.[62] Beef was not procurable, as the killing of a cow was regarded as sacrilege by the Sikh and the Dogra rulers—a crime which involved capital punishment.[63]

The water-nut or *singhara*, ground to flour and made into bread, formed the chief article of diet of *hanjis*[64] who lived on the margin of the

Dal, Nagin and Anchar lakes. Happily for such poor people nature was usually very bounteous in Kashmir. But unfortunately the Dogra rulers levied a heavy tax on *singhara*. It was a source of considerable amount of revenue to the Government.[65] It was considered state property, and the nuts were gathered anually and sold to the *hanjis* at exorbitant rates.[66] No wonder, Robert Thorp found the *hanjis* in a miserable condition. Their cottages were "windowless, fireless, lightless and bare".[67]

The Kashmiris, rich and poor, had a great taste for tea,[68] of which two kinds found their way into the markets of Srinagar, *surati* and *sabz*.[69] The tea reached Srinagar from three sources: Bombay tea from China, hill tea from Kangra in the Punjab, and green tea from China, via Lhaasa and Ladakh.[70]

Formerly guests were served superior quality bakery products called *baqir khani* or *kulcha*. But with the establishment of hotels and sweet shops in the city the food habits of the people began to change slowly. For the elite it now became impossible to treat the guests on traditional confectionary. In fact, the presence of European bakers in the city proved itself to be very obtrusive as is evident from the penetration of cakes, biscuits, pastries etc. in Kashmiri homes. Among the people of Srinagar the English bakery goods are now in extensive use on special occasions.

Lawrence says that the average daily meal of the Kashmiri was indicative of little of taste or culture.[71] But when the services of professional cook (*waza*) were sought on festive occasions some taste was "displayed in the preparation and arrangement of viands." It was on special occasions not only the ghee or fat was extensively used for mutton and vegetable preparation.[72] This practice still holds good.

Formerly the Kashmiri Pandits were in the habit of fasting two days in every month. During these days they ate nothing but a little flour made out of *gair* or water-chestnut, which was known as *gairwavgra* or *phalhar*.[73] According to Bates, *phalhar* was the term applied to this simple dish by the Pandits themselves.[74] But by 1899 the Pandits were seen taking freely *ganhar*, vegetable marrows and red pepper on fast days.[75] It is also remarkable to note that the Kashmiri Pandits who once avoided tomatoes, the red-fleshed kabuli vegetable marrow, carrots and red beans, gradually overcame their prejudices against these vegetables.[76]

Formerly there were no liquor shops in the city, but with the opening of the State distillery in Srinagar in Ranbir Singh's time, the number of wine shops began to increase.[77] Though drinking was increasing[78] rapidly among the Hindus and Muslims, rarely could one see a drunken man in the streets, as public opinion was against the use of alcohol and a drunkard was generally looked down upon.[79] The fact that people had started drinking is amply borne out by the resolutions passed by the Srinagar Municipality, *Anjumans* and *Sabhas* from time to time, which expressed concern at growing intemperance.[80] Even a temperance society came into being, though it was short-lived.[81]

LEISURE AND RECREATION

We may now turn our attention to another aspect of social life, namely the various ways in which recreation was organized in the city.

Before the time of Maharaja Gulab Singh the various wards of Srinagar "used to turn out with slings and stones, and played a very earnest and serious game."[82] This would lead to broken heads and limbs, and even deaths.[83] But Gulab Singh is said to have looked at this fighting spirit disapprovingly and interdicted the mimic warfare.[84]

Tipcat, which was common all over India, was played in Srinagar, and the loser had to give the winner a ride on his back.[85]

Hop-scotch was also a favourite game of the children, and one of the seven compartments was known as 'hell'.[86]

Wrestling and *kabadi* also found favour with the Kashmiris.

Little girls had their rag dolls, and carried them in toy palanquins, playing at marriage.[87]

On other occasions children played the game *kaneh marven* (*stone striking*). The game needed two participants each holding a small stone in his hand. One of the boys threw his stone over a distance of four to five yards and the other was required to make it a target by striking it with the stone in his hand. If he succeeded, the first player was required to lift him bodily on his shoulders and carry him to the place where the striking stone lay. If he failed, it was his turn to throw the stone and of the first player to strike it.

The boys also played hide-and-seek (*zhep zhep*) late in the evening particularly in moonlit nights.

Among the many amusements on the river banks was the sight of three or four women or girls sitting back to back.[88] This was known as *tulay-langun-tulan-chas*.

On seeing this favourite sport of the girls, Biscoe remarked:

"Each one seems to be scratching the head of the one in front, but, as a matter of fact, they have reverted to type, to their ancestors of the forests, and are relieving one another of irritating lodgers — in fact, according to Scout Law, each doing a good turn."[89]

During the closing days of the month of *Ramazan* and immediately before and after the *Id-ul-Zuha*, young women in each neighbourhood assembled after dusk in the compound of one of the houses and celebrated the functions by singing in standing rows the traditional songs called *rov*. Two rows were formed one facing the other and each women extended her arms over the shoulders of her two neighbours. One of the rows kept on singing a song verse by verse and the other repeated the first line of the song every time, the singing of a verse was completed by the other. No musical instruments were used during this process but the women kept on moving their bodies forwards and backwards as they went on singing in chorus. The song was "pretty and the dance graceful."[90]

In fact, all such amusements were those which the people[91] themselves provided. But in point of fact "there was no game and no pastime in Kashmir proper."[92] Little girls had many games of their own, but they married so early that frivolity after marriage was strongly discouraged. After they had passed their babyhood most of their recreations were closely connected with social and religious ceremonies. In fact, there was no society in the city, and the only gatherings were at weddings or at the fairs at the shrines of the saints. The life of the artisan class was terribly earnest, and the poor artisans' children had to work from a very early age. Besides, the atmosphere was full of the supernatural-evil-minded ghosts and bogies and the kindly spirits of the ancestral dead which sat round the homes of Kashmiri boys. It was seldom that *bhands*[93] (professional troupe of acrobats), *bachhas* (dancers), or snake-charmers found it worth their while to give a performance in the city of Srinagar.

From the 'eighties of the last century, however, new games like football, cricket, hockey, polo-vault, regatta, etc. began to be introduced in Srinagar. This took place with the establishment of Mission schools in the city. In addition to this, various kinds of games, debates, lectures and occasional picnics were also encouraged. This made school life attractive, besides strengthening the bond between the students and their school. The scout movement was another important feature of the extracurricular activities. Games such as cricket, football and hockey were also regularly organized in government schools and colleges and their standard gradually improved. Physical instruction was given in every school.[94] Football became a popular game with the school boys. Maharaja Hari Singh organized various football matches in the newly opened playgrounds.[95] Hundreds of people used to witness these matches. Amar Singh was very fond of cricket and Amar Singh Club which is the best cricket ground in Srinagar, is named after him. Maharaja Hari Singh was a lover of polo and he used to play this game twice or thrice a week on the pologround. It is reported that a large number of spectators visited the pologround to see Maharaja Hari Singh play polo.[96]

One good result of these activities was that the people of Srinagar, particularly the artisans spared time to see the games. In fact, football became the *hashish* of the city people.

During the reigns of Maharaja Pratab Singh and Maharaja Hari Singh many parks were laid out in the city, which in course of time attracted people from different quarters of the city. The result was that the people who assembled in these parks during leisure hours engaged themselves in chatting and discussing all sorts of matters ranging from their domestic problems to the political affairs of the State. These parks were provided with some sports equipment for children. The progress amidst the higher circles was greater.[97] It now became a fashion for the well-to-do to take their wives with them to the cinemas or for outings on Sundays to the Nishat and Shalamar gardens.[98]

Another characteristic feature of Srinagar's changing life was the growth of various clubs. The Srinagar Club, the Amar Singh Club, the Harison Club, the Golf Club etc. became new centres of amusement and recreation. Formerly the circle of friendship was narrow because the opportunities for people to get together were few. But in the changing social life the circle of friendship grew. The clubs and associations tended to follow the lines of economic and community demarcation. As such the principle of social stratification and linguistic limits seem to have operated in the organization of leisure.

Walking on the Bund and the Boulevard was a new feature that entered the leisure time pursuits. It was characteristic of the city life. After the busy hours of a day's work, the educated class resorted to walking for pleasure.

Formerly during their leisure people went to the mosques or temples, but now they began to visit tea-shops, theatres, cinemas parks and playgrounds to while away their time. Even public lectures were attended for diversion.

The printing press heralded an era of wider dissemination of knowledge. Besides books, newspapers and periodicals were the outcome of the printing press. Doubtless the newspapers greatly influenced not only the educational but also the recreational aspects of life. A wealth of information came through the press and thus contributed to the general knowledge. Libraries and Museum were other agencies which helped the growth of knowledge.

MUSIC AND DANCE

Sufiana kalam is said to be the classical music of Kashmir. It was during 'Muslim rule' in Kashmir that Kashmiri music absorbed certain influences from Iran,[99] Arabia, Samarqand and Tashqand. *Muqams*, musical modes equivalent to *ragas*, and rhythmic patterns like *neemdoor* and *turki zarb* were introduced into Kashmiri music at this time. "Music and dancing the Sufis believed to be essential in bringing about the state of ecstasy which enabled men to see God face to face, thereby moulding Kashmiri and Persian styles into a few synthesis."[100] The very names, *sufiana kalam* and *hafiza* dancing, point to the Sufi influence. In many travel accounts we find references to the troupe of professional *nautch* girls of Srinagar.[101] Dancing was confined to them and no respectable person, Hindu or Muslim, would dream of allowing his women-folk to perform in public.[102] The *nautch* girls sang *sufiana kalam* and Kashmiri *ghazals* to the accompaniment of *hafiz naghma* "a dance the purpose of which was to express visually the meaning of the song."[103]

Amir Khan Jawan Sher, an Afghan Governor of Kashmir, maintained a large troupe of dancing girls at State expense. He would pass most of his time in the gardens of the Dal, enjoying the graceful dance and music of his favourite *hafizas*.[104] Similarly, the Sikh Governors of the Valley were enchanted by these dancers.[105] Maharaja Gulab Singh[106] and Maharaja Ranbir Singh maintained a large number of *nautch* girls to entertain themselves and their Indian and European guests.[107]

The *hafizas* were professional dancers who had to undergo severe training under skilled masters. "The orchestra accompanying them was invariably of the *sufiana kalam* type—*santur, saz-i-Kashmir, sitar* and *tabla*. They sang Kashmiri and Persian couplets and *ghazals*, explaining the meaning with appropriate gestures and the movements of hands, feet and eyes, swaying the body at each step half-way around to left or right."[108]

The dress of *hafizas* was identical with those of the classical dancers of northern India—"a tight fitting short blouse and a skirt of enormous width which was worn gathered tightly about the waist. A *dupatta* of filmsy gauze-like silk was draped about her head and shoulders. She wore the traditional Kashmiri jewellery, large *kundlas* or earrings, talraz, balis and necklaces."[109]

It was the usual practice to see only two *hafizas* taking part in a show. The dance would commence with music, "the *hafizas* taking up the refrain with suitable movements and gestures. They would move in a semi-circle with short steps gliding effortlessly across the floor. The movement of feet required great agility and long practice."[110] The *nautch* girls also brought into play their eyes as much as any other part of the body which required skilful muscle control so as to give expression of various moods and emotions.

As late as 1920 the *hafizas* of Srinagar were greatly in demand at weddings, *melas*, and out-door parties. It was through them that Prinsep, visiting Srinagar in 1877, managed to go to a wedding. They were Muslims, remarks the traveller, "yet had they all the caste feeling of the Hindoo. Of moral sentiments they were entirely innocent but they would never permit any one to drink out of their cup or smoke from their hookah, as they always went about with these two utensils, for smoke and tea are the two things necessary to a Kashmiree."[111] Prinsep got translated many of the distiches sung on the occasion. The following song gives us a good picture of the manners of the city people, and the way that the Muslim and Hindu customs have acted on each other.

Mother of the Bridegroom to the Bridegroom.

"Urge on thy steed in every direction.
I will prepare thy seat in the garden pavilion.
On the right the Koran, on thy left the necklace.
Thou art worthy to be called Lalla Gopal."

On hearing this song the traveller was wonder-struck and remarked: "Lalla Gopal, one ot the names of Krishna, who was supposed to have been the type of loveliness. Curious, this, when sung by a Mohammedan."[112]

It should be remembered that *hafiza* dancing was not only suited to the tastes of the upper classes of the city population but it was also popular with the common people. There was hardly any festive ocassion in which music did not play its part. It was indulged in and cultivated because of its charm and aesthetic values. We are told about public gatherings which were embellished by the presence of the sweet-voiced singers. Such public concerts were usually arranged with funds collected by voluntary subscription.[113]

It was after 1920 that the *hafiza* art rapidly declined. The growing popularity of the film dance and 'Hindustani' songs contributed in no small measure to its decline. With the growth of vulgar tastes owing to the advent of the cinema and theatre in Srinagar, women ceased to get into this profession. Morality is also said to have become lax among the *nautch* girls. This deprived the *hafizas* of the patronage of the better class people of Srinagar, who used to engage them on occasions of festivals and marriages. Though *hafizas* are no longer to be found in Srinagar, their graceful skill in dancing and peculiarly melodious voices are still within the living memory of many old men of the ancient city.

The growing influence of the theatre and motion pictures, however, shows that they occupied a prominent place in the changing context of leisure activities. By 1946 there existed three cinema halls in Srinagar. Various *Anjumans* and *Sabhas* are said to have expressed their concern at the growing popularity of the cinema, particularly its dance and songs among the public. Thus resolutions[114] were passed against the new favourite places of entertainment. Not a few of the local newspapers indulged in vehement propaganda against what they called the "moral degeneration" caused by films. This shows the mood of the time.

FAIRS AND FESTIVALS

With their long and chequered history and rich cultural background, Kashmiris have been taking great pleasure in celebrating festivals with elaborate colourful ceremonies.[115] Some of these festivals were celebrated in honour of the advent of spring and summer. For instance, they greeted the spring with exultation and went in flocks to *Badamwari* (Almond garden) and paid homage to the sweet lilacs.[116] Lawrence very significantly remarks: "It is not mere love of beauty of colour that impels them, but a spirit of thanks-giving that the winter with its miseries of cold and its dreary monotony of white snow has passed, and that the earth has come to life again with all her bright flowers and promise of kindly fruits."[117] The following saying in Kashmiri gives us a fair idea of how the Kashmiri looked forward to the spring.[118]

Wandae chali shin galli bayi yi bahar

If winter comes, can spring be far-behind!

The people of the city celebrated the *Badamwari* festival collectively without any consideration of class and creed. Out in the almond gardens, one generally found Hindus and Muslims sitting side by side, drinking tea from their steaming *samavars*[119] On this occasion the songs of spring were also sung.[120]

The wandering *watals* celebrated a special festival once a year when they flocked to Lala Bab's shrine near the Dal lake. It was called *Watal Mela* (fair of watals) or 'the feast of roses.'[121] On this occasion the *Watals* settled many matters affecting their tribe and marriage alliances were made.

One popular feature of the *Watal Mela* was the dance[122] which was known as *Watal dumbael*. These *watal* dancers[123] carried tall banners, the emblems of the *Mela*, to the shrine of Lala Bab.[124] They travelled on foot and gave performances on the way.

The Kashmiri Pandits held customary ceremonies on many religious festivals. Most popular among their festivals[125] were the *Shivratri* or *Herat, Nawreh* or *Navratra, Har Navmi, Ram Navmi,*[126] or *Maha Navmi, Janam Ashtami,*[127] *Pun, Raksha Bandan* and *Baisakhi*. Of these *Shivratri* was the most important. Fish was an important article of diet on this day. On the eve of *Baisakhi*, the Kashmiri Pandits assembled at Ishbari, a locality about half a kilometre from Nishat Bagh and bathed in the sacred water of Guptganga spring. Like the first *Navratra*, the *Baisakhi* festival was also celebrated during the spring season and the devotees used the occasion for relaxing in the Nishat Bagh. Some of them engaged *doongas*, a day ahead of the festival and after the performance of religious rituals at the spring, spent the whole day in recreation.

With the influx of the Punjabi Hindus, the *Dusserah* began to be celebrated in Srinagar with great *eclat*. During the Dogra rule, Hazuri Bagh in Srinagar became a centre of attraction for the city population on the eve of the *Dusserah*.[128] Effigies of Ravana, Kumbhakaran and Meghnad were burned at sunset on this day. Other festivals celebrated by the Punjabi Hindus were the *Holi*[129] and the *Diwali*.[130] Unlike the *Dusserah* these two festivals were not celebrated by the Kashmiri Pandits.

Maharaja Gulab Singh celebrated the festival of *Holi* on a grand scale.[131] On this day he used to enjoy himself by sprinkling coloured water on hundreds of the *hanjis* seized for the purpose.[132] Rich Pandits of the city also took part in this festival on the Maharaja's orders.[133] Colourful functions organized in Bagh-i-Colonel Mehan Singh[134] were graced by the presence of Kashmiri and Punjabi dancers and musicians.[135]

Maharaja Gulab Singh is said to have introduced the *Ankut* or harvest-home festival into Srinagar. The festival took place on the second day of *Diwali*, when the people of the city were "fed at the expense of the State on the first fruits of the autumn harvest."[136] Sir Walter Lawrence has given the following description of the *Ankut* festival in Srinagar:

"Huge feasts of rice and other autumn cereals are prepared at six appointed places for the better class Pandits, the common Pandits, the better class Musalmans, the common Musalmans, the Shias and the Dogras. The Dogra feast takes place in the Basant Bagh, to which the idol of the royal temple is carried in the morning. No flesh of any kind is eaten at the *Ankut*. The feasts for the better class Pandits and Musalmans are very prettily arranged. The guests sit down to their white rice and other dainties, salt and sweet. For the common herd there are platters of red rice with a portion of vegetables; but their feast is a scramble, and the hungry scavengers rush in and sweep up broken platters, dust and rice."[137]

Fairs and festivals have played a very vital role in the life of the Kashmiri Muslims.[138] Among their religious festivals may be mentioned *Moharram*,[139] *Id-ul-Fitr*,[140] *Id-ul-Zuha, Milad-un-Nabi, Shab-i-Barat, Shab-i-Qadr* and *Shab-i-Miraj*.[141] *Nouroz* was celebrated by the Shias only.

The Shias took out processions on the eve of *Moharram*. They recited the verses which extolled the heroic deeds of the hero of Karbala. The mourners beat their breasts and sometimes caused even serious injuries to their persons. With the spread of modern education, most of the westernized Shia families gave up the practice of breast-beating. It was also during the month of *Moharram* that the Shias called meetings where mourners recited elegies. Feasts were arranged for the participants. The Sunnis did not take out processions on the occasion of *Moharram* but they distributed cooked rice (*tahar*)[142] and *sharbat* among the poor. On *Id-ul-Zuha*, the devotees sacrificed sheep.

Among other popular festivals of the Muslims of Srinagar must be mentioned *Urs-i-Shah-i-Hamadan, Urs-i-Batmaloo, Urs-i-Charar-i-Shariff, Urs-i-Makhdoom Sahib, Urs-i-Pir Dastgir, Urs-i-Naqshaband Sahib* and *Urs-i-Hazratbal*. The various *mohallas* of Srinagar like Batmaloo, Khawaja Bazar, Khanqah etc. are named after different saints. It should be remembered that the Hazratbal festival[143] was a joyous and a memorable day in the dull lives of the Muslims of the Valley. *Shikaras* and *doongas* were engaged by the devotees on the eve of the *Miraj Shariff*, the *Id-i-Milad* and the *Urs-i-Chahar Yar*, when the holy hair was exhibited at the Hazratbal shrine.[144] Tea and sumptuous dishes were served in the boats, those musically inclined played on guitars and drums to the accompaniment of singing.[145] Writing about the participation of the villagers in the Hazratbal festival, Dr. Neve remarks:

"These are the great days to which the people, especially women and children look keenly forward; for not only is there the display at the shrine, but the opportunity of showing off their best clothes and jewellery, and of seeing the shops of the city and making their frugal purchases. A bundle on the man's back contains a few day's rice and condiments, and the wife carries a fat cock as a present to the moullahs."[146]

Importance of the festivals

The annual fairs held at the shrines were a "red letter day in the dull lives of the Muslims."[147] Thousands flocked to these shrines and spent the day eating and buying goods, such as pretty *kangars*, wooden patterns, glass bangles, necklaces, and painted clay toys.[148] Fairs and festivals drew together the people of the neighbourhood, and community ties were strengthened by common participation. Also the one good result of these shrines was the role they played in the integration of different communities and castes and in cementing the social relations of the inhabitants of Srinagar and other parts of the Valley. It is remarkable to note that the Hazratbal shrine attracted the Hindus[149] and the Sikhs[150] and this speaks of the communal harmony of the Kashmiris. From the economic point of view, fairs and festivals offered opportunities for buying and selling special kinds of commodities. They attracted merchants and artizans and good business was done.[151] There were fairs which drew people from remote parts of the Valley.[152] Indeed, a fair covered a very large hinterland. Some businessmen found it difficult to sell their goods all through the year; the annual fairs offered them a suitable outlet for their surplus products.

But there was another side of the picture. The people believed that a visit to the shrines would secure the object of their wishes.[153] Thus the custodians of the shrines like the *Babzadas*, the *Pirzadas* and the *Sayyids*[154] played a very important role in the life of the Muslims of Kashmir. In fact, priests officiating at the various ceremonies and rituals at home and at shrines became an important exploiting agency in an organised manner. Among the Muslims the services of a priest were required at every step and the conception of a family priest grew to such an extent that the priest was almost a permanent member of the household. It should be remembered that the ignorant masses hovered around the house of their *mullahs* to seek redress for their troubles. The *mullahs* would give them an amulet (*tawiz*)[155] and he received some gift (*nazrana*) in lieu of the services rendered by him. The *mullahs* were also invited by their disciples (*murids*) to recite *khatam-i-shariff* at their residence. On this occasion they were treated to feast and a few coins were doled out to them.

Notwithstanding the spiritual and historical significance of the *ziarats* and *khanqahs* for sensitive souls, they were converted into chief centres of superstition and charlatanism by their custodians. The crafty, hypocritical and materialist *mullahs* kept the common folk in the dark. They were made to believe that the disease was caused not by the germs, filth etc. but by certain supernatural factors. No wonder, the Kashmiris regarded cholera as a wrath (*qahar*) of God. It is also worthwhile to note that the *mullahs* gave birth to various kinds of superstitions. For instance, the credulous masses were taught to believe that smallpox was caused by the *gini* of smallpox (*shootilbud*). Thus the *mullahs* at once assumed the function of a doctor, a physician, a judge,[157] and what not because of his connections with the *ziarats* and the *khanqahs*. It is, therefore, not surprising that the people obstinately opposed modern medical practices and ideas of sanitation.[158]

SOCIAL CUSTOMS

Both the Hindus[159] and the Muslims of Srinagar have an elaborate code of rituals and ceremonies with regard to birth, marriage and death. A careful study of the old customs[160] and traditions reveals that they still continue to be practised by a great majority of the people. Western impact has not been felt in regard to these rituals and except for few highly westernized sections of the people, the rest of the city population continues to perform the old ceremonies.

The Muslims differed from the Hindus in many of their customs with regard to birth, marriage and death,[161] but they had resemblances in certain respects. Both were superstitious. For instance, when there was a cholera or smallpox epidemic in the city, its occurence was attributed to the *ginis* and God or goddesses.[162] While the Muslims consulted the *mullahs*,[163] the Pandits performed some regular ceremonies when smallpox[164] attacked their children. These ceremonies, however, ceased to exist owing to the spread of modern education.[165] Similarly, the old system of having a grass bed[166] for the mother at the time of her confinement was gradually being discarded, thanks to the efforts of the medical missionaries and practitioners who brought home to the people the dangers of this insanitary practice.

Till very recently the Muslims of the Valley observed a very curious custom in times of natural calamities. As Lawrence writes: "Musalmans from all parts of the Valley flock to Chrar Shariff, and when scarcity is imminent, where calamities such as earthquake, cholera, and drought occur, thousands gather there and sit silent on the hills around, confessing their sins and begging pardon."[167] This impressive ceremony was called *Noufal*. The great place for the confession of sins in the city was the Idgah,[168] to which were carried an emblem and the holy relics by the Muslims of Srinagar in a procession. Special prayers were offered in congregations at the Idgah for protection against the ravages of several calamities.[169] It is of interest to note that during the period under review, *Noufal* processions in the city were often taken by the *mullahs* at the command of the rulers.[170] This was due to the fact that Gulab Singh and Ranbir singh also believed in the efficacy of *Noufal* prayers. The Hindus too were required by the Maharaja's to invoke God's help at the time of distress. On such occasions they would visit Sharka Devi's hill.[171]

Both among the Hindus and the Muslims offerings were made to the dead on prescribed occasions. While the Hindus performed the *shradha*[172] ceremonies, the Muslims organized *khatam-i-shariff*. This concern for the dead was an indication of the fact that they considered themselves to be in continued connection with those whom they could not see any more. With such a support, even if it was of an imaginary nature, life, perhaps, became somewhat easier to bear.

In certain respects, the rituals of the Hindus and the Muslims were similar. For example, for childless parents it was customary to visit shrines, call the aid of saints and *darveshes* and to keep fasts in order that they might be blessed with children. Though the majority of the population of the Valley embraced Islam in the fourteenth century, they did not seem to have given up their old customs, rituals and beliefs. Devotion to, reverence for, and implicit trust in the shrines and *mullahs* played a larger part in the religious life of the average Kashmiri Muslim. And although Prophet Muhammad was venerated by the people, their knowledge of his teachings was meagre. For them it is the shrines which protected the believers from disease and disaster. They looked to it for aid in any enterprise. A Muslim woman who had no issue went to a priest or a *darvesh* for a charm or visited a shrine, where she tied a piece of string (*daesh*) to the inner entrance, pledging thereby that if she bore a child, she would make suitable offerings at the shrine.[17]

RELIGIOUS REFORM

It is clear from the above that religion with the majority of the people in Srinagar was nothing more than the observance of a certain set of rituals.[174] Until the beginning of this century, there was not a single religious association in Srinagar, where people could discuss religious affairs and raise their voice against the superstitious practices. It is not, therefore, surprising that Srinagar did not see any religious reform movement worth mentioning till the dawn of this century.[175] However, in Maharaja Ranbir Singh's reign Husain Batku, a resident of Srinagar, attempted to preach what was termed 'Wahabi' doctrines.[176] He raised a cry against *pir-mureedi*, superstitions, rituals and denounced the worship of *asthans* (shrines). But the opposition of the local *mullahs* was so strong that the Maharaja was compelled to give orders for Husain's expulsion from the city.[177]

Husain Batku's mission was carried on by Sabzar Shah and Sidique Hasan Khan.[178] They made the *mohalla* of Narwara in Srinagar a centre of their religious activities.[179] Later, in the 'twenties of this century the 'Wahabis' founded the *Anjuman-i-Ahl-i-Hadith*[180] which came in the limelight under the inspiring leadership of Moulvi Ghulam Nabi Mubaraki and Moulvi Nur-ud-din. The *Anjuman's* official organ was the *Muslim*. The paper aimed at the extirpation of social evils among the Muslim community.[181]

It should be remembered that the '*Ahl-i-Hadith*' represented an advanced school of Muslim thought. They confined themselves to the text of the Quran and *Hadith* (tradition) and relied upon individual judgement for their interpretation. They disowned the doctrine of *Hayat-i-Nabi* (the Prophet being still alive and in touch with his followers). They believed that there could be no communion between the living and the dead, who could not consequently benefit each other. They stood for reform in Muslim manners, customs and life and aimed at the elimination of superstitions and rituals. They laid emphasis on the unity of Godhead, denounced the worship of *pirs* and advocated the abolition of anti-Islamic practices among the Muslims.

The preachings of the '*Ahl-i-Hadith*' brought them into conflict with a great majority of the conservatives. For many years a heated debate took place in some mosques of Srinagar among the adherents of the shrines and the '*Ahl-i-Hadith*' with regard to the religious issues. It is interesting to note that the '*Ahl-i-Hadith*' were dubbed contemptuously as *kutas*[182] by the devotees of the shrines and *mullahs*. So devoted were the Muslim masses to the priests that even the leaders of the Kashmir political movement had to seek the support of Mir Waiz Muhammad Yusuf Shah[183] while using the religious places for the furtherance of their political objectives. Besides the '*Ahl-i-Hadith*', Ahmediyas[184] under the leadership of Moulvi Abdullah[185] also did a lot of propaganda against the rituals.

Though a very large majority of the Muslims of Srinagar remained uninfluenced, the religious reformers[186] brought about a change in the attitude of many. Even many custodians of shrines admitted that '*Ahl-i-Hadith*' ideas were gaining ground in Srinagar.[187] This leads us to the inference that the practice of tying knots at the gates of shrines must have died down among the '*Ahl-i-Hadith*' families. Participation in the festivals in one way or the other was (and is still) current to a great extent though side by side growing indifference towards them also existed.

As regards Kashmiri Pandits, no religious reform took place among them during this period. Even the Arya Samaj which had denounced in the strongest terms the worship of idols, the performance of *shradhas* and old customs and beliefs outside the Valley could not achieve much in this direction in Srinagar owing to the hostility of the Brahman priests. It should, however, be remembered that the Samaj did much to improve the social position of Kashmiri Pandit women.[188]

MARRIAGE

As regards marriage, boys and girls did not enjoy the freedom of selecting their spouses.[189] The selection was the exclusive privilege of parents[190] or the guardians as it was believed that the children, however, grown up they might be, would not, because of their inexperience, be able to make the correct choice. The unmarried people did not even participate in the discussions about the offers received from various households as this was regarded as an act of misbehaviour.

Among the Muslims each class would prefer to enter into matrimonial alliances with persons belonging to the same class. The Sayyid families in particular endeavoured to marry only in the Sayyid families. But if suitable matches were not available, they did not hesitate to marry in other classes.[191] The *hanjis* and the *watals*, however, married only in their respective class, because they ranked last in the social hierarchy.[192]

As compared to the Pandits,[193] the Muslims of the city spent little on marriages. Their main item of expenditure on marriage was on the *wazwan*[194] (feast). Both the Muslims and the Hindus gave sumptuous and prolonged feasts on the occasion of marriage. Dowry was practically non-existent among the Muslims,[195] but among the Pandits the system of dowry had almost attained the force of law.[196]

The system of dowry seems to be largely a result of the rapid progress of western education among the Pandits; for a youngman who had done well at college was a most desirable bridegroom, and naturally the price had tended to rise as steadily as the demand. The tyrannical custom which compelled a father to spend huge sums upon feastings, processions and dowry on the occasion of a daughter's wedding, pressed heavily on the poor. Most fathers were compelled to borrow huge sums of money and in consequence, passed the remainder of their lives in debt and worry.[197]

There was yet another evil custom prevalent among the Pandits. Everytime the father wished to see his married daughter he had to pay some cash. Lawrence observes: "This sum varies from eight annas to five rupees, and as it has to be given by the bride's father whenever he invites his daughter to his house, and on all great holidays, anniversaries. domestic events, and birth-days, it is a severe tax on the Pandit who is blessed with daughters."[198] This practice still continues.

POSITION OF WOMEN

The occupations of women furnish a subject of much interest and importance.[189] Besides preparing food women's most laborious work was that of husking and grinding grain.[200] The rice was cleaned in a wooden mortar, in which it was pounded with a heavy wooden pestle. It was a healthy work, which produced a fine physical development in those accustomed to the exercise.

The women of the artisan class supplemented their husband's work. For example, the potter's wife dug the clay for her husband and painted the pots with streaks of colour before they were baked.

The shawl industry gave work to a number of women in their homes. The 'pashm'[201] was given in its raw state to these women who spun it into the reed to different degrees of fineness. They sold it in small quantities to shopkeepers in the bazar, from whom it was bought by the *karkhanadars* and others. The decline of shawl industry, however, rendered hundreds of such women destitute and helpless.

The beginning of industrialism gave scope to the labour of women. It is interesting to note that the silk factory employed a large number of women.[202]

The women of the *hanji*[203] class deserve special mention. From early dawn to nightfall, she was kept busily employed in preparing food, looking after babies, fishing in the river, selling vegetable products of the lakes and the floating gardens and doing such filed work as she was able to perform. Her only relaxation was the chat with her friends at the river or with her customers who used to joke with her, and the *hookah* which she loved as much as her husband. She was a cheery, hard-working creature, devoted to the care of her household. If her moral sense was vague, her language foul, her person less clean than might be desired — these faults were largely due to her environment and those who knew her best learnt to respect her many virtues.

It should be remembered that the *doonga hanji's* house provided no facilities for privacy or for the isolation of the sexes. Gossip and petty squabbles of husband and wife, or wives, were conducted in the open air, and became the common property of the neighbourhood. Such incidents gave occasion for shameless indecency or abuse which the children learnt at an early age when they were too young to understand anything.

Another class of women was known as *gaan* (prostitutes). There were two ill-famed centres of prostitution in Srinagar e.g. Tashwan and Maisuma. The sale of young girls in Kashmir to established houses of ill-fame in Srinagar and India was both protected and encouraged by the Dogra rulers.[204] According to Robert Thorp, the license granting permission for the purchase of a girl for this purpose, cost about 100 *chilkee* rupees in Ranbir Singh's time.[204] The traveller lamented that such sales took place because the very poorest and lowest classes of the people sold their children.[206] In 1880 the Maharaja received from 15 to 25 per cent of the whole revenue of his State from the gains of his licensed prostitutes.[207] It is also said that there were 18,715 State prostitutes in Kashmir in 1880.[208]

Though the Maharaja derived a lot of income from the prostitutes, no amount of money was spent on their benefit. Mr. Henvey, Officer on Special Duty in Kashmir in 1880, writes that no care was taken of the sick prostitutes.[209] In consequence, syphilitic disease was spreading terribly throughout Kashmir. This is evident from the Srinagar Mission Hospital report which says that during 1877-1879 the total number of new cases treated was 12,977. Of these 2,516 were entered as 'venereal diseases.'[210]

There was yet one other misery to which the prostitutes were subjected—they could not marry and settle down as respectable women.[211]

It is a sorry commentary on the leaders of the religious reform movements in Srinagar that the sad plight of the innocent young girls did not engage their attention. Never did they raise any voice against the houses of ill-fame and immoral traffic in women. Credit, however, goes to a gallant barber of Srinagar who waged a crusade against many houses of ill-fame situated in Maisuma. He was popularly known as Muhammad Subhan Naed. He lived in Maisuma and like his neighbours, he "was continually disturbed at night by the ribald songs accompanied by musical instruments such as the harp and zither, and also by men wrangling."[212] But, writes the founder of modern education in Kashmir, what really upset Subhan Naed "were the cries of anguish from the unfortunates, recently forced into this cruel life, many of them quite young, who had been sold by their relations under the pretence that marriages had been arranged for them."[213] Moved by the cries of these poor creatures, the energetic young barber sought the help of some decent men in fighting this evil. "He wrote pamphlets to show up this cruel traffic, and distributed hundreds of them in the city. He would stand up in the streets and preach, and at night, with some of his friends, would stand outside those houses trying the men visitors from entering (Sic)."[214]

The selfless services of the valiant Subhan Naed ultimately bore fruit, when, in 1934, the State Assembly passed an Act suppressing immoral traffic in women.[215] It provided penalties for persons who kept, managed or allowed the use of any place as a brothel or procure women or girls for prostitution or live upon the earnings of prostitutes or traffic in women and children. Those who solicited in public places, encouraged or abetted seduction or prostitution of minor girls were also penalized.[216]

The suppression of immoral traffic Act of 1934 had a disastrous effect on a very large number of prostitutes. It now became difficult for them to eke out their existence. While some prostitutes made good their escape to India, there were many who took to *charka* on Subhan's advice. It is also remarkable to note that some of the prostitutes earned a decent living by working in the Silk factory.

The position of middle and upper class women was not good. There was no more variety in their life than that of their menfolk. Marriage was the great event of their life. To arrange the marriage of daughters[217] was the most pressing duty of a *kori-moul* (father of daughters). No scandal was so grievous as that which resulted from the presence of an *anharish* (virgin) daughter in the house. Biscoe says: "Self-respecting women are obliged to wear dirty garments, for if they wore clean ones they might be taken for women of loose life."[218] Almost all the upper class women were never seen in the streets of Srinagar.[219] *Pardah* was common among the Muslims.

Child-marriage was prevalent among the Pandits and the Muslims. While widow-remarriage was practised by the Muslims, it did not find favour with the Kashmiri Hindus. Among the latter, the number of widows was appalling.[220] Many of them were young and innocent girls, exposed to temptations, and often led unhappy lives.[221] From Mr. Biscoe's autobiography we get some idea of the sad plight of young Brahman widows. Remarks Mr. Biscoe: "As there was no restriction to early marriage there were numbers of child widows who were obliged to live in their father-in-law's house, and do as they were told. I came to know of the cruelties practised on these girls, especially by the Brahman priests, who were often the fathers of the drowned babies. The infants were thrown either in the river or to the Pariah dogs at night so that the Hindu religion should not be disgraced."[222]

SOCIAL REFORM

The social evils that had crept in Srinagar society did not escape the notice of Christian missionaries.[223] Inspired by evangelical zeal they attempted to reform the society. At the same time Arya Samajists, Ahmediyas and 'Wahabis' made their appearance in Srinagar to counter the missionary propaganda. Thus committees and associations rapidly came into being in Srinagar.

The Arya Samaj was represented in Srinagar by those Hindus who had come from Punjab as State employees and by those who had settled permanently or semi-permanently in the city for business purposes. To begin with, the Samaj did not register any success[224] on account of the hostility of the Kashmiri Pandits and their priests. But with the passage of time some Kashmiri Pandits extended their support to the Samaj in its social work. Among the local reformers may be mentioned Shri Ram Chandrji Abhay who worked hard to remove the disabilities of Pandit women. Even attacks were made on his life by the orthodox, but he did not give up the struggle. The evil effects of child marriage were publicised. Propaganda was also conducted in favour of widow remarriage.[225] It is remarkable that during 1920-30 the Arya Samajists celebrated the marriages of half a dozen widows in Srinagar.[226]

The Arya Samaj in Srinagar was also engaged in educational propaganda. It maintained a girls school of the middle standard in Wazir Bagh wherein the number swelled to about 100 in 1931.[227] Under its auspices ran Vanit Ashram at Rainawari where widows were given lessons in the three R's and were also taught embroidery and weaving work to enable them to earn a living.[228]

A more important influence than the Arya Samaj was provided by a group of young educated Kashmiri Pandits who organized themselves into a body known as the Fraternity in 1930.[229] Among the prominent persons who were directly or indirectly associated with the Fraternity were Damodhar Bhat, Dina Nath Hanjura, Mohan Kishen Tikku, Dina Nath Kachru, T.N. Koul Jalali, Dina Nath Parimu, Dina Nath Dilgir and Dr. Saligram Koul. Prem Nath Bazaz was the senior member of the group. The Fraternity became an important medium for propagating the ideas of those who wished to change Hindu society. The conception of social reform visualised by the Fraternity included not only a check on wasteful expenditure at weddings but also the spread of education among girls, freedom for widows to remarry, revival of cultural activities, improvement in communities health, and change in 'national' dress to make it decent, graceful, dignified and suitable for the climate of Kashmir.[230]

The Fraternity launched a campaign to mobilise public opinion in favour of the proposed social reform. Frequent public meetings were held at which women were assembling in large numbers to hear speakers. The movement for reform caused a reaction among the orthodox Pandits who had organized themselves into a group known as Sanatan Dharam Sabha earlier in 1923.[231] The members of this group were opposed to any social reform and indulged in a vehement propaganda against the reformers. "For weeks", writes Bazaz, "it became difficult for the young enthusiasts to move freely in the city. They were nicknamed as *munda kath* (progeny of widows) and were contemptuously addressed and sneeringly looked down upon."[232]

The political movement started in July 1931 by Muslims brought about a great change in the outlook of Kashmiri Pandits. One reaction of the Muslim movement was an intense social reform among Kashmiri Pandits.[233] It should be remembered that in the changed environment, the Fraternity rechristened itself in July 1931, as the Sanatan Dharam Young Men's Association (or Yuvak Sabha) with the sole purpose of safeguarding the interests of the Pandit community. To begin with, the Yuvak Sabha confined its activities to the political issues of the time;[234] its leaders frequently displayed "their ultra loyal attitude towards Dogra

Raj."[235] But the success of the Muslim movement soon taught them that a very small minority which identified its interests with those of the despotic rulers would have little political future.[236] Under the changed political conditions the Yuvak Sabha leaders deemed it proper to devote themselves to the internal reforms of their own community.[237] It is significant that even the orthodox members of the Sanatan Dharam Sabha who had previously hampered the reform found refuge in the Yuvak Sabha which now "acquired the halo of saviours."[238]

The Yuvak Sabha and its activities brought about a number of changes in Hindu society, thereby adding much to the emancipation of women. Under the auspices of the Sabha meetings were held by the Kashmiri Pandits in various parts of the city at which women's participation was significant.[239] Under Pandit Kashyap Bandhu's leadership, this organization became very popular by rallying public opinion to its view. Not only women's freedom and women's education were ceaselessly advocated, but also the reformers were successful in popularising widow remarriages among Kashmiri Pandits. It was due to the efforts of the reformers that the number of widow remarriages began to increase day by day. More important, even the Sanatan Dharam *purohits*, the standard bearers of orthodoxy, recognized the validity of widow remarriage.[240]

It was the courage and perseverance of the reformers that brought about the Widow Remarriages Act of 1933 which legalised marriages of Hindus. Maharaja Hari Singh made these observations in the preamble of the Act: "Whereas bearing in mind the advance in ideas recently made in Hindu Society, the recognition by the majority of Hindus that the incapacity of Hindu widows to contact a second valid marriage is harmful to Hindu Society and the progress made all over the world as also in other parts of India towards the enfranchisement of women, we consider that the removal of obstacles to remarriage of Hindu widows in the State will lead to the promotion of good moral and to the public welfare."

Pandit reformers of this period like Kashyap Bandhu, Hargopal Koul, Gopi Kishen and Uma Razdan also raised loud and bitter complaints about the extortionate payments demanded by the bridegrooms' family from the father of the bride. In 1944 *Samaj Sudhar Samiti* came into being. Several cases of ruined families were publicised.[241] It is significant that dramas written in Kashmiri depicting the social evils were staged. Squads of youth were organized who picketted homes where wealth was lavishly spent on marriages and other festivals.[242] All these efforts proved futile.[243]

For various reasons the movement for social reform was confined to the Hindu community. They had made good progress in education, "achieved a bit of political power by capturing subordinate jobs in the administration and were beginning to extricate themselves from the effects of long and deep slumber."[244] The Muslims, on the other hand, were still backward. It was, however, in the late twenties of this century that the Ahmediyas made their appearance in Srinagar. Feelings ran very high among the orthodox when Moulvi Abdullah courageously opposed *pardah*, supported girl's education and launched a crusade against the *mullahs*.[245] He also denounced the evil customs such as ritual worship which hampered the progress of the Muslim women. Abdullah's success was, however, short-lived since the movement of 1931 turned the attention of the entire Muslim community of Kashmir to the more vital issues of the time. Thus the movement for reform among Muslim women receded into the background on account of changed political conditions. It should, however, be remembered that the social, economic and political changes which occured after 1931 contributed greatly to the emancipation of Muslim women. In was in 1931 that the women of Srinagar made their first steps in the struggle for Kashmir's freedom.

IMPACT OF THE NATIONAL MOVEMENT

"The horses of the military were trampling the crowds down, and in front of them dashed a group of women with tin boxes filled with stones. Rattling them loudly, they made the terrified horses rear and hesitate."[246] Later it was the women again who sat outside Sheikh Abdullah's prison walls for three days until they had, perforce, to release him.[247] It is remarkable that the illiterate women of Srinagar were guiding the men. Again when the Quit Kashmir Movement was launched in 1946, the women of Srinagar "hid the undergrounds leaders, even when they knew that discovery would mean the arrest of their menfolk and harrassment for months afterwards ... They lent their clothes to disguise runaway leaders. They brewed tea and cooked food for those in hiding. They shouted slogans after curfew hours; they congregated at Dargah Shariff every week in spite of military trucks and police guards."[248]

The contribution of the illiterate and poor women to the freedom movement was great indeed.[249] Among many numberless and unnamed poor women who suffered for the cause of Kashmir may be mentioned Zoni and Mukta.[250] After the tribal raid, the women's army came into being. It is significant that the first battalion of the army was named Mukta battalion.'[251]

HINDU-MUSLIM RELATIONS

A perusal of the writings of the period shows that there existed good neighbourly relations between the Hindus and Muslims of Srinagar. The period of mutual jealously and antagonism between the two religious groups in which political and economic reasons were as much as, and perhaps more, responsible than the religious factor was a temporary phase. In fact, the process of mutual assimilation and interaction of thought and culture had started as early as the establishment of 'Muslim Rule' in Kashmir.

The friendly relations between the two religious communities of Srinagar are testified to by many accounts. The *Gham Khawar-i-Kashmir*[252] (Lahore) in its issue of August 17, 1895 wrote that the Hindus and Muslims in Srinagar lived like brothers. The same view was expressed in the *Amrit Bazar Patrika* on August 19, 1931. Munshi Ganesh Lal visiting Srinagar in 1846 found 'very little distinction' between the two religious groups.[253] Dr. Ernest Neve who had an intimate knowledge of Kashmir observed: "In Kashmir there is very little fanaticism. In some respects the toleration is surprising. The friendly relations existing between Mohammedans and Hindus are remarkable, and partly to be explained by the fact that many Hindu customs have survived, even among Mohammedans."[254]

The Kashmiri Pandits were not very particular about matters of defilement or pollution by touch. They would, for instance drink water brought by a Muslim and eat food cooked 'on the boat of a Muslim.[255] Even foster-mothers were permitted by them for their infants,[256] and it is said that the foster-brothers often obtained 'great power in a Hindu household.'[257] Maharaja Gulab Singh is reported to have made a vain attempt to stop the practice of drinking water brought by a Muslim. "But it was all to no effect", observes Lawrence, "and when it is remembered that there is no caste of water-carriers in Kashmir it is not to be wondered at that the Hindus failed to comply with Maharaja Gulab Singh's edicts."[258]

We get references to the services rendered by the Muslims to the Hindus in connection with the latter's marriage ceremonies.[259] The task of carrying and delivery of cooked eatables and sweetmeets etc. prepared for distribution among the relatives on the ceremonial rites was performed by the Muslims. This practice was known as *bhaji*.[260] However, this custom slowly died down. It is said that one of the chief causes of its decline was 'hostility and disfavour' with which it was looked by Maharaja Pratap Singh.[261]

It appears from the foregoing account that the Dogra rulers looked askance at the social intercourse between Hindus and Muslims. This is also proved by the fact that an attempt was made in Gulab Singh's reign to prevent the Pandits from eating *halal* meat.[262] New meat shops allotted to the Hindu butchers were opened in the city and the local Hindu population was persuaded not to buy meat from the Muslim butchers.[263] But to the bigoted ruler's chagrin, the Kashmiri Pandits persisted in consuming the *halal* meat as is evident from their petition submitted to Wazeer Panoo.[264] Ranbir Singh did his utmost to stop the practice of buying meat, cheese, rice and milk by the non-Muslims from the Muslims,[265] but to no avail.

Causes of Religious Tolerance

Sir Walter Lawrence gives two reasons for the religious tolerance in Kashmir. "In the first place". observes he, "the strict prohibition of kine-killing, removes one of the principal causes of ill-feeling, and in the second place, the strong rule under which the people lived for generations would not brook any quarelling between Hindus and Muslims. A Government which maintained State Mullahs to celebrate marriages and formed out the right of celebration was not likely to allow any signs of intolerance and fanaticism, and a revivalist in the old days would have met with short shrift."[266] But Lawrence's thesis seems to be hardly convincing. It must be remembered that condign punishments were meted out to the persons found guilty of killing cows.[267] "Often they were boiled in oil and then hung from a hook which was fixed on to a pole in a public place."[268] In the Sikh as well as in the earlier part of the Dogra rule in Kashmir Fateh Kadal presented a ghastly picture. There was a pole and hook on this bridge, "on which used to swim the bodies of those who had been convicted of killing cows, as a warning to the citizens.[269] These brutalities would have filled the Muslims of the city with horror. Not very rarely, the Muslims expressed their resentment against the acts of terrorism,[270] though not against the ban on cow-slaughter.[271] The result was that the Government had to modify rules so as to make the punishment appear less severe.[272]

As to the Government's policy of suppressing the acts of intolerance and fanaticism, we need not stress the point beyond saying that the Sikh as well as the Dogra rulers were more responsible for fanning communal feelings than their subjects themselves. It will be no digression to observe here that the great mosque of Shah-i-Hamadan would have fallen victim to the sadism of the Sikh Governor, but for the timely intervention of Pandit Bir Bal Dhar.[273]

The spirit behind tolerance and goodwill may be found in the social structure and cultural pattern of Srinagar which is characterized by unity as well as diversity. Even when the political conflicts were raging round the Valley in medieval times, the masses were receiving instructions from their two great saints, Lalla Ded and Shaikh Nur-ud-din Wali. They sang the songs of mutual love and affection which "stirred the souls of Hindus and Muslims alike to their deepest depths." Besides, the *Rishi* order of the Sufis did much to foster feelings of love in Kashmir as it had imbibed some elements of *Vedantism*. The *Rishis*, for example, would abstain from taking meat and even now many of the Muslim and Hindu families in Srinagar do not cook meat on the anniversaries of the *Rishi* saints.[274] The participation of Hindus and Muslims in each other's festivals also cemented the bond of friendship between the two.[275]

In conclusion, it may be said that certain similarities in social customs of the two divergent groups must have also contributed to the growth of religious tolerance in Srinagar. *Menzrat*, or use of the *mehandi* dye, *gandun* or *lagenchir* or fixing of the marriage day; *phirsal*, the visit paid by the bridegroom to the bride's house after marriage; *gulimiut*, the giving of money etc. are only some examples to show how the interplay of various cultural forces has shaped the society of Srinagar during its period of history. Even at present, when the bases of society have undergone a radical change, the old order survives to a considerable degree.

It would be wrong to think that there never arose feelings of vengeance between the two. Such feelings were aroused in 1931, when the Muslims rose in rebellion against the autocratic rule of the Maharaja. But these were only passing storms. The responsibility for creating misunderstanding goes always to the vested interests. These were not wanting. Thus the political leaders of 1931 fighting no doubt for safeguarding the interests of the Muslim community, were painted in lurid colours. But it is the so-called 'communalists' of 1931 who came to the rescue of their non-Muslim brothers when the Valley was shaken by the tribal raid in 1947.

NOTES:

1. The raw material required for the manufacture of *wagu* was grass which was obtained from paddy plants after husking.
2. Lawrence, *op. cit.,* p. 250.
3. Ibid.
4. Ibid. Younghusband, *op. cit.,* p. 220.
5. Lawrence, *op. cit.,* p. 250.
6. Writing in the 'sixties of the last century, Torrens observed that when he questioned the Kashmiris about the Russian tea-urn (*samavar*), "they acknowledged that its shape had been imitated from a Russian model brought by some travelling merchants years ago from the north. This dodge for keeping tea hot had evidently impressed them with a great respect for the Muscovite; and they may be said the imbibe with each cup of comfort a spice of Russian influence. Muscovite intrigue may lurk in the aroma of each demestic teapot; and methought the very hiss of the steaming 'Samavar' breathed a covert warning, prophetic of the future." (Torrens, *op. cit.,* p.309); See also Bates, *op. cit.,* p.39.
7. Knowles. 'Kangar', *Indian Antiquary* Vol. XV, 1885, pp. 265-66; Hultzsch, 'Kangar', Ibid., Vol. XV, 1886, p. 57; Stein, *Rajat*, verse 106 and note; Bates, *op. cit.,* p.38; Sufi, *op. cit.,* II, pp. 589-90; Torrens, *op. cit.,* p. 310.
8. Bates, *op. cit.,* p. 38.
9. Sufi, *op. cit.,* II, pp. 590-91. The famous Urdu poet, Chaudri Khushi Muhammad Nazir, has also sung in praise of *kangri*. See *Nagma-i-Firdous*, part I, pp. 139-140.
10. Sufi, *op. cit.,* II. pp. 590-91; Bates, *op. cit.,* p.38; See also Carus Wilson, *Irene Petrie*, pp. 178-181.
11. According to the findings of a recent study, an "overwhelming majority of cases of deformities resulting from burns reported in Kashmir are attributable to the Kangri ..." A group of doctors, who made a statistical study of 1,500 cases at the Shri Maharaja Hari Singh Hospital, Srinagar, said in their report: "*Kangri* was the cause of post-burn contracture deformities in 95 percent of the cases. Only five percent of the contractures resulted from electricity of disel burns." The doctors further reported that all the patients came from the low and middle income groups. This, they claimed, "was probably because the more affluent use iron stoves or electric heaters." *The Indian Express,* June 15, 1976, p. 7; See also J. N. Sathu's article on 'Kangri,' *The Consumer Gazette* (Independence Day Kashmir Special). August 10, 1975, p. 28.
12. Lawrence, *op. cit.,* p. 250.
13. *The Indian Antiquary*, October 1885, p.265.
14. *Makar Sankranti* falls at the end of frost in the month of *Magh* every

year. It is the time of hope for Kashmiri Pandits who tortured by the infernal cold of winter look to *Makar Sankranti* as a Day of Deliverance.

15. Lawrence, *op. cit.*, pp. 250-53; *Beyond the Pir Panjal*, p. 240; Moorcroft, *op. cit.*, II, p. 131; Bates, *op. cit.*, pp. 35-36; Dugsal, *op. cit.*, p. 177; Dermot Norris, *op. cit.*, p. 10; Wakefield, *op. cit.*, pp. 105-106; Marion Doughty, *op. cit.*, pp. 124 and 131; *Kashmir in Sunlight and Shade*, pp. 138-139; *Schonberg, op. cit., II*, p. 100; *Where Three Empires Meet*, p. 26; *Parbway, Emerald Set with Pearls*, p. 64; *The J & K Territories*, p. 18; Newell, *JASB (V), 1854*, p. 433; Knowles, *Indian Antiquary*, Vol. xiv, Oct. 1885, p. 266; Hasan, *Tarikh* (Persian), I. pp. 452-54.
16. *The Ranbir*, Dec. 19, 1932. The original name of Kashyap Bandhu was Tara Chand Koul. He left Kashmir for India in 1921 in search of fortune. In the course of his travels he came into contact with the leaders of the Arya Samaj movement. Having been influenced by the movement, Tara Chand Koul changed his name to Kashyap Bandhu at Quetta and studied Sanskrit and the holy scripures under Vishwa Bandhu in a Samajist educational institution at Lahore. He preached the Samajist doctriness and edited the *Arya Gazette*, an Urdu weekly devoted to the cause of Arya Samaj movement. "He fell in love with and married, in 1921, Vimaladevi, daughter of Vishnudutta, a Kashmiri Pandit who had settled at Ferozpore." In response to the call given by the Yuvak Sabha Kashyap Bandhu returned to Srinagar in August, 1931 and took an active part along with his wife in the field of social reform. *Daughters of Vitasta*, p. 251.
17. *Daughters of Vitasta*, p. 250.
18. *The Ranbir*, 19 Dec. 1932.
19. *Census*, 1931, I. p. 102.
20. Gordon, *Work and Play in India and Kashmir*, p. 232; *Pataw* was also used by Maharaja Gulab Singh's soldiers. See Mirza Saif-ud-Din, *op. cit., Vol.* VI, f. 180a.
21. *Census*, 1931, I, p. 102.
22. Lawrence, *op. cit.*, p. 252; *Beyond the Pir Panjal*, p. 240 ; *Census*, 1931, I.p. 102.
23. *Census*, 1931, I, P. 102; *Kashmir in Sunlight and Shade*, pp. 142-143.
24. *Daughters of Vitasta*, p. 199; Marion Doughty, *op. cit.*, p. 124; Dugsal, *op. cit.*, p. 177.
25. Ibid.
26. Ibid; pp. 243, 250; Moulvi Majid, *op. cit.*, p. 70; *Census* 1931, I, p.102.
27. *Census*, 1931, I, p. 102; *Daughters of Vitasta*, pp. 252-253.
28. *Daughters of Vitasta*, pp. 252 -253; *The Ranbir*, Dec. 19, 1932: *The Tribune*, Sept. 25, 1931.
29. Kilam, *History of Kashmiri Pandits*, p. 279.
30. Ibid; Parimu, *op. cit.*, p. 437.
31. Kilam, *op. cit.*, p. 279.

32. Ibid.
33. Ibid; See also The *Ranbir*, May 1, 1928.
34. Wakefield, *op. cit.*, p. 106: *Census*, 1911, I, p. 106.
35. *Beyond the Pir Panjal*, p. 240.
36. Bates, *op. cit.*, pp.35-36: Wakefield,*op. cit.*, p. 106.
37. Bates, *op. cit.*, pp. 35-36.
38. Ibid., p. 36; *Kashmir in the Sunlight and Shade*, p.150; Lawrence, *op. cit.*, p. 252.
39. Bates, *op. cit.*, pp. 34-35.
40. *Kashmir in Sunlight and Shade*, p.150; *Census*, 1921, I, p. 90.
41. Petrocokina, *op. cit.*, p. 84; *Census*, 1921, I, p.90.
42. *Census*, 1931,I, pp.102, 141; See also Moulvi Majid, *op. cit.*, p. 23.
43. *Daughters of Vitasta*, p. 243.
44. *The Khidmat*, February 11, 1948.
45. Moulvi Majid, *op. cit.*, pp. 23,70
46. *Census*, 1921, I, p. 102, 141.
47. Bates, *op. cit* ., pp. 35; Joshua Duke, *Ince's Kashmir Handbook*, p. 22; Lawrence, *op. cit.*, pp. 253-254; see also Khan Bahadur Ghulam Ahmad Khan, *Note on High Prices of Shali in Srinagar*, p. 8.
48. Joshua Duke, *op. cit.*, p. 22; Bates, *op. cit.*, pp. 35.
49. Ibid.
50. Ibid.
51. Bates, *op. cit.*, pp. 49.
52. Ibid., p. 45.
53. Ibid.
54. Lawrence, *op. cit.*, p. 254; See also *Where Three Empires Meet.*, p. 73.
55. Lawrence, *op. cit.*, p. 254.
56. Ibid.
57. Mir Saif-Ullah, *op. cit.*, pp. 75-76; Mirza Saif-ud-Din, *op. cit.*, 1853. Vol. VI, f. 22a; *Census*, 1901, I, p. 84.
58. Lawrence, *op. cit.*, p. 254; *Census*, 1901, I, p. 84.
59. *Census*, 1901, I, p. 84.
60. Lawrence, *op. cit.*, p. 254.
61. The Muslims as a rule abide by the prohibitions of their religion in regard to food, for instance, it is forbidden to eat the flesh of an animal not properly slaughtered. The Muslim practice of slaughtering animals is called *halal*.
62. Lawrence, *op. cit.*, p. 254. n.
63. *The India We Served*, p. 135; *Where Three Empires Meet*, pp. 15-16; *Cashmere Misgovernment* (typed copy), Chapter IV, p. 32; Joshua Duke, *op. cit.*, p. 22; Gugsal, *op. cit.*, p. 172; Mirza Saif-ud-din, *op. cit.*,Vol. VI, ff. 101 b, 102 a; Vol.VII, f. 85 b; NAI/Foreign, Oct. 4, 1853, Secret, Despatch to the Secretary of State, No. 67.
64. Bates, *op. cit.*, p.35; Joshua Duke, *op. cit.*, pp. 22 and 24; Schonberg,

op. cit.,II.,p. 103; Richard Temple, *op. cit.*, II, p. 55; Wakefield, *op. cit.*, pp. 154-155; *Where Three Empires Meet*. p. 86.

65. Ibid; *Cashmere Misgovernment* (typed copy); Chapter IV, p. 33.
66. Schonberg, *op. cit.*, II, p. 103; Wakefield, *op. cit.*, pp. 154-55; *Cashmere Misgovernment* (typed copy); Chapter IV, p. 34.
67. *Cashmere Misgovernment* (typed copy), chapter IV, p. 34.
68. Torrens, *op. cit.*, p. 308; Bates, *op.cit.*, p. 39; Lawrence, *op. cit.*, p. 254.; Schonberg, *op. cit.*, p. 127; Honiberger, *Thirty five Years in the East*, p. 181.
69. Bates, *op. cit.*, p. 38.
70. Lawrence, *op. cit.*, p. 254.
71. Ibid., p. 253.
72. Ibid.
73. Bates, *op. cit.*, p. 50.
74. Ibid; Temple, *op. cit.*, II, p. 55; See also Moulvi Hasan, *op. cit.*, Vol. I, p. 454 and n.
75. Lawrence, *op. cit.*, p. 300.
76. Ibid.
77. Ibid., p. 281; *Kashmir in the Sunlight and Shade*, p. 127.
78. Marion Doughty, *op. cit.*, p. 166; Lawrence, *op. cit.*, p. 281; See also Moulvi Hasan, *op. cit.*, I, p. 456.
79. *Kashmir in Sunlight and Shade*, p. 127.
80. *The Ranbir*, Sept. 21, 1936; June 3, 1940.
81. *Kashmir in Sunlight and Shade*, p.127.
82. Lawrence, *op. cit.*, p. 255; *Imperial Gazetteer*. p. 41.
83. Knowles, *A Dictionary of Kashmiri Proverbs and Sayings*, p. 3.
84. *Imperial Gazetteer*, p. 41; Lawrence, *op. cit.*, p. 255.
85. Ibid.
86. Ibid.; Denys, *Our Summer in the Vale of Kashmir*, p. 142.
87. Lawrence, *op. cit.*, p. 255; *Imperial Gazetteer*, p. 41.
88. *Kashmir in Sunlight and Shade*, p.106.
89. Ibid.
90. Lawrence, *op. cit.*, p. 266.
91. The Kashmiris are full of fun and not a few of them know how to enjoy themselves. Sometimes it is the *charas*-sodden, fantastically skipping, howling, and evil-featured naked *faqirs* covered with filth, who cause amusement to the humourous city population. One wonders to see the young and old men poking fun at these people by pelting stones at them. But equally important is the stark reality that such paupers are held in great veneration by some families in the city. The people like gatherings and wherever a crowd congregates it is sure to be a merry one. Very often there is much ado about nothing in the bazars and streets of this ancient city.
92. *Imperial Gazetteer*, p. 40.

93. Ibid., p. 41; Lawrence, , *op. cit.,* p. 256.
94. *Administration Report of J&K State* (1901-1904), p. 554; 1913-1914, p. 108.
95. *The Ranbir,*Sept. 16, 1924; Sept. 30, 1924; Sept. 7, 1926; Aug 30, 1927; Sept. 20, 1927.
96. Ibid.,Aug. 30, 1927; Maharaja Hari Singh was also a good golfer and tennis player. Denys, *op. cit.,* 128.
97. *Census*, 1931, I, p. 141.
98. Ibid.; *The Ranbir*, July 20, 1926.
99. For a detailed discussion on the impact of Persia on Kashmir, see Ishaq Khan, "Persian Influences in Kashmir in the Sultante period, 1320-1586," *Islamic Culture*, January 1977, pp. 1-9.
100. *Kashmir,* June-July, 1954, Vol. iv, No. 6, p. 137.
101. Forster, *op. cit.,* II, pp. 24, 25, 32; Hugel, *op. cit.,* p. 146; Honiberger, *op. cit.,* p. 183; John Knight, *Diary*, pp. 82 and 85; Wakefield,, *op. cit.,* p. 170; *The J & K Territories*, p. 182; Prinsep, *op. cit.,* pp. 227-28.
102. Parbway, *op. cit.,* p. 68.
103. *Kashmir*, June-July, 1954, Vol, iv, No.6, p. 137; See also Wakefield, *op. cit.,* p. 170.
104. Moulvi Hasan, *op. cit.,* III *(Ibrahim's tr)*, p. 641.
105. While describing the condition of the dancing girls in the Sikh rule, Baron Hugal writes:
"These poor creatures are doomed to a hard fate; they are not allowed either to sing or dance without permission, and if they get this, an officer of the Government always accompanies them, who grasps whatever the receive." *op. cit.,* p. 146.
106. Mirza Saif-ud-din's voluminous *Akhbarat* are full of information in regard to the performances given by the *hafizas* before the European guests of the Maharaja. Vol. vii, 1854, f. 202a; Vol. III, 1850, dd. 566, 906, 95a; Vol. Vii, 148 a; Vol. viii, 1855, ff. 59b, 66a, 74a, 82ab, 92a, 107b.
107. Wakefield, *op. cit.,* pp. 170-71; *The J&K Territories*, p. 182; Honiberger, *op. cit.,* p. 183; John Knight, *Diary,* pp. 82, 85.
108. Bamzai, *History of Kashmir,* p. 524; See also *Kashmir*, June-July, 1954, Vol. iv. No.6, p. 137.
109. Ibid.
110. Ibid.
111. *op. cit.,* p. 228.
112. Ibid., pp. 227-228.
113. *Kashmir*, June-July, 1954, Vol. iv, No. 6, P. 137.
114. *The Ranbir,* Sept. 21, 1936.
115. Miss Florence Parbway who visited Srinagar in the beginning of this century remarks: "The natives (*Kashmiris*) are very fond of a Timasha or fete, when they wear gorgeous clothes and sprinkle scent upon each

other and in Kashmir they often celebrate great occasions by a trip on the river." (*op. cit.*, p. 67); see also Wakefield, *op. cit.*, pp. 157-58.

116. Stuart, *op. cit.*, p. 174. Lawrence, *op. cit.*, p. 26.
117. *op. cit.*, p. 26.
118. Arthur Neve writes, " In Japan there is an old-time national custom of the *Nagm*i or Beholding, when all go out to view the successive spring blossoms and to make holiday. In the same way the pleasure-loving Kashmiris pour out of the city in thousands on the fine days in March, when the almond gardens which extend round the slopes of the fort hill are in blossom. The trees are planted rather close together, and all bloom simultaneously. The effect from a little distance is rather that of a sun-lit cloud than of anything more earthly and substantial. There is not a leaf on the trees, but the dense masses of white or delicate pinkish flowers give ample shade, in which groups of people gather, drink tea, and sing the songs of spring." *(Picturesque Kashmir*, p. 36).
119. Ibid.; Lawrence, *op. cit.*, p. 279-80.
120. *Picturesque Kashmir*, p. 36.
121. Bates, op.cit., p.375; Lawrence, *op. cit.*, p. 315; *Imperial Gazetteer*, p. 38; Wakefield, *op. cit.*, p. 157-158.
122. Bates, op.cit., p.375.
123. The Kashmiris call these dancers *dumbal-i-maet* or *Lal-Bab Saebin-Maet*.They are still seen performing *dumbael* (a kind of folk dance) on the occasion of the *Watal Mela*.
124. Lt. R.G. Taylor records in his diary that a 'grand fair' on the lake at the *ziarat* of Lal Bab was celebrated on 25th June, 1847. See *Lahore Political Diaries*, 1847-49, Vol. vi, (P.G.R.), p.41.
125. For a fuller description of festivals, see Lawrence, *op. cit.*, pp.265-266.
126. Mirza Saif-ud-din, op. cit., Vol. vii,1854; f. 92a.
127. Lt. Taylor was in Srinagar in 1847 when this festival was observed. He writes: "The *Junum Ushtomee,* and no work done. The moment of Sri Krishna's birth announced by a salve from the Hurree Purbut guns in the middle of the night." *Lahore Political Diaries* 1847-49, Vol. vi, 91; See *Mirza Saif-ud-din, op. cit.*,1852, vol. v, f. 69a.
128. The *Ranbir*, Oct. 11, 1927; Oct. 31, 1932.
129. *Census*, 1911,1, p. 98; Mirza Saif-ud-din,*op.cit.*, Vol. 111, 1850, f. 39a.
130. *Census*, 1911, 1, p. 98.
131. Mirza Saif-ud-din, *op.cit.*, Vol. V11, 1854, ff.79 ab. 80a.
132. Ibid.
133. Ibid., f. 79a.
134. It is now called Basant Bagh.
135. Ibid., f.77b.
136. Lawrence, *op, cit.*, p. 271.
137. Ibid., pp.271-272; See also Mirza saif-ud-din, *op. cit.*, Vol. v, 1852, f 87b; Vol.VII.1855, ff.135b, 137a.

138. For a detailed account of festivals of the Kashmiri Muslims, see Lawrence, op.cit., pp. 292-93. It should, however, be remembered that Islam "sanctioned only two festivals in which some elements of rejoicing was present and these were the two '*Eids*. (Nizami, *Some Aspects of Religion and Politics in India during thirteenth Century*, p.297).
139. Mir Saif-ullah; op.cit., p. 85.
140. Ibid., p.86, Mirza Saif-ud-din, op.cit., Vol. VII, 1854, ff. 153ab.
141. Mirza Saif-ud-din. op.cit., Vol. III 1850, ff.51a, 56b.
142. The practice of distributing *tahar* among the relatives, children and poor still obtains in Srinagar. This custom is observed not only on the eve of *Moharram* but on several other occasions. It is interesting to observe here that the dreams have often played an important role in the life of the average Kashmiri Muslim. Even now a dreadful dream is sometimes followed by the distribution of alms. Until very recent times, special beneficiaries of this custom used to be such people as were addicted to smoking hemp *(charas)*. *Shodas,* as they are called in common parlance, would, not long ago, assemble in petty large numbers in a specific meeting place *(takia)*. Some of them are said to have been persons of high spiritual calibre. With the spread of modern education, however, the practice of entertaining *shodas* with *tahar* and sumptuous meals has become extinct in most of the Muslim families of the city. *Takias* existed in Srinagar at many places till late 1970s. The rendezvous of *shodas* at Batmaloo presented a very colourful scene during the festival of Batmalloo Sahib. On this occasion the *shodas* held a feast and organized musical concerts by voluntary contributions.
143. Ibid., Vol. III, 1850, ff. 51a, 56b; Vol. V, 1852, ff. 58 b, 60 b, 90 b; Vol, VII, 1855, ff. 146 b; *Beyond the Pir Panjal*, p. 231; Arthur Neve, *Thirty years in Kashmir*, pp. 301-2; Wakefield, *op. cit.*, p. 157; *Census*, 1911, I, p. 102; Bates, *op cit.*, p. 375; Mrs. Stuart, *op. cit.*, p. 160.
144. *Census*, 1911, I, p. 102; See also Mirza Saif-ud-din, *op. cit.,* 1852, Vol. V. ff. 58 b, 60 b, 90 b, Vol. III, 1850, ff, 51 a, 56 b.
145. *Census*, 1911, I, p. 102.
146. *Thirty Years in Kashmir,* pp. 301-302.
147. Lawrence, *op. cit.*, p. 289.
148. Ibid.
149. Mirza Saif-ud-din, *op. cit.,* 1850, Vol. III, f. 51 a.
150. Bates, *op. cit.,* p. 375; *The Amrit Bazar Patrika,* August 19, 1931; Wakefield, *op. cit.,* p. 157.
151. Lawrence, *op. cit.*, p. 289.
152. *Thirty Years in Kashmir*, pp. 301-2. Hazratbal festival, for example, attracted thousands of villagers from various *parganas*. See Mirza Saif-ud-din, *op. cit.,* 1850. Vol. III, f. 51a, 56b; Vol. V, 1852, ff. 58b, 90b.
153. Lawrence, *op. cit.*, p. 289.
154. Ibid., p. 287.

155. Bates, *op. cit.,* p. 36.
156. Lawrence, *op. cit.,* p. 293.
157. As late as 1911 most of the disputes were seldom referred to the courts, but were settled by the *pirs* (Census, 1911, p.211). Lawrence, *op. cit.,* p. 296.
158. Dermot Norris, *op. cit.,* p. 45; Shephered, *op. cit.,* p. 101.
159. Mr. Ernest Neve remarks: "The Hindus' whole life from the hour of his birth till the day when he dies and his son sets light to his funeral pyre, is regulated by an elaborate code of religious rites, ceremonies and customs. These involve daily worship with ablutions and offerings to idols of flowers and food, frequent fastings, and the observance of a very large number of holy days." *(Beyond the Pir Panjal,* p. 240).
160. For details, see Lawrence, *op. cit.,* pp. 257-71; *Kashmir in Sunlight and Shade,* pp. 153-168; A. K. Bamzai, *The Kashmiri Pandit,* pp. 21-27.
161. Ibid.
162. *Kashmir in Sunlight and Shade,* p. 63.
163. To the custodians of local shrines the plague provided a unique occasion for trading upon the superstitions of the people. It is they who were the greatest obstacles to the success of Dr. Arthur Neves' efforts. Shephered, *op. cit.,* p. 101.
164. *Kashmir in Sunlight and Shade,* p. 63.

Lawrence observes: "It is a sad fact that the occurrence of smallpox has become one of the accepted customs of Kashmir, and the Hindus have regular ceremonies which must be observed when the disease attacks their families. When it appears that a child is sick with the smallpox, the first thing to be done is to sew rupees into his headdress. He is then placed in a separate room, and is surrounded by clay toys of horses, elephants, palankins, fans and sugar cakes, water-chestnuts and shells. Until the pustules are developed the child is kept on rice and curd, and no salt may be given to the child or used by the mother or wet-nurse. A little fish or a piece of meat is always hung up in the sick room *(chhai ratan),* but while the smallpox lasts no meat may be eaten and no prayers may be repeated in the house. When the disease abates the rupees are taken out of the headdress, and are spent on rice boiled in milk, which is distributed to relations and friends. The room is cleaned and the toys and a plate full of rice are flung into the river. If the smallpox is very severe, Sitla Mata, the smallpox deity, must be propitiated, and offerings of sheep, goats, horses or donkeys, and eyes of gold or silver are made to her priests on Hari-Parbat. Forty days after the smallpox first makes its appearance *(chat-jihun),* rice boiled in milk is again distributed to relations and neighbours." (*op. cit.,* pp. 263-64).

165. *Kashmir in Sunlight and Shade,* p.160.
166. Lawrence, *op. cit.,* p. 258.
167. Ibid., p. 288.

168. It is here that the Muslims assemble for prayers on the two *Eids*.
169. Mirza Saif-ud-din, *op. cit.,* 1852, Vol V, ff. 37ab, 63ab; Vol VIII, 1855, ff. 129ab; *Wajeez-ut-Tawarikh* (MS.), f. 69b.
170. Mirza Saif-ud-din, *op. cit.,* Vol. VIII, 1855, ff. 129ab; *Wajeez-ut-Tawarikh* (MS.), f. 69b.
171. Ibid.
172. Lawrence, *op. cit.,* p. 263.
173. Ibid., p. 270.
174. *Census*, 1901, I, p. 32.
175. Ibid., 1921, I, pp. 60-61; also Ibid., 1911, I, pp. 32-33.
176. Moulvi Hasan, *op. cit.,* I, p. 442.
177. Ibid.
178. Ibid.
179. Ibid.
180. The Census of 1921 (Part I, p.64) points to the existence of the *Anjuman* in Srinagar even before 1920. But during my conversation with Moulvi Ghulam Nabi Mubaraki I came to know that the *Anjuman* was founded in about 1925. Among its founder members were Haji Muhammad Shahdad, Ghulam Shah Naqeeb, Ahmed Ullah Shahdad, Abdul Aziz Chikan and Moulvi Ghulam Nabi Mubaraki. I was told by Mubaraki Sahib that the establishment of the *Anjuman* was opposed by the *mullahs* and *the muftis* of Srinagar. They issued a *fatwa* against the organisation, debarring its members from attending the mosques. This did not upset the apple-cart of the religious reformers who now filed a suit against the decision of the *mullahs*. The court pronounced its verdict in favour of the *Ahl-i-Hadith*. As the 'Wahabis' carried the day, they began to preach against the *mullahs* courageously. The mosque of Zaldagar became a stronghold of the 'Wahabis' under Moulvi Anwar Shah. The Moulvi was dauntless in his criticism of the *mullahs* and what he termed the "superstitious" practices of their followers.
181. *The Muslim,* Shaban, 1359 H; July 2, 1941; Sept. 16, 1943; Oct. 2, 1941; Safar 1360 H; Moharram, 1360 H ; Sept. 16, 1944; March 2, 1942.
182. Before 1931 two chief *mullahs* of Srinagar, Mir Waiz Jama Masjid and Mir Waiz Hamadani, wielded great social and religious influence on the Muslim society (*Daughters of Vitasta*, p. 242; *The Statesman*, June 11, 1946; *The Ranbir*, Nov. 16, 1942).
183. It is worth noting that in December 1930, the Muslims of Srinagar did not, in the absence of Mir Waiz Ahmed Ullah's directive, actively respond to the call of the Muslim Conference of Lahore to rise against the Government. This startled some educated youngmen who had manifested designs of shaking off the Maharaja's authority by forming the Reading Room Party. But after the death of Ahmed Ullah in March 1931, his successor, Mir Waiz Muhammad Yousuf Shah supported the aims and objectives of the Reading Room Party.

184. See Farquhar, *Modern Religious Movements in India,* pp. 137-38.
185. *Daughter of Vitasta*, p. 243.
186. Among them must be mentioned Moulvi Hasan Sahib, Moulvi Ghulam Nabi Mubaraki, Moulvi Anwar Shah and Moulvi Nur-ud-din.
187. Lawrence, *op. cit.,* p. 285; Moulvi Hasan *op. cit.,* I, P. 442.
188. *Census*, 1911, I, pp. 148, 210-211 ; *Census*, 1931, I, pp. 296-97.
189. Parbway, *op. cit.*, p. 67.
190. Ibid. See also Petrocokina, *op. cit.*, pp. 84-85.
191. *Beyond the Pir Panjal,* p. 83; See also *Where Three Empires Meet,* p. 22.
192. *Beyond the Pir Panjal,* p. 83; See also Drew, *op. cit.,* p. 179.
193. Lawrence, *op. cit.*, p. 282.
194. Among the Muslims of the city, food is wasted on a lavish scale on such an occasion. There can be no denying the fact that many of the woes of certain sections of the Muslim society in Srinagar, including indebtedness, have arisen from the social compulsion of organizing massive feasts at the time of marriages and deaths. This is why the State Government has, from time to time, incorporated guest control rules to curb ostentatious spending at weddings and funerals. But, unfortunately, guest control orders are being flouted. It is regrettable that the attitude of treating social crimes as nominal receives sanction from higher authorities too.
195. At present the Muslims of the city consider daughters a matter of expense to them, as they generally have to give dowries. *Kori-malen Satar* (May fathers of the daughters be protected !) is on the lips of an average city Muslim when he offers prayers in congregation. The system of dowry among the Mussalmans of Srinagar dates back to the days of Bakshi Ghulam Mohammad former Prime Minister of the Jammu and Kashmir State, when such families as received untold money and favours from the ruling party, gave dowry in order to move up in the social hierarchy. Since then this evil custom has been followed with all impunity by the city Muslims. It can hardly be denied that the dowry system has reduced the institution of marriage to a barter. The practice of giving motor cars, scooters and television-sets in dowry by some neo-rich in the city has assumed dangerous proportions. It is distressing to note that the Muslims of the middle class are between Scylla and Charybdis; for not unoften the bridegroom's family demands luxurious items from the other party. Owing to this fact, the number of spinsters seems to be growing. The concern that the people in general have is reflected in the sad fact that the attempts of the social reform committees have proved to be abortive and there is hardly any study worth the name, except one, of this social evil which continues to wreck Muslim families year after year.
196. Lawrence , *op. cit.,* p. 262 ; *The Ranbir*, Jan. 15, 1940; *Daughters of Vitasta*, p. 253.

197. *The Ranbir*, Jan. 15, 1940; *Daughters of Vitasta*, p. 253.
198. Lawrence, *op. cit.*, p. 262.
199. "The men stand idle, and watch the women toiling up and down the ghats with heavy waterpots, believing that their wives were born to be the burden-bearers." C. Wilson, *Irene Petrie,* p. 220.; See also Wakefield, *op. cit.*, pp. 92-93, 114-115; *Where Three Empires Meet*, p. 35.
200. Dermot Noriss, *op. cit.*, p. 11; Petrocokina, *op. cit.*, p. 85;.Wakefield, *op. cit.*, p. 115.
201. Schonberg, *op. cit.*, II, pp. 131-132 ; Dugsal, *op. cit.*, p. 206; Wakefield, *op. cit.*, pp. 143-145; *Cashmere Misgovernment (Kashmir Papers, p. 62).*
202. Census, 1921, I, p. 179.
203. The *hanjis* or boatmen form a separate class in Srinagar. They are fine-looking atheletic and hard-working. The boats form also their homes, for the greater part of them pass their lives entirely on board and know no other dwelling-place. According to the Census of 1911, the *Hanjis* numbered 3,798 in Srinagar alone.
204. *Cashmere Misgovernment* (typed copy, Chapter IV, p. 35.
205. Ibid.
206. Ibid.
207. NAI/ Foreign, Sec, E, Mar. 1883, No. 86.
208. Ibid.
209. Ibid.
210. Ibid.
211. *Cashmere Misgovernment* (typed copy), Chapter IV, p. 35; See also *Wrongs of Kashmir (Kashmir Papers*), p. 32.
212. Biscoe, *Autobiography*, pp. 259-60.
213. Ibid.
214. Ibid.
215. Ibid., p. 238; *Victory After Defeat* (Mission School report, 1934-1935, p. 6).
216. *J & K Information* (issued by the Bureau of Information, His Highness's Govt., March 1947), pp. 10-11; *Census*, 1941, p.6.
217. Till very recently the barbers of Srinagar were very fond of arranging matches for others. See, for example, *Kashmir in Sunlight and Shade,* p. 131.
218. Ibid., p. 106.
219. Ibid., p.60; James Milne, *The Road to Kashmir,* p.126.
220. A.K.Bamzai,*The kashmiri Pandit,* p.32.
221. Ibid*; Beyond the Pir Panjal,* p. 240.
222. *Autobiography,* p. 96; See also *Beyond the Pir Panjal,* p. 240.
223. *Vide* Chapter V, *Christian Missionaries and the Western impact.*
224. *Census,* 1911, l, pp. 148, 211.
225. Based on the author's interview with Shri Ram Chandrji Abhay.

226. *Census,* 1931, I, p .297; See also *The Hamdard,* May 15, 1938.
227. *Census,* 1931, I, p.297.
228. Ibid.
229. *Daughters of Vitasta*, pp. 232-233.
230. Ibid., p.233.
231. J&K (G.R), F.No. 46/G-39, 1923.
232. *Daughters of Vitasta,* p.240.
233. *The Tribune,* Sept. 25, 1931.
234. Ibid., Nov. 21, 1931.
235. *Daughters of Vitasta*, p.249.
236. Ibid.
237. Ibid.
238. Ibid., p.251.
239. *The Tribune,* Sept. 25, 1931.
240. *Daughters of Vitasta,* p.252; *The Ranbir,* May 29, 1928; June 5, 1928.
241. *Daughters of Vitasta,* p.253; *For the role of Samaj Sudhar Samiti,* see also *The Tribune*, Oct. 16, 1946.
242. *Daughters of Vitasta,* p.253.
243. Ibid.
244. Ibid., p.241.
245. Ibid., pp.242-243.
246. *The Khidmat* (Eng), Feb 11, 1948; See also Kh. Ghulam Mohammad's article on freedom movement in Kashmir in *Daur-i-Jadeed*; July 8, 1955. p. 19.
247. *The Khidmat* (Eng.), Feb 11, 1948.
248. Ibid. The following extract from a report on Kashmir situation cabled by Mr. Norman Cliff, Foreign Editor, News Chronicle, London, on June 21, 1946, testifies to the leading role played by the women of Srinagar in the struggle for freedom:

     A feature of the meeting at Khanqah-i-Mualla (Headquarters of the National Conference) was the "the presence of a solid phalanx of women with their babies, in a State where Purdah prevails. They cast aside the face coverings of their Purdah hoods, challenging identification by the police. When the meeting ended, women shouting `Down with Dogra rule' led the procession defying the troops to open fire. I saw only lathis used." Ibid.
249. *Daughters of Vitasta,* p.262.
250. *The Khidmat*, Feb.11, 1948.
251. Ibid.
252. *Report on Native Newspapers,* Punjab, 1895, p. 499.
253. *Op. cit.*, p. 32.
254. *Beyond the Pir Panjal*, p. 164; See also *Where Three Empires Meet,* p.76. Lawrence wrongly says that the Sunni Muslims of Kashmir are Hindus at heart. *op. cit.*, p. 286.

255. *Beyond the Pir Panjal*, p. 82; Lawrence, *op. cit.*, p. 300; See also Ganesh Lal, *op. cit.*, p. 32.
256. Lawrence, *op. cit.*, p. 300 *Beyond the Pir Panjal*, p.82.
257. Lawrence, *op. cit.*, p. 300.
258. Ibid.
259. *Census*, 1901, l, p.84.
260. Ibid.
261. Ibid.
262. Mirza Saif-ud-din, *op. cit.*, 1853, Vol. VI,f.22a; Mir Saif Ullah,*op. cit.*, p. 75-76.
263. Mirza Saif-ud-din, *op. cit.*, 1853, Vol. VI, f. 22a;.
264. Ibid.
265. Mir Saif Ullah, *op. cit.*, p. 75,76,94. Gulab Singh is also reported to have "severely interdicted the eating of cheese" among the Kashmiri Pandits, Lawrence, *op. cit.*, p. 300.
266. *Op. cit.*, p. 286.
267. Mir Saif Ullah, *op. cit.*, p.80; *Cashmere Misgovernment* (typed copy), Chapter IV, p. 32; *Where Three Empires Meet*, pp. 15-16.
268. *Kashmir in Sunlight and Shade*, p.123.
269. Ibid., pp.113, 123.
270. See, for example, Mr Brailsford's remarks in the *Hindustan Times* June 2,1946; See also Spencer Lavan, *The Ahmediyah Movement*, p. 150.
271. Writing in the reign of Pratap Singh, Knight observes: "Until recently, the killing of that sacred animal, the cow, was punishable with death. Imprisonment for life is now the penalty and many an unfortunate Mohammedan, I believe, is lying immured in Hari Parbat because that in time of famine he has ventured to kill his own ox to save himself and family from starvation." *Where Three Empires Meet*, pp. 15-16; See also *Cashmere Misgovernment* (typed copy), Chapter IV, p.32; The *Hindustan Times*, June 2, 1946.
272. The Mussalmans of Srinagar do not like beef and rarely do they attend the marriage functions of their village brethren, where the flesh of ox is eaten in great quantity on such occasions.
273. Moulvi Hasan, *op. cit.*, (urdu tr.), p. 521. "It is to the lasting credit of Birbal Dhar that when a deputation of Muslims headed by Sayyid Hasan Shah Qadiri Khanyari approached him to dissuade the Sikhs from the destruction of the *Khanqah* he moved in the matter, used his influence and saved this historic structure from vandalism." Sufi, *op. cit.*, II, p. 726.
274. The Kashmiri Pandits have great veneration for the Muslim saints, particularly Dastgir Sahib (Sayyid Abdul Qadir Jilani of Baghdad). The name of this great saint is often invoked by the Pandits of the older generation. Among them he is popular as *Kah no*.
275. See *The Martand*, June 27, 1934; Feb. 12, 1936.

CHAPTER V

CHRISTIAN MISSIONARIES AND THE WESTERN IMPACT

Srinagar society was more or less static until the advent of Christian missionaries in Kashmir in the second half of the last century, when a significant change came about. Besides the educational development which resulted from the activities of the missionaries in Srinagar, the different administrative methods of the British affected the social structure and social institutions of the city.

Before describing the impact of Western ideas on Srinagar society and culture, it is pertinent to refer to the causes that attracted the missionaries to Kashmir. A careful reading of these causes will give us useful and correct clues to the state of things in the past.

First, Kashmir was a remarkably suitable region by its geographical position, by its salubrious climate, and by its beauty and fertility, to become a great Christian missionary centre for the surrounding countries of Tibet, China, Yarqand, Afghanistan and Turkistan.[1] Secondly, the sweltering heat of many parts of India was very distressing for many missioners; so Kashmir was regarded as the best place for missionary personnel to recuperate. Thirdly, the missionaries cherished the hope that if the people of Kashmir were converted to Christianity, they might become great evangelists in Asia. Moorcroft expressed the same view when he visited the Valley in the early nineteenth century. He observed: "I am convinced that there is no part of India where the pure religion of the Gospel might be introduced with a fairer prospect of success than in Kashmir."[2] Fourthly, from the dawn of history Kashmir had been a religious centre. Hinduism, Buddhism and Islam had flourished in the Valley. As students of the history of Kashmir, the missionaries very well knew that it was formerly a great missionary centre for Buddhism. Might not Christianity receive an equal welcome from the people! Might not the Gospel there fall on fertile soil! Such at least was their longing and prayers.[3]

Last but not the least, an important cause was a moral one. The missionaries were not oblivious of the deplorable condition of the people of Kashmir who had suffered a great deal at the hands of both rulers[4] and priests. There was, in addition, ignorance, disease, poverty and deterioration of morals[5]. It was a call, which the missionaries could not resist.

Such were the causes which motivated the Christian missionaries to come to Kashmir. There aim was to win the country for Christ, and they cherished the belief that the spread of the Gospel would provide a panacea for the sufferings of the people. Their policy was to extend the knowledge of Christianity, and they saw in Kashmir a duty and an opportunity. But to make use of this opportunity and to fulfil the duty was not an easy task. In fact, there were serious obstacles in the path of the missionaries.

GOVERNMENT'S HOSTILITY TO THE MISSIONARIES

Though Maharaja Gulab Singh was apparently on good terms with the British, he was at heart dead against any Western penetration in Kashmir. A special order was issued in 1854 by the Governor General Lord Dalhousie, at the request of Maharaja Gulab Singh, forbidding European visitors to remain in Kashmir during the winter. He established a rule that Europeans were to be admitted to Srinagar by prescribed routes only; and from the time of their entrance to their exit, they were to be under vigilant supervision and were not to be allowed to mix with the people.[6] For an ordinary visitor, who wanted merely to spend the summer amidst the natural beauties of the Valley, this presented no difficulty. But it put a spoke in the wheel of the missionaries. They were not allowed to rent a house in the city of Srinagar, where they could pursue their activities. Under no circumstances could a European or a British subject own landed property in the dominions of the Maharaja.[7] Guest houses were built outside the main city for the convenience of European visitors, and a special quarter in the environs of Srinagar was set apart for them. Agents were appointed to look after their requirements, and all business was transacted through a *babu*, deputed for the purpose.[8] Thus the Europeans were completely isolated from the people of the city. This put difficulties in the way of the missionaries, whose task lay with the masses, and whose success depended upon close and constant contact with them.

This deliberate isolation was prompted by the understandable fears of Maharaja Gulab Singh, his officials and his great land owners.The Maharaja was, no doubt, actuated by low and selfish motives in not allowing the European visitors to the Valley to mix with other people. He had no wish that the missionaries should take back to British India details of the treatment of a people,[9] in whose welfare he showed very little interest.[10] To the British he owed his throne and he feared their interference should his manner of rule become known.

It should be remembered that the missionaries first made their appearance in 1854, when Colonel Martin, a retired Army officer of Peshawar, Rev. Robert Clark[11] of the Punjab Missionaries and two Indian Christians entered Srinagar. This preliminary exploration was followed by another one eight year later in the summer of 1862. It was in 1864 that a permanent mission was established in Srinagar.[12] But the establishment of a permanent mission in Kashmir was not a bed of roses. The withdrawal during the winter season and the renting of a house for missionary purposes presented difficult problems for them. In fact, there were houses for European visitors but they were outside the city. The missionaries objected to residing among the visitors. Clark very well knew that to live among them was to sacrifice his work. This is evident from a memorandum which he drafted when the Maharaja wanted him to reside in European quarters.[13]

In view of the attitude of the authorities and the ruling prince, the missionaries adopted the ruse of renting a house through the resident French shawl merchants of Srinagar.[14] In April 1864, the attempt of Rev. Robert Clark, accompanied by Mrs. Clark, to enter the rented house in the city seemed nearly impossible. From the missionary journal we know that on their arrival to Srinagar they were mobbed by a crowd of 1,000 to 1,500 people,[15] who threatened to set the house on fire, some of them coming within the compound and throwing stones.[16]

But Robert Clark had an indomitable will. On 18th April, 1864 he opened a school in Srinagar despite the opposition of the authorities.[17] It was an important event in the history of Srinagar. Such parents as sent their children to the missionary school received domiciliary visits from the police.[18] They were told if their children went to school, they would be banished to Gilgit.[19] It is also worth noting that on 2nd May, 1864 Mrs. Clark opened a dispensary in the city which "speedily attracted patients in crowds and the homes of the people began to open to her."[20]

It must, however, be pointed out that the people of Srinagar were not hostile to the mission. We are told that Robert Clark got in touch with the chief *Moulvi* of Srinagar when the disturbances took place. But the *Moulvi* professed himself unable to deal with the uproar, for no one dared interfere with a riot goaded by the authorities.[21] Thus the oppositions of the people to the missionaries was not spontaneous, but, as they themselves admitted, engineered by the authorities. In fact, the opposition to the mission school came from the Government.[22] Equally important to note is that the *Moulvis* did not see the missionaries as competitors with a consequential financial or influential loss to them. With no vested interest in education, they were lackadaisical about the activities of the missionaries. Clark wrote in his journal that it was not people who opposed the missionaries but the Government.[23] He further remarked that the people were friendly enough.[24]

On November 2, 1864, Clark had to leave Srinagar along with his family as the question of a winter residence in Kashmir presented another serious problem.[25] With their departure, the dispensary and the school also closed.

KASHMIR MEDICAL MISSION

As early as 1862 attaching a medical missionary to the new C.M.S. mission in Kashmir was considered at the Lahore Conference. Kashmir was specially referred to in the general resolution as being a country where medical aid was not available and where deep prejudices might be resolved by this means. It should be kept in mind that Rev. Clark, a staunch advocate of Medical Missions, was the moving figure so far as the establishment of the Kashmir mission goes.[26] Not only did he advocate its need before the Committee, but he also seems to have entered into correspondence with Dr. Elmslie, the designated doctor to the Kashmir Medical Mission. He kept in touch with him and informed him about the difficulties which he was to face, and thus helped to prepare him for his future field.

It was on May 8, 1865 that Dr. Elmslie opened his dispensary in Srinagar.[27] It was a memorable day in the history of Kashmir Medical Mission. Only 10 persons visited the dispensary that day. Dr. Elmslie used to visit the city and its environs, and while giving medical advice, distributed religious tracts, but no bazar preaching was attempted. Slowly the patients started to visit the dispensary, and the number of patients increased, until by August and September it had risen to 90 daily.

Dr. Elmslie was not allowed to have a roomy house for performing his duties. "His life was hard and difficult", writes Mr. Biscoe, "for he had no hospital, his operations being performed under the trees; also orders were issued that the people were not to visit the doctor, and sepoys were stationed around to keep them away, as the sick persisted in coming for relief. Several patients suffered imprisonment for disobeying the order of the authorities."[28] But instead of showing some appreciation of the medical relief work he had rendered, the authorities remained hostile.

In 1866, unable to obtain adequate accommodation, a tent had to be set up for the use of patients. Despite the opposition of the local officials, the sick persons flocked to Dr. Elmslie.[29] The number of patients treated that year was 3,365. The number shows a healthy change in the outlook of the people. In 1867,[30] during Dr. Elmslie's summer campaign a cholera epidemic broke out in the city. From his writings, we know that his offer to the Government for help was spurned.[31] Nevertheless, Dr. Elmslie carried on these summer campaigns of the medical missions up to 1870. In 1870 the Rev. W.T. Stores[32] did the work during Dr. Elmslie's absence on furlough. In 1872, he returned, and worked during the summer. He died in the same year in Gujarat on his way back from Kashmir to the Punjab. For four seasons, Dr. Elmslie cured thousands of Kashmiris and thus "did an immense deal of good work in Kashmir."[33]

DR. ELMSLIE'S CONTRIBUTION TO SRINAGAR

The pioneering efforts of Dr. Elmslie bore some fruit when immediately after his death the Maharaja allowed the missionaries to stay in Srinagar for the whole year. It was the effect of Elmslies' appeal for medical missions which roused the spirit of service in the women of England to help their sisters in India. It was because of his appeal that Fanny Butler devoted her life to the task of uplifting women in India and Kashmir. And, indeed, it was the result of his efforts, and those of his successors, that henceforth the medical missionaries were able to carry on their work in Kashmir without much difficulty.

While commenting on the influence of Dr. Elmslie's work in Kashmir, Dr. Ernest Neve writes:

"The opposition of the State authorities had been, to a considerable extent overcome, the confidence of the Kashmiris had been won, and an immense amount of relief had been afforded to sufferers. Four Kashmiris had become Christians. One of these for many years continued to render faithful service in Kashmir as a Christian teacher. As an indirect result of the Medical Mission, the first Kashmir State dispensary had been started, and this was the fore-runner of the present extensive Medical department."[34]

Another important result of Dr. Elmslie's struggle was that the State started to give aid to an Arabic School in 1868 which, in a way, was the first Government school.[35] It was started solely with Government aid. The result was that not only was the Government committed to one of its major responsibilities, but it helped to start a revival in the indigenous system of education. The story of how this school came into being is described by Dr. Elmslie. It is said that Sher Ali, a father of two sons, requested Dr. Elmslie to teach English to his sons. As the doctor was on the go all day because of medical service, he directed one of his assistants to teach English to his sons. When the matter was reported to the Maharaja, a vigorous effort was made to get the father to give up sending his sons to the mission bungalow to learn English. Thereafter the Maharaja gave orders for the opening of a school for the teaching of Arabic which was "intended exclusively for the sons of those who may be called the nobility of Kashmir.[36]"

Despite this reaction, Elmslie's teaching resulted in a demand for English education, though on a small scale. Elmslie himself contributed to Kashmiri literature, and prepared the Kashmiri-English dictionary, the first of its kind.

Dr. Elmslie lamented the want of proper schools in Srinagar where a scientific medical education might be obtained. He remarked that every year an epidemic, either of smallpox or cholera, carried off thousands of people. It was he who awakened the Government to the need of encouraging vaccination and sanitation in the Valley, but especially in the city, to save people from sudden death.[37]

CHANGE OF GOVERNMENT'S POLICY

After Dr. Elmslie's death in 1872, the medical work was continued by Dr.. Theodore Maxwell.[38] By this time the conditions had changed. The local officials' prejudices were overcome by the selfless labour and dedication of the missionaries. This had also endeared them to the people of Srinagar. So great was the impact of the Kashmir Medical Mission that the Government also opened the first State dispensary in Srinagar in 1870.[39]

It is also noteworthy that whereas in the early days of 1860 Maharaja Ranbir Singh would not grant the doctor an inch of ground, in 1874, the Maharaja granted a site for the Mission Hospital on the hill called Rustum Gaddi, beneath the *Takht-i-Sulaiman*.[40] The State Government constructed a building at this place at its own expense. The hospital was known as Drugjan Hospital. The State also gave a yearly donation to the Mission Hospital including free electric light. The Maharaja also visited the hospital on several occassions. Equally remarkable to note is that whereas in the early days, the officials tried to intimidate the doctor and patients in every way, now they and their families willingly made use of the medical help and skill which the Drugjan Hospital offered.[41] The statistics regarding the attendances in the hospital[42] are indicative of the significant changes which Srinagar was witnessing under the pressure of Western impact. Never could any hospital in Srinagar earn such reputation as did the Drugjan Hospital. It was a boon to the poverty-stricken people of the Valley. No doubt, Dr. Arthur Neve[43] described it as a second pilgrimage centre, the first being Hazratbal.[44]

Another hospital, exclusively for women, was established at Rainawari by the Church of England Zenana Missionary Society. Among the lady missionaries whose dedication to the cause of women's health earned approbation were, Miss Butler, a lady doctor, Miss Irene Petrie[45] and Miss Robinson, trained nurses, "who laid down their lives on duty in the Valley." Miss Kate Knowles was yet another noble doctor who earned deep affection for her services to the women of Srinagar.

The medical missionaries also did a great deal of work during famines. Indeed, "the only bright spot in the dreary history of the Kashmir famines was the devoted and unselfish conduct of the missionaries."[46] During 1877-1880, Rev. Mr. Wade[47] and Dr. Downes[48] opened an orphanage where 150 children were fed with wheat imported from the Punjab.[49] They also employed many hundreds of starving labourers on famine relief works, and made and repaired roads, dug and cleaned canals, filled up foul holes, levelled uneven ground and planted trees.[50] "Many of the most familiar landmarks in Srinagar", writes E. Neve in about 1912, "such as the lines of poplar trees, roads and canals in and around the Munshi Bagh, the European quarter of Srinagar, date back to this time."[51] Thus it was the missionaries who awakened the State Government to the necessity of grappling with the moral and physical evils of Srinagar.

Epidemics were more rampant then and combined with the insanitary conditions of the city, took a heavy toll of life. The fatal years were

1888, 1892, 1900, 1907 and 1910.[52] These epidemics give us an idea of how people were steeped in superstition and also show how the ignorant masses were terribly scared: "offices and schools closed, and the people sat in their houses, as they said, waiting to die."[53] They would only take the medicine of their *hakims* or "trust to the prayers and incantations of the priests," who would write some sacred words on pieces of paper (*tawiz*) which the patients would swallow.[54] Mr. Biscoe's account of the cholera epidemic shows that the people took no precautions, for they were not considered to be of any use. "You would see a man washing in the river the clothes of a relation who had just died in cholera," remarks Biscoe, "and a few feet down-stream a man would be drinking the water of the river. It was useless remonstrating, for your words had no meaning to them. Cholera was the will of Allah, or of the gods, what had water or anything else to do with it?"[55]

Credit thus goes to the missionaries for saving thousands of people who would have otherwise died. A large number of workers combined with the Church Missionary and Church of England Zenana Society did their best to "lift the veil over the moral condition of this miserable and diseased city."[56] The staff and boys of the C.M.S. School saved 73 lives when cholera appeared in the city in 1902.[57] It is remarkable to note that they even carried the filth in baskets on their shoulders.[58] The devotion and skill of the medical missionaries brought about a great change in the outlook of the people who now recognized the benefits of the Western system of treatment. With the progress of education, remarks Biscoe, the people gradually attributed sickness to germs.[59] By the second quarter of the present century, allopathic treatment had become very popular among the people.[60]

IMPACT OF CHRISTIAN MISSIONARY SCHOOLS

Social Service

Tyndale Biscoe instituted a regular system of social work[61] in the C.M.S. High School. This met with marked success and induced a spirit of manliness among his pupils, who did yeomans service during floods, rescuing families which were stranded "on the roofs of rickety houses or small patches of dry ground."[62] His system was combined with the inculcation of moral and physical courage e.g. in cholera outbreaks,[63] fires,[64] floods, boating accidents etc. A sanitation corps was formed in the school. The plan was to get boys and masters to volunteer for this work, to persuade citizens to allow the corps to visit their homes, clean their compounds and fill the cesspits with sand from the river beds This was strongly opposed both by pupils and parents. Such work was regarded as fit only for coolies and Biscoe was attacked for deliberately making the Brahman boys do so. But Biscoe made the boys do the job of cleaning the streets and compounds in the city. As a result a very powerful campaign was organized against the school. The popular resentment was clearly shown in the papers.[65] They stated that "Mr. Biscoe makes his Brahman boys drag dead dogs through the streets of Srinagar."[66] The school faced a crisis when the discontented men stirred the staff to a mutiny.[67] The result was that a Hindu School was opened just in front of the Mission School.[68] The sponsoring authority of this school was Mrs. Annie Besant, the President of the Theosophical Society of India. The Mission School Report of 1901 points out that in a fortnight three hundred boys left the Mission School and joined her school.[69] Biscoe was, however, brave enough to hold his ground. His tenacity of purpose and determination was crowned with success when the boys started coming back again after some time.[70] Commenting on the importance of C.M.S. High School, Sir Henry Sharp remarks:

"Under the management of Rev. C.E. Tyndale Biscoe the school has developed a remarkable *esprit de corps*, and the utmost care is devoted to physical instruction, to the encouragement of manliness and to the cultivation of the civic virtues. With its record of life-saving and other public benefits, the school is an important asset to Srinagar and holds a unique position."[72]

Under Biscoe the school became a pioneer of social work in Srinagar. The policy of training boys in social service was later followed by the State schools, and "the influence of the mission schools not only reached the corners of Kashmir Valley but also the State schools of Jammu."[72]

Change and Reform in Curriculum

Owing to the isolated position of Kashmir most of the boys or people never left Kashmir, and many had not even been out of Srinagar. It was difficult to explain and describe objects and conditions which lay outside this limited experience. To overcome the difficulty, pictures were often used and Biscoe says that in order to make the local staff believe that sea was made of salt water, a party of masters had to be sent to Karachi, in order that they might see, feel and taste the sea.[73]

The following subjects[74] were included in the curriculum in addition to the subjects required for entrance to the Punjab University.

1) A knowledge of the geography of their own country and especially of the city of Srinagar.
2) A knowledge of the different kinds of boats, houses, agricultural implements, etc. which were in Kashmir.
3) A knowledge of the differences between the common trees by their leaves and to know their uses.
4) A knowledge of everyday events that were taking place in the world around them.

All this was introduced, so that boys would get really interested in their own country, would have their hobbies instead of staying indoors, and would realise something of the vastness and variety of the world, and so their eyes would be taken away from the narrow limits of Kashmir.

Social Reforms

The missionaries were the pioneers of the reform movement in Srinagar. It has elsewhere been noted that the people of Srinagar had gained notoriety for their filthy habits. The most important reform which Biscoe brought into the school concerned cleanliness. Its introduction was very difficult, not because of the dress or climate, but because of the attitude of the pupils. The Brahmans of Srinagar cherished the illusion that they were the cleanest possible persons on earth. Biscoe points out that 'if by chance one of the European staff should touch them, they would squirm in utter disgust at such defilement.'[75] So before they could become clean they had to learn that they were dirty. To this were added three more great enemies—parents, custom and public opinion.

The parents believed that if a boy looked clean and tidy then the devil might become fond of him and run off with him. Personal cleanliness was further intimately connected with economic and social factors. On the economic level, a person who was clean and tidy had generally been more highly taxed from the days of Afghan rule, since the Government had based its taxation scale upon the rather simple assumption that anyone who was clean was also rich.[76] Lack of cleanliness was thus a protection not only against the rigours of Kashmir weather but also against extortions by the State. On the social level, cleanliness was equally ill-advised. The Kashmiri women were known for their beauty throughout India and they were often abducted and sometimes, even sold.[77] This explains why the

Kashmiri women put on dirty dresses.[78] Once when a Zenana missionary was forced to say, "O dear Kashmiri women, why won't you wash? " they looked with surprise at her and replied, "we have been so oppressed that we don't care to be clean."[79] To a superficial observer it may appear that Biscoe was crusading against the dirty habits of his pupils, but in reality he was attempting the extremely hurculean task of changing the attitude of his pupils and their deeply rooted social opinions. Notwithstanding these difficulties he made his way. In carrying through this reform some harsh methods were used, but without their use, it seems, success would have remained a mirage. "We have been able to raise the standard of cleanliness to a degree that I never thought possible two or three years ago," writes Biscoe in a letter, "we not only fine the dirty boys, but their form masters also, are held responsible for the uncleanliness of the boys."[80]

The next important reform pertained to dress.[81] In 1890 the dress of Biscoe's pupils consisted of *pheran*, nosering, heavy earrings, and a pair of wooden clogs.[82] No vigorous action seemed possible on account of this dress. To Biscoe, boys who could neither run, play nor walk fast, were strange indeed. This eccentricity in dress demanded change. Before embarking on a plan of reform, he justified his determination to alter dress. Writes Mr. Biscoe, "... The School is not intended to westernize the boys, and wherever the habits of the people are harmless or commendable, they are encouraged to preserve their national custom and dress. But wherever the customs have harmful effects every means is employed to try to alter them ..."[83]

The method which the founder of modern education in Srinagar used to accomplish this reform was the introduction of games, which were made compulsory. In one of the Mission School Reports[84] it is clearly mentioned how games served to emphasize the need for changes in dress. The nosering and earrings, for instance, were found to be a painful accessory when boxing was introduced.[85] The *pheran* disappeared because of the horizontal bars, wooden clogs were hardly serviceable for playing football.[86] Thus Biscoe was able to use games as a powerful instrument of change and reform.

Of all the many evils the missionaries attacked, the remarriage of Brahman widows required "great pluck and perseverance."[87] Mr. Biscoe struggled against the custom which forbid Hindu widows (often mere girls) from remarrying.[88] It was in 1928 that the first widow remarriage took place in Srinagar.[89] The Sanskrit teacher of the Mission School Mr.

Shanker Koul was the only "priest" who had the courage to set his face against orthodox opinion and to perform the rites in the teeth of opposition.[90] By 1947, the Mission School staff had arranged over one hundred remarriages of Brahman widows.[91] Indeed, Mr. Biscoe was greatly moved by the sad plight of the young Brahman widows. In order to save them from being forced to live impure lives, he started a pension fund for the widows. Every master had to pay a portion of his monthly salary into this fund. The school treasury also contributed to this fund. With this pension a widow was able to free herself of her late husband's family and could live the life she chose. She no longer lived in perpetual fear and bondage. It is worthwhile to note in the late 1940's the fund helped thirty widows.[92]

Emergence of a New Class of Learned Men

Before Srinagar came under the influence of mission schools, its social system and school organization was geared to Hindu and Muslim thought. The indigenous educational institutions known as *maktabs* and *patshalas* provided only religious instruction of a very limited type and they cannot, therefore, strictly speaking, be classed among institutions which were engaged in promoting general education. There can be no denying the fact that the Hindu and Muslim education has never kept pace with changing social conditions. Only when the influence of English education was most strongly felt was this traditional social and religious matrix loosened. The advent of the Christian educators resulted in the breakdown of Srinagar society and laid the foundations of a new one. A new, previously unknown, class of people was created. Members of this new middle class chiefly resided in Srinagar and had a good knowledge of English which proved useful for government and other services. From this class of people many of whom received their education in mission schools also came a great number of teachers, doctors, lawyers and leaders. Thus a new élite of learned men was created.

Cultural Changes

Modern education initiated certain cultural changes which have been both intensive and extensive. The influences extended to domestic institutions such as wedding customs. For the élite it now became impossible to entertain the guests on the traditional confectionary. The hiring of a jeep or motor car for the bridal procession through the city, or the provision of a Western style suit and shoes for the bridegroom's outfit, were examples of the cultural impact of the British on the new class of learned men. That the influence of new ideas was mostly displayed at weddings, which otherwise were celebrated in the traditional manner, indicates an assimilation of new types of behaviour, rather than a displacement of old by new patterns of behaviour.

The education of the boys along modern lines and the influence of European teachers were changing taste and fashion. Illustrative of the change in fashion were the wearing of trousers, jacket and waist-coat by the educated community. The prestige accorded by expenditure on sundries also reflects the impact of new ideas on the English educated people. For instance, the Westernized class frequently visited restaurants, theatres, cinemas and parks. The Western influence was also noticeable in the number of English words used by the city people particularly by the *Hanjis* and the business community.[93] By using English words those who had contact with the English visitors wanted to distinguish themselves from mere country yokels. Thus as a result of contact with the British many English words found their way into Kashmiri vocabulary. The people of the city dopted English words for foreign innovations, such as *redu* for radio, *bus* for bus, *car* for car, *houzboat* for houseboat etc. People used the same English terms to denote foreign words. For example, *meem* for madam, *milut* for minute, *lumber* for number, were picked up by the people. Thus the use of English words became a criterion of prestige in Srinagar, because of its main links with the English, whereas this was not true of the villages with their concentration on peasant values and activities.

Another interesting thing to note about the western impact is that the traders of Srinagar deliberately chose anglicised names for themselves and their boats[94] with a view to get the foreigners interested, such as 'Suffering Moses', 'Sunshine Ally', 'Anemeda', 'Chota Sultana', 'Walnut Willie' and *shikaras* and boats are called 'Peddington Station', 'Buckingham Palace', 'Victoria the Great', 'Churchills Cigar', 'Lady Love', 'Under my Quilt' etc.

Of all other factors which helped the position of the C.M.S. the utilitarian value of education[95] they provided was no doubt, the most important. In the long run this feature of educational provision dominated all aspects of policy. In fact, it was then the English education which strengthened the position of the privileged groups in society. Only an English education could produce an élite and only members of the existing élite could make the best use of the education that was provided. It was under such circumstances that English education was provided. It was under such circumstances that English education acquired a position of dominance in the city.

The European travellers and businessmen in the city also promoted new ideas. All the Europeans lived in Sheikh Bagh, which was known as the European quarter. Social intercourse between the Europeans and the city people was by no means uncommon. We hear of the Europeans treated to a *wazwan*[96] by the wealthy merchants of Srinagar. Some of the foreigners found their apartments furnished after the European fashion. Thus Srinagar provided the convenient social and cultural setting for the meeting of East and West.

The greatest imapct of the mission schools was on social mobility. It benefitted the mission and non-mission boys alike although the former were often at an advantage because of good schooling. An English education helped to raise the status of all those who could benefit from it.

Another consequence of modern education was the emergence of a group of people, often described as Westernized. It was an influential group with considerable wealth and prestige. The members of this class were eager for Western knowledge by their excessive admiration of the West, and coupled with an increased necessity for education in English in order to enjoy the best fruits of Western culture, tended to ignore their own Kashmiri culture. It is this class which discarded the Kashmiri dress and put on the dress in European fashion. More important, it was this section which rejected traditional values and institutions. In the highly Westernized sections of Srinagar society ritual seems to have played a minimum part. Indeed, it was contact with the British and the study of English that led this group to be critical of many of their customs, manners and ideas.[97]

Growth of Private Enterprise in Education

The influence of missionaries was not religious. But the social influence of the Christian missionary activities particularly in the field of education was indeed considerable. The liberality of their conduct produced the most favourable impression on the Muslims as well as the Hindus of the city, and led to great educational activity and enterprise. One result of their activity was that an element of private enterprise in education was stimulated. The Muslim education movement, the result of private enterprise, was started in the 'nineties of the last century. It was initiated by Mir Waiz Moulvi Ghulam Rasul Shah[98] as a safeguard against Muslims being driven towards Christianity. He believed that ignorance of the principles of Islam was dangerous for the Muslims. The climax of his efforts was the creation of a primary school in which religious instruction was imparted. With this initial purpose, the school slowly developed into a High School[99] and began to follow the mission school pattern. In the 1930's the *Aujuman-i-Nusrat-ul-Islam* started two primary girls schools.

The establishment of a network of private schools by the Hindus was also a direct result of missionary activities. After 1930 the education of Pándit girls received great impetus through the establishment of the 'Women Welfare Trust.'

Later in the 'thirties of this century the Roman Catholic Mission opened a high school in Srinagar which still flourishes.

Changes in the Position of Women

The mission schools helped a great deal in emancipating the Kashmiri women. Through the activities of the mission, the quality of family life was considerably improved. It is a recognized fact that to a certain extent social change hinges for its success on the participation in social affairs of enlightened women with opportunity and responsibility. The missionaries recongnized this and left no stone unturned for attracting the girls to their schools. Towards the close of the Dogra rule, there were girls' schools in different parts of the city, preparing if not a large number but a few, at least for higher education in the universities, others for professions such as teaching and medicine, and still others for domestic work.

Missionary Impact on the State

The impact of the social service rendered by the missionaries during famines, floods and cholera is judged by the fact that the Government also evinced a great interest in the welfare of its subjects. The State's concern for the welfare of its subjects is clearly indicated by the various ameliorative measures taken from time to time to combat famine, disease and prejudice. The establishment of the Public Works Department, Industries Department, Cooperative Department, Fire Brigade Department, Cooperative Credit Societies etc. marked an important step towards progress.

Another important result was that the state began to take an interest in education. The opening of government schools, the creation of the system of grants-in-aid to encourage private schools, and, above all, the appointment of educational committees and organization of educational conference point to a change in the policy of the Government.

The Birth of the Reform Movement

Last but not the least, one of the results of Christian missionary activity was to make sensitive Kashmiris critical of their own society and some of its institutions. It is important to realise that some missionaries were also men of closed minds who failed to understand or appreciate the Kashmiri point of view or character. They started with a somewhat naive assumption that everything in Kashmiri society and religion was bad and that Christianity was the only true religion that could save the afflicted soul. The missionaries launched indiscriminate attacks upon Kashmiri society through various kinds of publications. One positive, if indirect result of such hostile criticism, was to produce a new sense of awareness among many people regarding the necessity of change and reform.

Thus *Anjumans* and *Sabhas* came into being. Meetings took place and resolutions were passed on a variety of matters. Newspapers, journals and conferences had as their main aim the safeguarding of the interests of a particular group they represented. Matters such as the age of marriage of girls, girl's education,[100] high dowry, widow remarriage, high cost of wedding[101] and funeral ceremonies and other matters were discussed in conferences.

An Estimate of Missionary Impact on Society and Culture

In spite of their great service to the people of Kashmir, the Christian missionaries made only a few converts in Srinagar.[102] The reasons for the missions failure in this respect are not far to seek. In the first instance, converts to Christianity were persecuted by the Maharaja's Government.[103] Besides, conversions were also greatly opposed by the Hindus and the Muslims alike. For instance, the conversion of a Muslim boy to Christianity caused great uproar among his co-religionists, who besieged the C.M.S. School and demanded that the convert be handed over to them.[104] However, the new convert stood firm and came to be known as Samuel Bakal.[105] Similarly, some Brahmans who embraced the new faith were persecuted by the Hindu population.[106] The Brahman priests and the Brahman Dharma Sabha were also very active and the latter carried on a vehement propaganda against the C.M.S.[107] Thus the formation of Hindu *Sabhas* and Muslim *Anjumans* during this period should be regarded as an attempt to counter the religious propaganda of Christian missions. In fact, the missionaries generated a sense of awareness among the local religious leaders. We have seen that the attitude of the Brahman priests towards the missionaries was hostile. It is they who prevented children from attending schools regularly. So great was the effect of their propaganda that at first the work of the missionary school was disrupted by parents who withdrew their children.[108]

If public opinion had supported the Brahmans in their hostility to the activities of the C.M.S. in Srinagar, the cause of modern education would have greatly suffered. But things turned out differently. In the first place, there were no effective government or private schools able to compete with the mission schools. The lack of competition alone, however, does not account for the unrivalled educational success of the mission schools. One main reason which can be advanced for this was the great change the mission teachers had brought about in the outlook of the parents. This, indeed, was the utilitarian value the people attached to the education of their children.

In the second place, the policy of Anglicizing education helped the C.M.S. to consolidate its position in Srinagar and other parts of the Valley. The progress of Western education induced people to judge education mainly in terms of its usefulness for social advancement. English was the gateway to higher education. It offered the greatest material prospects. Though Urdu was the official language of the Government, a knowledge of English was desired of all who wished to seek employment in the various branches of the administration.

NOTES:

1. Robert Clark, *The Missions of C.M.S. and C.E.Z.M.S. in the Punjabi and Sindh,* p.167
2. *Op. cit.,* II, p. 129.
3. Some of the high British officials are reported to have made an appeal to the C.M.S. for the introduction of the words of God into Kashmir. See Eugene Stock, *The History of the Church Missionary Society, its Environment, its Men and its work,* Vol. II, pp. 572-73.
4. NAI/John Collett to Sir J. Wallace, Foreign, Extl. B, Oct. 1887, Nos. 223/226 (MS); Foreign, Sec. E, March 1883, Nos. 81-84, p. 3; Nisbet to the Secretary to Govt. of India, Foreign, sec. E, April 1889, Nos. 80-98, p. 7; Lawrence to Nisbet, Foreign, Feb. 1891, Sec. E, 295-326, pp. 22-

23; Henvey's note, Foreign, Sec. E, Mar. 1883, No. 86; Foreign, Sec. 28 Jan. 1848. Nos. 41-42; Despatch to Secret Committee Foreign, 22 Jan. 1848, Sec. No 10. (MS). *The India We Served*, p. 128; Schonberg, *op. cit.,* II, p. 8; *Wrongs of Kashmir* (typed copy), Chapter III, p. 24; Torrens, *op. cit.,* p. 301; Temple, *op. cit.,* I, p. 302; *The Hamdard-i-Hind*, Lahore, 16 Sept., 1895 *(Report on Native Newspapers,* Punjab, 1895 p. 590).

5. See Ishaq Khan, "Some Aspects of Corvee in Kashmir" (*Research Biannual,* Vol. I, No. II, 1976. pp. 58-71).
6. Martyn Clark, *Robert Clark of the Punjab*, p. 190.
7. Ibid; *Kashmir in Sunlight and Shade*, p. 178; *Where Three Empires Meet.* p. 37.
8. Martyn Clark, *op. cit.,* p. 191; Davidge, *Travellers Companion and Guide to Kashmir*, p. 25.
9. See Stock, *op. cit.,* II, p. 575.
10. NAI/Foreign, Sec. Jan. 28, 1848, Nos. 41-42; Despatch to Secret Committee (MS.), Foreign, Jan. 22, 1848, Sec, No. 10.
11. Robert Clark, *op.cit.,* p. 167; Clark died on 16th March 1900 "universally honoured and revered." See Stock, *op. cit.,* p. 203; *C.M. Intelligencer*, July, Oct, Nov. 1900 and *C. M. Review*, Dec. 1907. His life was written by his adopted son, Dr. H. Martyn Clark, under the title *Robert Clark of the Punjab*.
12. Robert Clark, *op. cit.,* p. 168.
13. Martyn Cark, *op. cit.,* p. 192.
14. Ibid.
15. NAI/Robert Clark to F. H. Cooper, Officer on Special Duty in Kashmir, dated 25th April, 1864 (Foreign and Pol. July 1864, Nos. 79-81).
16. Ibid; See also Robert Clark, *op. cit.,* pp. 168-69; Martyn Clark, *op. cit.,* p. 195; Ernest Neve, *op. cit.,* p. 68; Shephered, *Arthur Neve of Kashmir,* p. 12.
17. Martyn Clark, *op. cit.*, p. 213.
18. Robert Clark, *op. cit.*, p. 169.
19. Ibid.
20. Ibid., p. 168; Martyn Clark, *op. cit.*, p. 213; *Cashmere* (E. Bickersteth, *Pamphlets India,* p. 8); See also F. Cooper's letter dated 20th May, 1864 to R.H. Davies (Foreign and Pol. July 1864, Nos 79-81).
21. R. Clarks' letter dt. 25th April, 1864 to F.H. Cooper (Foreign & Pol. July 1864, Nos. 79-81); Robert Clark, *op. cit.,* p. 169; Martyn Clark, *op. cit.,* pp. 195 and 197; See also Mrs. Ashley Carus - Wilson, *Irene Petrie, Missionary to Kashmir,* p. 119.
22. Robert Clark, *op. cit.,* p. 169.
23. Clark's Letter dt. 25th April 1864 to F.H. Cooper (Foreign and Pol. July 1864, No. 79-81; Robert Clark, *op. cit.*, P. 169; Martyn Clark *op. cit.,* pp. 203-205 and 208.

24. Martyn Clark *op. cit.,* 229. Robert Clark's conducts and acts were appreciated by the people of the city. See NAI/No. 76 (Foreign and Pol. A, Sept. 1864, Nos. 74-76) Mrs. Clark also won unbounded respect and gratitude from all classes of people in Srinagar for her "humane exertions and truly Christian charity and demeanour." Cooper's letter dt. 19th July, 1864 to Clark (NAI/Foreign and Pol. A., Sept., 1864, Nos. 74-76).
25. Martyn Clark, *op. cit.,* p. 229; See also NAI/Foreign and Pol. A. Sept. 1864, Nos. 74-76.
26. Martyn Clark, *op. cit.,* p.236.
27. Elmslie, *Seed Time in Kashmir,* pp. 96-97; Carus-Wilson, *op. cit.,* p. 120; *Cashmere (Pamphlets India),* p. 11.
28. *Kashmir in Sunlight and Shade*, p. 240; Robert Clark, *op. cit.,* pp. 170-171; *Wrongs of Kashmir (Kashmir Papers,* pp. 7 and 18).
29. See *Friend of India (Kashmir Papers*, pp. 36-38).
30. In 1867 Maharaja Ranbir Singh appointed intelligence men to enquire into the working of the missionaries. J&K (P.R.) File No. 368 to 1867.
31. Elmsile, *op. cit.,* p. 195; *Friend of India (Kashmir Papers*, pp. 36-38).
32. Carus-Wilson, *op. cit.,* p. 121.
33. Wilson, *The Abode of Snow,* p. 354; Bates, *op. cit.,* p. 17.
34. *Beyond The Pir Panjal,* p. 71.
35. Elmsile, *op. cit.,* pp. 222-223.
36. Ibid. We are told that in the time of Rev. J. Hinton Knowles three old boys of the C.M.S. School were arrested in Srinagar for learning English. For more interesting details, see *Fifty Years Against the Stream*, p.1.
37. Bates, *op. cit.,* p.17.
38. Robert Clark, *op. cit.,* pp. 171-172; Shephered, *op. cit.,* pp. 12-13; *Thirty Years in Kashmir*, p.29.
39. *Beyond the Pir Panjal,* p. 71; *Imperial Gazetteer*, p. 12.
40. *Kashmir in Sunlight and Shade,* pp. 240 and 242.
41. Ibid., p. 242.
42. Ibid; The total attendance at this hospital was 38, 954 in 1922 as against 34, 815 in 1920. *Census,* 1921, I, p. 64.
43. Dr. Arthur Neve devoted his life to the service of God and humanity in Kshmir for thirty eight years (1882-1920). His death in 1920 enveloped Srinagar in a pallor of gloom. See Shephered, *op. cit.,* p. 132.
44. *Thirty Years in Kashmir*, pp. 301-302.
45. For the life of Irene Petrie, see Carus-Wilson, *Irene Petrie. Missionary to Kashmir.*
46. NAI/Fanshaw's note on famine (1877-79), Foreign, Sec. E, Mar 1833, Nos. 81-82, p.12.
47. Robert Clark, *op. cit.,* pp. 172-73; *Thirty Years in Kashmir,* pp. 29-31.
48. Dr. Downes who joined D. Maxwell in 1877 played an important role in the permanent establishment of the Kashmir Mission. It was he "who

obtained final permission to remain for the winter, by stirring public opinion on the subject through the newspapers, and during six years without any college or trained assistant or nurses conducted the medical mission, seeing sometimes as many as three hundred patients in one day." *Vide Kashmir Mission* (C.M.S.), 1901, p. 25; See also Carus-Wilson, *op. cit.*, p. 123; Shephered, *op. cit.*, p. 13 *Thirty Years in Kashmir*, pp. 31-32.

49. NAI/Foreign, Sec. E. March 1883, Nos. 81-82, p. 12; Foreign, A Pol. E, Sept. 1882, Nos. 253-65, p. 2.
50. Ibid., *Beyond The Pir Panjal,* p. 266.
51. *Beyond The Pir Panjal,* p.266.
52. Ibid., pp. 272-73.
53. *Kashmir in Sunlight and Shade,* p. 306.
54. Ibid.
55. Ibid.
56. *Beyond The Pir Panjal,* pp. 242-243.
57. Biscoe, *Autobiography,* p. 117.
58. Ibid; See also Shephered, *op. cit.,* p.99.
59. *Kashmir in Sunlight and Shade,* p. 63.
60. Ibid., p. 232; Biscoe, *Autobiography,* p. 60. With the introduction of allopathic system of medicine the indigenous schools of *vaids and hakims* declined (Bazaz, *Inside Kashmir*, p.240). Formerly barbers performed minor surgical operations, but later they began to lose much of their influence (*Beyond The Pir Panjal,* p.242).
61. For more details, see *Social Service in Kashmir; Rock Shifting in Kashmir*, p.13; *A School in Action,* pp. 8-14; *With Pick and Shovel in Kashmir,* pp. 12-13; *It can't Be Done, Then Do It* pp. 7-8.; *Still Pegging Away in Kashmir,* pp. 11-20. *Victory After Defeat,* pp. 12-13; *Digging Foundations in Kashmir*, p.10.
62. *Beyond The Pir Panjal,* p. 253.
63. Biscoe, *Autobiography*, p.117.
64. Mr. Biscoe "was the first to organize fire brigade work in Srinagar, himself leading his boys and masters in many a fiery combat." *Thirty Years in Kashmir,* p. 306.
65. *Against the Current*, p. 9.
66. *Fifty Years Against the Stream*, p.58.
67. Ibid., Bisoce, *Autobiography*, p.77.
68. Bisoce, *Autobiography,* p.77.
69. Ibid.
70. Ibid ; *Fifty Years Against the Stream*, p.58.
71. *Sharp's Report* (1916), p.66.
72. Ibid., p.23.
73. *Fifty Years Against the Stream*, pp. 32-33.

74. Ibid., pp. 34-35.
75. *Against the Current,* p.6.
76. Sufi, *op. cit.,* pp. 23-24. Dermot Norris very significantly observes: "Good clothes, or even a neat appearance would have been construed to indicate that the wearer (Kashmiri) was in easy circumstances and would have attracted tax-gatherers as surely as honey-scented flowers attract the bee." (*Kashmir,* p.9); Dugsal *op. cit.,* p.179.
77. *Cashmere Misgovernment* (typed copy), Chapter IV, p.35.
78. Arthur Brinckman writes in his *Wrongs of Kashmir* (p.33) that every Kashmiri who wore "ornaments beyond the common or clothes better than the roughest," was "marked down for plunder by the rapacious officials."
79. Carus-Wilson, *op. cit.,* p. 111.
80. Quoted in Brain Holmes, *op. cit.,* pp. 166-67.
81. *Grinding Grit into Kashmir,* p.10.
82. *Fifty years Against the Stream,* pp. 3-4; *Kashmir in Sunlight and Shade,* pp. 263-64.
83. *Fifty years Against the Stream,* p.13.
84. *Still Pegging Away in Kashmir,* pp. 9-10; *It Can't be done*; *Then Do It,* pp. 3-4.
85. Ibid.
86. Ibid; *Fifty years Against the Stream,* pp. 3-4
87. Biscoe, *Autobiography,* pp. 93-97; See also *Riding the Storms in Kashmir,* p.13.
88. *Against the Current,* p.11.
89. It was in May 1928 that two young Brahman widows of the city were remarried through the efforts of Shankar Koul, the Headmaster of the C.M.S. School, Srinagar. Biscoe writes that this marriage caused "a great uproar in the city. But like all storms, this one blew itself out in time." (*Autobiography,* p.97).
90. Ibid.
91. Ibid., p.100.
92. Ibid., p.97.
93. "The shopkeepers and *hanjis* who have English speaking customers speak English though broken and full of solecisms." *Census,* 1931 I, p. 102) ; Majid, *op. cit.,* pp. 77.
94. *The Khidmat* (Eng.), April 17, 1946, p.4.
95. It is interesting to note that owing to the establishment of the Mission School in the city, the number of boys studying in the Government Middle School, Srinagar, fell from 227 in 1888-89 to 160 in 1889-90. From Colonel W.F. Prideaux, Resident in Srinagar, to W.J. Cunningham, NAI/Foreign, May 1892, Sec. E, Nos. 6-7.
96. Eckenstein, *The Karakorams and Kashmir,* pp. 238-239.

97. Dermot Norris who visited Srinagar in Maharaja Hari Singh's reign remarks: In the past Kashmiri Pandits "were extremely bigoted and the social evils ... were rampant in their society. But today, largely due to the efforts of a few devoted Englishmen, who have worked among them for many years there are signs that some of them are becoming modern in their ideas, and are preferred to cast aside the more harmful of the conventions which guided their forefathers in every direction." (*op. cit.*, p.9); See also *Beyond The Pir Panjal,* p. 254.

98. Moulvi Rasul Shah came of the Mir Waiz family of Srinagar. He was the first who like Sir Syed Ahmed Khan, was bestirred into action by the backwardness of his community . Imbued with some progressive ideas, he realized that without modern education the Muslims will remain always backward. He believed that a good education on western lines, supported by wise religious teachings from the Quran, would produce young Muslims of capacity and character. In this he was greatly helped by some outside Muslims who were in State service. Among the outsiders who helped the Moulvi was Munshi Ghulam Rasul Shah, the then Revenue Minister of Kashmir. It was through the efforts of the latter that the school received grant-in-aid of Rs.50 per month from the State. The school was then raised to the middle standard. English was also taught. In order to mobilise public opinion in his favour, the Moulvi founded as association called *Anjuman-i-Nusrat-ul-Islam*. It was devoted to religious and educational subjects of the Muslims.

The Muslim officials encouraged Moulvi Rasul Shah in a courageous spirit, but the local Muslims under the leadership of fanatic *Mullahs* raised violent agitation and even attempts were made on the life of the Moulvi. Despite this opposition, the school progressed and soon became a High School, the fore-runner of the present Islamia College, Srinagar. It was unfortunate that the successors of Mir Waiz dabbled in petty politics and did nothing for the social and moral uplift of the Muslim community. Their narrow outlook on religion and politics did much to promote faction and rivalry.

99. *Fouq, Mashahir-i-Kashmir*, p. 123.

100. J&K (G.R.), F.N, 209/45-C of 1920.

101. *The Ranbir*, 15th January, 1940; 3rd June, 1940; 22 Oct. 1945.

102. Biscoe, *Autobiography*, pp. 115-122; The *Ranbir*, Dec. 30, 1940; *Census*, 1921, I, p.6. "The words of the Book are good", was often said by the *Mullahs*, "but each man must keep his own religion, If God had meant me to be a Christian, he would have made me one." *op. cit.*, p. 97.

103. NAI/Foreign, Genl B, Aug. 1867, Nos. 119-120 (MS); See also Martyn Clark, *op. cit.*, pp. 231 -232; *Cashmere (Pamphlets India,* p.9). Neither Gulab Singh nor his successor gave full religious freedom to the missionaries. NAI/Foreign Pol. July 1864, Nos. 79-81; *Wrongs of*

Kashmir (Kashmir papers, pp. 7 and 16); C.M.S. Reports (*Kashmir Papers*, pp. 42-43).

104. Biscoe, *Autobiography*, pp. 115-122.
105. Ibid.
106. Ibid., pp. 267-269.
107. Ibid.
108. *Kashmir in Sunlight and Shade,* pp. 110 and 262.

CHAPTER VI

EDUCATION

Ancient Kashmir is said to have been the seat of Sanskrit learning and "from this small Valley have issued master pieces of history, poetry, romance, fable and philosophy."[1] It remained for centuries the home of the great Sanskrit scholars and at least one influential forms of Hinduism, Saivism, "has found some of its most eloquent teachers on the banks of the Vitasta. Some of the greatest Sanskrit poets were born and wrote in the Valley and from it has issued in the Sanskrit language a world famous collection of folklore."[2] "Kashmiris," writes Sir George Grierson, "are proud and justly proud of the literary glories of their land."[3]

With the coming of the Muslims, Islamic influence penetrated deep into the valley. The 'Muslim rule, saw the promotion of learning, both Persian and Sanskrit. *Madrasas*[4] and *Maktabs* were founded. Sultan Zain-ul-Abidin is said to have founded a University at his capital, Nau-Shahr. The Mughal rulers encouraged vocational training in carpet, shawl-making, papier-mache and other handicrafts. Thus at "the end of the seventeenth century Kashmir stood as a pioneer of progress and a beacon of enlightenment to the surrounding territories. From this position, it declined under the tyrannies and extortions of subsequent rulers, until, by the early years of the nineteenth century, the cultural glories of its past had disappeared, and it was known abroad chiefly for the desolation of its land and the misery of its people."[5]

Modern education does not seem to have existed in Srinagar until the advent of Christian missionaries in Kashmir when a changed outlook gradually came into being. The *maktabs* of Srinagar and of other parts of the Valley were generally affiliated to the mosques, where the boys were taught to read Arabic so that they might be able to read the Quran. Likewise the Kashmiri Pandits had their schools called *patshalas* where Sanskrit was taught to enable them to read the sacred books. Persian, introduced in Kashmir by the Muslim rulers, continued to remain the official language till 1907 when it was replaced by Urdu.[6] Thus Persian was also taught in *maktabs* and *patshalas* and both Hindus and Muslims showed a keen interest in learning Persian. Both boys and girls were entrusted to the care of the *moulvi* or of the Pandit by their parents who taught them the fundamental rituals and principles of their religion.

In 1872 the following were the leading *patshalas* and *madrasas* in Srinagar.[7]

	Sanskrit readers	Veda readers	English readers	Persian readers	Arabic readers	Number of Students
Pathshala of Srinagar	...	75	...	...	...	75
Madrasa of Nawakadal	...	...	...	192	...	192
Madrasa of Maharaj Gunj	...	...	...	68	68	
Madrasa of Rainawari below Hari Parbat	...	...	...	71	...	71
Madrasa of Basant Bagh	...	...	...	154	...	154
Madrasa of Aisha Kaul	...	....	...	51	...	51

From this it is obvious that the city was very backward in education. Even the *Administration Report* of 1873 which is the first of its kind in the Jammu and Kashmir State testifies to the educational backwardness of the city population. The report makes mention of Government schools only in the city and these are named as Pathshala, Nawakadal School, Maharaj Gunj School, and the Basant Bagh School.[8] It is further stated that the expenditure on education in Srinagar amounted to the petty sum of Rs. 36,372. Out of this amount Rs. 11,875 were spent on the pay of teachers, Rs. 1,567 for the maintenance of institutions, Rs.2,268 for free rations, Rs. 18,661 for scholars, Rs. 40 as reward, Rs. 1,137 for the purchase of books for the use of scholars.[9] Besides, it is stated that the then Maharaja Ranbir Singh spent Rs.17,737 on translation work.[10] Regarding his educational policy, Sir Aurel Stein writes that the translation "into Hindi of standard works, selected from the whole range of the Dharsanas, the Dharma, and other Sastras,were executed and partly printed,with the object of spreading a knowledge of classical Hindu learning among the Maharaja`s Dogra subjects. Again Persian and Arabic works on historical, philosophical and other subjects were translated into Sanskrit with the assistance of competent Maulvis in order to facilitate the exchange of ideas which the Maharaja in a spirit of true enlightenment desired to promote between the representatives of Hindu and Mohammedan scholarship in his dominions."[11]

While Maharaja Ranbir Singh patronized Arabic, Persian and Sanskrit learning, the education of the masses remained in an extremely low state. The educational institutions classed as *maktabas and patshalas* often provided only religious instruction of a very limited type and they cannot, therefore, strictly speaking, be classed among institutions engaged in promoting general education.[12]

It was during this period that the missionaries made their appearance in Srinagar. The travel accounts published by the European visitors to Kashmir in the first half of the 19th century awakened the western philanthrophists to the vast scope for missionary work in the Valley. In 1854, Colonel Martin, a retired Army Officer of Peshawar, Rev. Robert Clark of the Punjab Missionaries and two Indian Christians came to Srinagar. They were cordially received by Maharaja Gulab Singh. "My subjects in Kashmir are very bad." The Maharaja is reported to have told the missionaries, "I am sure that no one can do them any harm. I am rather conscious to see whether Padri Sahibs can do them any good."[13] But this attitude of the Maharaja did not last. Though the Christian Missionary Society of London started its acitivities in Srinagar in the `sixties of the last century, it had to face serious opposition from the State authorities.

At first the missionaries thought it prudent to administer medical relief to the people of Srinagar during periods of epidemics. The useful services rendered by the medical missionaries made them popular among Kashmiris and this encouraged them to fight illiteracy. These was not a single school in Srinagar,where the right type of education could be imparted. Maharaja Ranbir Singh's school established in 1874 was the only State school but here the media of instruction were Sanskrit and Persian. It cannot be denied that the Dogra Government's attitude towards education of their subjects was indifferent.

The proposals of the Christian missionaries to found schools in Kashmir were approved by the C.M.S. in London. The founder of the modern Schools in Srinagar was Rev.J.H.Knowles.[14] It was in 1880 that Knowles laid the foundation of the C.M.S.School on the hospital premises in Srinagar.

In its infancy the C.M.S.School had to face a number of problems. The most pressing problem was that of school building. It was owing to this difficulty that Clark's first school was abandoned in 1864.[15] Between 1864 and 1880 the Kashmir Medical Mission had succeeded in bringing about 'good relations and understanding' among the people. But the official's attitude towards the mission had shown little change. The Government's orders prohibiting the missionaries from renting a house for a school building were still in force. Thus the C.M.S. had no alternative but to start the school on the hospital premises. [16]

In 1880 there were only five pupils reading in the C.M.S School.[17] Perhaps the problem of accommodation accounts for this small number of pupils. In those days there was no bus or *tonga* service in the city As such, pupils could not be attracted in large numbers on account of the hospital buildings being outside the city. It is said that those who attended complained of distance.[18] To remove this obstacle the missionaries obtained in 1883 a building at Sheikh Bagh in Srinagar. This act is said to have given rise to opposition and suspicion. Wrote Knowles:

"During the past year the mission school has been terribly opposed by the Government of this country. The reason for the increased opposition was our renting a large house by the city, and transferring our school there. His Highness the Maharaja will not permit any person to rent a room or possess a stick in the Valley."[19]

It is clear that in the beginning the attitude of the State authorities towards the missions was hostile.

In 1883 the number of boys on the school roll fell from 47 to 30.[20] Knowles attributed this decrease to distance.

It was in 1890 that the Government permitted the C.M.S. to shift the school down to the city, and it was moved from the hospital premises to a large house and compound on the river bank in the middle of the city (*Fateh Kadal*). As a result of this, the number of students increased to about 200 in 1890.[21]

While describing the future objective of the C.M.S. Mr. Knowles wrote:

"Our desire and intention is to bind Kashmir with a girdle of mission schools. It will be a very expensive business and already we are spending from our slender store, but we are determined to go on, assured that He who has opened wide the door, will furnish us with the means. We put our trust in Him."[22]

Mr. Knowles had to undertake ten-year's spade work in laying the foundation of the C.M.S. School.[23] He was assisted by Rev. C.L.E. Burges, A.B. Tyndale and also by some Kashmiri teachers in the work of building up the school.[24] Rev.C.L.E. Burges taught Mathematics. A.B.Tyndale of the Magdalen College, Oxford, started a Technical School and taught Brahman boys carpentry.[25] But the experiment came to nought owing to the social customs of the Kashmiri Pandits which prevented them from learning this trade.[26] We hear of a Brahman boy who worked hard for two years in the smithy shop of the school. Later, he opened his own bicycle repairing shop.

Miss Helen Burges was the first lady who established the kindergarten system in Srinagar. It is interesting to note that in the beginning the system generated doubts in the parents' minds, for several among them are reported to have removed their boys from the school because of it, for they said, "we send our children to school to learn and not to play."[27]

The opening of the Mission School in Srinagar heralded the dawn of a new era in the annals of modern Srinagar. Times change, so that when Rev. Tyndale Biscoe joined the school in 1981, there were 250 pupils on the school's roll.[28] Mr. Biscoe, who had come to assist Knowles, was amused to find boys wearing a very dirty nightgown in the class room. Not only that, their foreheads were plastered with red paint. Many boys wore huge golden earrings which, as Mr. Biscoe observes, "would have torn the lobes of their ears off if they had not been supported with a string over the tops of their heads."[29] It is also interesting to note that in the beginning the mission boys were permitted to bring *kangri* with them in winter.[30]

At first, nearly all 250 boys receiving instructions in the C.M.S. School were Kashmiri Pandits.[31] They were "the sons or grandsons of those officials who had bullied and squeezed the Mohemmadan peasants for years past, and their large houses in the city, with all their wealth, were standing witness to their looting powers, for the salary they received from the State was quite insignificant."[32]

Mr. Biscoe had to strive very hard to make his mission a success. In the beginning he found himself beset with numerous difficulties in imparting a new type of education to the Brahman boys. Biscoe's was a herculean task but ultimately he succeeded to some extent in dispelling ignorance. He himself says that he had come to Kashmiri to learn rather than to teach. How and what to teach the advanced pupils was the immediate question which exercised his mind. So, before embarking on any big plan, Biscoe made a thorough study of Kashmir's people. This study revealed to him that oppression, corruption, exploitation and superstition had robbed the people of their very spirit.

To these oppressed and enslaved people Biscoe was determined to give an education, "which would revive their spirit, which would help them develop character and become active citizens."[33] To him the goal of education was "to produce good citizens, imbued with the spirit of serving the universal Father by following the example of Christ in serving their fellows who will thus be able to help the people of their country to cast aside the reproach which has been put upon them by their neighbours, until they become in character a worthy complement of their most beautiful country."[34]

As stated earlier, the majority of the boys studying in the C.M.S. School was that of the Brahmans. Many of them were twenty years old or more and married. It was difficult to convince such grown-up boys that change was desirable and prepare them for it.

We are told that for some years the school started at 11 a.m. but pupils did not attend till midday.[35] Punctuality was not insisted upon because it was not the rule in the indigenous school which the State had founded in the city.[36] The holidays were the holidays of the Hindu boys. While explaining the nature of his work and difficulties, Biscoe writes: "One never could tell whether all the school or only half, would be present on any given day, for some boys would think one god important and some another. How could there be discipline when boys could attend or stay away at their own whim."[37]

The first step taken by Biscoe, therefore, "was to insist upon punctual attendance by the pupils." For this purpose, he introduced regular hours of instruction. Also holidays were arranged on the western pattern. Thus started the process of westernization in the C.M.S. School.[38]

At the beginning these measures were opposed by the pupils. It was a startling innovation in the city, for the government school in Srinagar was not thus organized. To discourage absenteeism among the boys, the practice of fine was introduced. This was not enough. Sometimes the boys did not come to school pretending to be sick. To check this tendency Biscoe hit on a novel scheme of visiting the houses of the boys.

It is also recorded that the boys were reluctant to play games.[39] This shows how superstition swayed their minds. Why did the boys stoutly refuse to play games? "For" said they, "we shall grow muscles on our bodies and then we shall become low-caste folk like the boatmen and coolies. If we play games, we shall have to run about and be energetic and people will laugh at us for gentlemen must not hurry."[40] It is also interesting to note that the Brahman boys even refused to touch a football[41] when it was introduced in Kashmir by Biscoe.[42] "We cannot kick this ball," said the Brahman boys, "for it is an unholy ball and we are holy Brahmans."[43] An example of how superstition reigned supreme is evident from a parents' letter of Mr.Biscoe, in which he requested Biscoe to grant his son exemption from joining playing teams and boating etc. for the astrologers had advised his son not to take part in games.[44]

It is clear that parents were averse to what they regarded as waste of time in sports. The boys were sent to schools to get a degree and that seems to be their aim.[45] Games were useless to them, whereas passing examinations meant employment in Government service.[46] We are told that the Brahman boys in the school thought it beneath their dignity to propel a boat.[47] Biscoe even speaks of the antipathy of some Brahman teachers to row.[48] But the founder of modern education in Srinagar did not budge an inch from the path he had chosen. To him school meant an institution where citizen's mind and bodies were to be trained. The great task to which Mr. Tyd\ndale Biscoe addressed himself, writes Ernest Neve, "was to teach the boys manliness, loyalty, charity, manners, cleanliness, truth" and other virtues".[49] For bodily development he laid stress on social service, games and sports and for mental exercise he introduced subjects like English, Indian languages (Urdu and Hindi), classical language (Persian), Mathematics, History, Geography, Science and Art. The boys were taught swimming which formed a special acquatic sport of the school. In the Mission school it was a rule that everybody must pass the swimming test before reaching his thirteenth birthday and failing this, his school fees were so increased that it became impossible for him to remain in the school.[50] In fact, there was no room for non-swimmers in this school. "The healthy athleticism of the C.M.S. School in Kashmir under Biscoe," remarks Dr. Brain Holmes in his article on British Imperial Policy and Mission Schools, "is an example of the way in which the same kind of the extra-curricular activities as those in England were introduced into the local schools."[51]

From 1893 Biscoe undertook various social service programmes and accomplished a great deal. It may be true that social service formed a part of the missionary activity but there can be no gainsaying the fact that the character[52] of the boys was ennobled and they realised that Srinagar was tradition-ridden and needed lifting. Mr. Biscoe does not indulge in exaggeration when he says that the products of his school learnt to be sorry for those in trouble. They could now differentiate between their school spirit and the spirit of the city. It now dawned upon them that superstition, ignorance and stupid customs had dampened their nobler spirit. These boys must have realised that Srinagar was far behind the rest of the world. Thus they set themselves to the task of changing the life of Srinagar.

Biscoe's students thus acquired a different outlook on life's problems. They were "talking language and behaving in a novel, unorthodox and non-conformist manner."[53] Later, these young men distinguished themselves as teachers and officials. An intellectual revolution was deeply surging and "was imperceptibly bringing the whole society in its vortex."[54]

GIRLS EDUCATION

The success of missionaries in both medical and the educational fields encouraged them to take up the cause of the women's education in Kashmir. To the missionaries the education of girls was of utmost importance for the girls would be the mothers of the future generation. It was the women of Kashmir who, more than the men, hindered progress on account of their ignorance and superstition. They were much more under the influence of the materialist and ignorant priests than the men. Since the boys were being educated and having their minds liberated from the clutches of the superstition, it was earnestly felt by the missionaries that they should find "like-minded" wives.

With this object in view, some time between 1893 and 1895 a girl's school was opened in Fateh Kadal by the Mission ladies. The opening of the girls' school shocked the people of Srinagar. There were murmurs and whispers in streets. The people thought that the missionaries aimed at polluting the minds of young girls with impure ideas. "The girls who were brave enough to attend were very timid", writes Mr. Biscoe, "and their parents were somewhat on the shake (Sic!), as public opinion was very much against them."[55] On the eve of the first prize day of the school, some of the European ladies were invited to attend the function by the lady superintendent. This, she thought would encourage the girls and parents. All the girls were assembled in the school, when on the appearance of the English lady visitors, some 'mischief-monger' in the street shouted out that the Europeans had come to kidnap the girls. Others took up the cry and in the tumult that ensued the girls left the school.[56] This episode resulted in the closure of the first girls' school for some time. A few weeks later the school reopened and surprisignly the school registered an increase in the number of girls. This phenomenal success emboldened the Christian missionaries to open another school which was attached to the boys school at Fateh Kadal.

Among the heroic souls who made girls' education acceptable in Srinagar in the midst of severe odd were Miss Churchill Taylor, Miss Stubbs and Miss Goodall.

Role of the C. M. S. Girls School

When Miss Fitze started a girls school in 1912, the majority of the girls attending her school were Muslim. In her yearly school report, Miss Fitze remarked: "Our chief trouble is that Hindu girls are taken away from us early on account of its being considered improper for them to go about after the age of 12, until they are married. I have lost quite a number of promising ones in this way. And consequently the Hindus on the roll call number only 35, while Mohammaden run upto 40..."[57]

In the beginning Miss Fitze had to face opposition from various quarters[58] but by 1914, opposition seems to have calmed down when the number of girls' schools rose to 3 in the city. By 1916 the girls were seen "coming better than ever before and mothers actually eager about their learning."[59] While commenting on the progress made by the girls school, Mr. Biscoe remarked, "The education of girls is progressing much faster than that boys did at its commencement, and I believe that the atmosphere of the city will be changed beyond all conception, when the mothers of this rising generation have been educated, for it is they and the priests who are the great stumbling blocks on the road to light and truth at present."[60]

In 1918, the school was raised to middle standard and it received a grant of Rs. 700 from the State.[61]

The following statistical information[62] is available regarding the number of girls in the C.M.S. Girls School, Fateh Kadal:

Year	No. of Girl Students	Year	No. of Girl Students	Year	No.of Girl Students
1912	Not known	1915	85	1918	100 (approx.)
1913	70	1916	83	1919	Not known
1914	70	1917	91	1920	70

This table testifies to the increasing number of students from 1913 to 1918, but shows the number falling to 70 in 1920. This was, perhaps, owing to the failing health of Miss Fitze during her last years of life. One can understand and appreciate the keen and active interest which she took in the education of girls. Miss Fitzes' school would have registered a greater increase but unfortunately the early marriage of girls stalled the progress.

The C.M.S. Girls School underwent a radical transformation during the period that Miss Mallinson was principal (1922-61). It can hardly be overemphasized that it was Miss Mallinson who was instrumental in bringing about enough educational and cultural advancement among the women of Srinagar. Under her inspiring leadership the school became a hub of cultural activities. She introduced swimming, dancing, drill, picnics, camping and mountaineering. It was thrilling to see the girls moving about freely and enjoying fresh air during the picnic and camping time. The first mountaineering camp was organized in 1938 when about 40 girls sought written permission of their parents for participating in the Mahadev mountaineering camp. The Girl Guide Movement helped girls to think of others, and was certainly developing in them a sense of responsibility and some idea of self-respect and self-control.

The subjects taught were English, Urdu, Persian, General Knowledge, Mathematics and Nature study. It is reported that "Hindi was introduced in the lower classes in 1944 by arranging a master to teach this subject."[63] And "in 1947 Science was introduced in the 9th class, so far the subject was not provided in any other girls' School."[64]

Apart from these subjects basket-making was introduced. Embroidery on bags and cushions was taught.[65] Also, laundry and cooking received much attention. It is also said that the girls learnt to weave some woollen bags and mats.

GOVERNMENT'S POLICY

In spite of the noble work of the Christian missionaries, Srinagar continued to remain very backward in education.[67] Missionaries were faced with seemingly insurmountable odds and were unable to take up the educational work on an extensive scale. Had the Government been desirous of uplifting the masses, it could certainly have spread a network of schools. On the contrary, the Dogra rulers did not like the idea of making their subjects politically conscious by spreading education.[68] The reports appearing in the vernacular newspapers of the Punjab give us an idea of the educational backwardness of the Kashmiris and the apathy of the Dogra rulers in that respect. These papers repeatedly and earnestly requested the Maharaja to attend to the education of the State subjects.[69] Towards the close of the last century a High School was opened in the city by Maharaja Partap Singh. But no steps were taken by the State authorities to make it attractive or to get students enrolled in large numbers. The *Paisa Akabar* (Lahore) dated 30th, November,1901 records that the state authorities did not "encourage the people to attain efficiency even in the education imparted in the said school."[71] The Census of 1901 showed how little attention was formerly paid to education. In that year only 2 per cent of the population could read and write.[72]

But the decade after 1904 saw some advance in education. In 1905 a Hindu college was started by Mrs. Annie Besant[73] in the city with the support of some luminaries of the theosophical society and Pandit Bala Koul of the Sahib family. Later, this college was taken over by the state and came to be known as Sri Pratap College.

At first it was the Hindu community which took to modern education. Many Hindu young men who passed from Sri Pratap College occupied posts of importance in the various branches of administration.

EDUCATIONAL BACKWARDNESS OF THE MUSLIMS

But the Muslims of Srinagar were less influenced by modern education than the Hindus.[74] The schools which the Muslims could boast of in the city were the Islamic High School and some middle and primary schools. The High School was beset with many difficulties, largely financial.[75] Maharaja Patap Singh took the following measures for promoting education among the Muslims:-

a) Aid was given to the Islamic High School and other Islamic schools. The aid given to the High School was Rs. 3,000 a year.[76]

b) Some Muslims were appointed as inspectors of schools. Also, a Special Officer's post was created with an exclusive charge of Muslims education.[77]

c) Scholarships amounting to Rs. 3,200 were given to Muslim pupils in high, middle and primary schools. Muslims could also participate in open scholarships. A small sum was also allotted for scholarships to Muslim girls.[78]

d) The *mullahs* were attached to some primary schools in the city for the teaching of the Quran in the lowest classes. [79]

e) *Maktabs* were encourged by small grants.[80]

The above measures had some good effect. The total increase of pupils in public institutions in the State was recorded as 4,315 during 1912-1914.[81] Of these 2,895 were Muslims.[82] In the same period the number of Muslims in middle schools increased from 626 to 1,521. A notable feature was large increase which took place in 1914 among the number of Muslims in private institutions. This rose in a single year from 3,965 to 7,325 owing to the appointment of the *mullahs* in the state schools and aiding *maktabs*[83]

But in spite of this, the Muslims did not take any larger part in collegiate and secondary education. In 1914 there were only 32 Muslim students studying in two colleges of Srinagar and Jammu. As against this, there were 147 Kashmiri Pandits studying in Sri Partap College in 1914.[85]

Causes of Muslims Educational Backwardness

There were many factors which prevented the Muslims from taking to modern education. The bulk of the population of the city consisted of the artisans who were naturally little enthusiastic about education,[86] Besides, poverty[87] and a reactionary clergy[88] discouraged modern education among the Muslims. But added to these facts was the indifferent attitude of the State authorities towards the education of the Muslims.[89] Almost all the newspapers published in the Punjab deplored the paucity of Muslim students in public schools.[90] This paucity was ascribed to the smallness of the number of Muslim teachers employed in these schools.[91]

Thus the real cause of the backwardness of Muslims in the field of education lay in the indifference of the State Government towards this basic aspect of social progress.

At last the Muslims began to feel their backwardness. Time and again, petitions were made by their representatives to the State and the British Government.[92] These petitions mark a significant change in the outlook of the Muslims of Srinagar and thus point to the growth of public opinion in the city. These petitions also point to the indifference and apathy shown by the State authorities to the education of Muslims. It was alleged that the department of Education which had been working under Maharaja's officials had practically neglected to safeguard Muslim interest.[93] Further, the officials had all tried to adopt measures which would discourage education among the Muslims.[94] Moreover the backwardness was attributed to 'unsympathetic and cruel treatment' which the Muslim pupils received at the hands of Hindu teachers.[95] In two petitions, therefore, the Muslim representatives requested the Secretary to the Government of India to place the Department of Education under a European officer.[96]

It is also worthwhile to note that the question of education of Muslims in Srinagar caught the attention of their co-religionists in India.[97] An association called the Muslim Kashmiri Conference was started in the Punjab and it established schools in Srinagar.[98] In September 1913 a deputation of the All-India Muhammedan Educational Conference presented an address to Maharaja Pratap Singh.[99] Among the remedies which were suggested to remove the backwardness of Muslims of the State was a provision for religious education; assistance to enable the Islamic schools to be raised to the collegiate grade; the grant of special stipends and scholarships for Muslims; the employment of Muslim professors, teachers, inspectors etc. and the appointment of a Special Inspector for Muslim education.[100]

It is clear that the Muslims of Srinagar were growing conscious of their community's backwardness and were looking forward to a change.[101] The Muslims were now urging the Maharaja to grant them some facilities so that they could make rapid advance in education. Thus it was under the pressure of public opinion that in 1916 Maharaja Pratap Singh invited Sir Henry Sharp,[102] the Educational Commissioner, Government of India, to suggest various ways and means of extending educational facilities for the Muslims of Kashmir. Mr. Sharp made a thorough enquiry into the grievances of the Muslims, and after examining the Muslim demands, submitted a report.

Sir Henry Sharp's Recommendations

1) According to Mr. Sharp, the further expansion of the primary education was "a prime necessity." Hence he recommended that an "early attempt should be made to establish a school in every village of 500 or more inhabitants"[103]

2) The only institution in the State which gave practical training was the Amar Singh Technical Institute in Srinagar.[104] The institution was established by Maharaja Pratap Singh. In 1916 the total number

of students in this institution was 157. Of these 115 were Hindus and 42 Muslims.[105] In view of the paucity of Muslim pupils, Mr.Sharp recommended some scholarships for Muslims students.[106]

3) Mr. Sharp felt that technical education was partially provided for at the Amar Singh Technical Institute. He remarked that the problems of practical education was one of the most urgent and important with which the Maharaja had to deal. Hence, he recommended the starting of medical, mechanical, electrical, agricultural schools and also schools for horticulture, silk-worm breeding, cattle breeding, carpentry, basket-weaving etc.[107]

4) Mr. Sharp recommended a small increase in the scholarships for Muslim pupils. This, he remarked, was justified by the size and poverty of the Muslim community and its educational backwardness. This increase, Mr. Sharp thought, would enable the Muslim students to continue education in high schools, college and technical institution. He also urged the Government to create a number of very small scholarships in primary schools, each of which was not to exceed a few annas. It was felt that such scholarships would enable the recipients to purchase books etc. and encourage them to remain till they reached the top classes.[108]

5) The establishment of a few college scholarships of Rs.10 for Muslims was also suggested. Such a proposal was supposed to have a good effect on the Muslim community.[109]

6) Mr. Sharp suggested that it would do well if a Muslim teacher of good qualification could be added to the Sri Pratap College in Srinagar as opportunity offered and, as soon as possible, to the State High School in the city.[110]

7) It was also proposed that the State High School of Srinagar be entrusted to the care of a Muslim Headmaster.[111]

8) Further, Mr. Sharp advocated the appointment of Muslim headmasters in some of the middle schools of the city. In 1916, it was not possible for the Maharaja to obtain the services of Kashmiri Muslims for this purpose. "But", observed Sir Henry Sharp, "numerous outsiders of the Hindu faith have been appointd to offices, and however laudable is the desire of the Durbar to employ only subjects of the State, there seems a good case, in view of His Highness' Muslim subjects, for relaxing the rule in case of Mohammadan teachers until there is a supply of Mohammadan graduates in the state itself,"[112]

9) Owing to the poverty of the Muslim community, remarked Mr. Sharp, some special concession by way of grant was justifiable in the case of Islamic schools, whether primary, middle or high.[113]

SHARP'S RECOMMENDATIONS REGARDING THE FEMALE EDUCATION

The Census of 1901 registered only 140 females in the city as literate, out of which 49 were Muslims and 50 Hindus. In 1911, the total female literate population was 116. Mr. Sharp was unable to make any suggestion regarding girls education on account of the highly conservative character of the people. However, he recommended organized attempt to open primary girls schools at those places in Srinagar where boys High or Middle Schools existed and where there were as yet no girls schools.[114] Secondly, it was suggested that a small capitation grant be given to the girls who attended the schools.[115] Thirdly, it was suggested that the girls be induced to accompany their small brothers to school. Fourthly, at first, the instruction given in the girls' school was to be very light, but gradually an elementary knowledge of 3 R's (as imparted in the Ist and 2nd primary classes) was to be made a condition of the grant. Fifthly, it was recommended that small prizes in money or kind be given to such girls as regularly attended schools or classes. The number of scholarships was to be increased from time to time. Lastly, the Maharaja was asked to seek the services of C.M.S. ladies and other private agencies.[116]

Maharaja Pratap Singh accepted the recommendations of Sir H. Sharp, but his ministers did not implement them.[117] As a matter of fact, soon after its publication, the report was safely kept in the archives. In 1931, an official enquiry Commission, presided over by Mr. B. J. Glancy, Political Secretary to the Government of India admitted that "no one appears to be aware of the nature of the report submitted by the educational expert."[118] For years the Muslims lived in sullen resentment.

In the meantime, the Kashmiri Pandits had made great progress in education. According to the Census of 1921, the Muslims of Srinagar presented a sad contrast to their Hindu brethren, [119] as 988 Muslims out of 1,000 were still unable to read and write. [120] When Lord Reading visited Kashmir in 1924, the Muslims of Srinagar submitted a memorandum to him. Among other things they demanded that steps be taken to improve the condition of Muslim education in the State.[121]

The significance of the memorandum is evident from the fact that among others it bore the signatures of two chief religious heads of Kashmir.

Maharaja Pratap appointed a committee of three official members, comprising a European, a Hindu and a Muslim, to look into the grievances of the Muslims. The Committee examined the memorial and reported that there was "no substance in it." Some of the signatories to the memorial `were exiled and deprived of their landed property. The two religious heads were warned but all official privileges which they had hitherto enjoyed were taken away from them.'

With the accession of Maharaja Hari Singh in 1925 a new chapter opened in the history of education in the State. The new Maharaja was educated in the famous Mayo College, Ajmer. To him goes the credit of introducing compulsory education in all municipal areas in 1930.[122] By this measure 5,132 students were added to the number of primary school boys in Srinagar alone. During 1931-33 compulsory primary education continued to be in force in the city of Srinagar and other municipal areas. It was reported that attendence at the new schools opened for this purpose remained satisfactory.[123]

Regarding the progress of secondary education, the number of secondary schools increased in Srinagar during Hari Singh's rule. The rapid advance of secondary education is further illustrated by the fact that by 1938 the Government High School and S. P. High Schools, Srinagar, were sending the largest number of students for the matriculation examination. Even a cursory glance of the Administration Reports from 1924 to 1947 testifies to the progress of secondary education in Srinagar during the last years of the Dogra ascendancy in the State.

College education also showed some progress during the reign of Hari Singh. During 1926-27 there were 480 students studying in S.P College, Srinagar. Of these 7 were Muslims. The decade after 1927 showed an increase in the number of S.P. College students. In 1937 the number of students rose to 1,318 (819 Hindus, 461 Muslims) against 1,187 (756 Hindus, 379 Muslims) of the previous year.[124]

To encourage college education, scholarships were provided. The educationally backward classes, e.g. Muslims were granted special scholarships. This was in addition to the usual scholarships of merit, on the basis of poverty etc.[125]

Attention was also paid to the physical education of collegiates. During 1938-39 one more post of Physical Director was created in the S. P. College. As such, the college had two Physical Directors.

The progress of college education in Srinagar is further evidenced by the fact that it was during Hari Singh's reign that another college, viz.,the Amar Singh Degree College, was founded in the city. In 1943-44, the number of students in this college was 552 against 520 of the previous year. This included 11 women students.[126] During the same period, the number of students in the S. P. Intermediate College was 1,010 as against 1,033 of the previous year. Of these 32 were women students against 28 of the preceding year. The decrease in the total number of students was due to the restriction on the number of admissions.[127] At the close of the year (1944 - 45) the number of students in the S. P College was 1,062, including 34 women students.[128] The number of students in the Amar Singh College was 539 including 13 women students, against 522 of the previous year.[129]

Although the people had begun to realise the benefits of female education, it was still a vexed question whether it would be wise to educate girls on modern scientific lines or to give only religious education to them. Meanwhile, boys education had made some progress. For such literate or partly educated young men it was difficult to find educated wives.

Evidently the society was ailing. Srinagar was in a ferment; 'new forces were developing in the womb of the old society and sensitive people could not help seeing that girls education was the need of the hour.'

In 1927 Women's Welfare Trust came into being[130] in Srinagar with the object of "advancing the welfare of the Kashmiri women by imparting to them knowledge, by stimulating home industry among them and by promoting their physical health and well-being."[131] The founder members of the Trust were theosophists like Mrs. Margaret E. Cousins, Mrs. L. D. Van Gheel Gilde meester, Sri Kanthe Toshkhani, Shridhar Kaul Dulloo and Aftab Koul Nizamat. The most important of the plans formulated by the trustees for the advancement of Kashmiri women was the education of both girls and adults.[132]

The Trust started a Primary Girls School with five students on its roll.[133] Within four years, the number of schools managed by the Trust rose to ten of which six were primary and three middle. The number of students also rose to 575.[134] In 1929 the Trustees started a school for Muslim girls in the city. Later, the number of Muslim girls schools managed by the Trust rose to three. The Trust also made a provision for at least one *purohit* Hindi teacher in every Hindu school and one *mullah* as instructor in Arabic in every Muslim school.[135] It was in 1934 that a girls High School was started by the Trust.[136]

The girls schools of the Trust gained popularity. Even the Chief Inspectress of the Government Girls School admitted in one of her writings that "the teachings and the results of the Trust Schools are much better than I have found in the government schools."[137]

In the meantime, the Government policy towards girls education had not remained unaffected. The first reform which Hari Singh introduced for the advancement of women's education was the creation of a post of Chief Inspectress of Girls' School.[138] Miss E. Chawner, a highly educated and trained English lady was appointed to this post. A number of new girls school were established in the city. Also, the status of many primary schools was raised to the middle standard and the first girls high school was opened in Srinagar which prepared students for the matriculation examination of the Punjab University.

REPORT OF THE EDUCATIONAL REORGANIZATION COMMITTEE

The Educational Reorgansation Committee was appointed by Maharaja Hari Singh in June 1938, "for the reorganization of the existing system of primary and secondary education in the State."[139] The Director of Education, Mr. K.G. Saiyidain, was appointed the Chairman of the Committee. The Committee submitted its report after making a comprehensive survey of the educational conditions. The report attempted "to deal with two inter-related aspects of the problem of educational reconstruction in the state, the expansion of educational facilities and the consolidation of the existing facilities."[140]

The following were the chief recommendations made by the Committee "with the object of overhauling and reconstructing the existing system of primary and secondary schools."[141]

1. The new scheme of education propounded by the Committee aimed at the establishment of a system of free, compulsory and universal basic education for all the children in the State not below the age of 7. Regarding Srinagar, the Committee observed that there were adequate schooling facilities in the city.[142] This was due to the scheme of compulsory education which had been in operation since 1930.[143] Thus the Committee recommended, as an immediate necessity, the starting of one well-staffed and equipped basic school in Srinagar

so that it could serve "as a practising and demonstration centre for the provincial training schools as well as a model school to demonstrate the possibilities of the extension of new scheme to other educational centres."[144]

For this purpose, it was felt necessary to draw a 25 year plan, so that during this period education should be made universal and compulsory and the requisite provision of schooling facilities be made throughout the State.

2. According to the Report, the most important problem in educational reorganization was the improvement in the quality and the efficiency of the teaching personnel.[145] Hence it was recommended that the teachers should be equipped "both humanly and professionally", to become the pioneers of the educational crusade that the members of the Committee had in view.[146]

3. The Committee urged the Government to liberalise rules governing grants-in-aid to private institutions.[147] Such a policy was bound to encourage the growth and development of private institutions.

4. The Committee advocated a diversification of the secondary course and the introduction of more practical work. The reason put forward for this proposal was that the secondary schools would be otherwise hopelessly out of touch with the socio-economic situation and needs of the people, unless this principle of diversification was introduced.[148] As the report put it, the state required "the services not only of clerks and administrators but also of trained and skilful artisans, craftsmen, engineers, medical workers, teachers, agriculturists and others in order to improve the existing standard of efficiency, productivity and general prosperity of the people."[149] It was necessary, therefore, to provide secondary schools of different types which would "correspond generally to the main line of peoples occupations and equip the young men for different walks of life" where skilled knowledge and disciplined character were needed for success.[150] After judging the occupational needs of the people, the Committee urged the Government to take steps for the gradual establishment of secondary schools of the following types,[151] giving the requisite vocational bias in addition to the existing schools described in (a) below:

   a) Schools providing literary, scientific and commerical education.
   b) Schools providing education in Mechanical, Electrical and Civil Engineering.

c) Schools of Agriculture and Horticulture.
d) Schools of Medicine.
e) Schools of Arts and Crafts.
f) Schools of Home Craft and Nursing (for girls).
g) Schools for the training of teachers.

These schools with the vocational bias were designated as "schools of secondary education" which implied that "there will not be merely schools for technical and professional instruction but educational institutions whose intellectual and economic status will co-eval with that of good secondary schools of an academic type."[152] Arrangements were to be made in these schools not only for technical instruction in the selected profession or vocation but, as the Committee recommended, arrangements were also to be made "for providing an adequate background of general knowledge and culture through a study of some of the important scientific and social studies as well as languages, which constitute the distinctively human, cultural and intellectual heritage."[153]

There can be no doubt that the idea underlying this proposal had significant implications for the future of education and culture in the city. It is a well known fact that the artisans of Srinagar were celebrated for their excellent craftsmanship. Hence the Committee very rightly observed that if some of Srinagar's craftsmen had the benefit of this kind of general-cum-technical education in secondary schools, they would be able "to forge for themselves new lines and introduce new and attractive motifs in their work."[154] Moreover, such a type of education was bound to enable the craftsmen "to look after their civic and professional interests more satisfactorily."[155]

5. The Committee recommended "that in all schemes of future expansion, priority must be given to the question of girl's education."[156]
6. The appointment of Physical Instructors was recommended.[157]
7. The Committee suggested that steps should be taken to provide religious education of a more effective nature for all those who made a demand for it. It may be pointed out that there was "an insistent demand for the provision of religious education in schools, paricularly among the Muslims."[158] The demand for religious education was "particularly strong in the case of girls' schools mainly attended by Muslim girls."[159]

A critical examination of the salient features of the new scheme leads one to the conclusion that rapid expansion of educational facilities was imperatively called for on account of the low percentage of literacy in the State. The forces that were shaping modern life in Srinagar were so quick and insistent in their demands that no government could afford to remain content with the leisurely pace of advance. The Committee suggested ways and means for improving the efficiency and social significance of the existing system of primary and secondary schools. The Committee's recommendations to eliminate wastage and stagnation of the existing educational system and to bring it into vital union with the socio-economic as well as the cultural life of the people had far-reaching consequences.

The Government gradually accepted the Educational Reorganization Committee's report of 1938. Fortunately for the State, the newly appointed Director of Education, Mr. K.G. Saiyidain, saw to it that his suggestions were "vigorously implemented, both qualitatively and quantitatively during the next six years."[160] Under Mr. Saiyidain's inspiring guidance the State marched on the road to success.

A RESUME

We have seen that the spread of modern education in Srinagar was obviously beset with innumerable difficulties. But the success of the private and the government schools, established in Srinagar after 1880, makes it clear that the demand for education was increasing. At first, the Pandit community took to modern education, but later the Muslims also evinced a great zeal in education.[161] In 1941, the total number of the literate Muslims in the city was 17,497.[162] The demand for girls education was also increasing, though slowly. This is evident from the considerable increase in the growth of female literates during 1921-1941. In 1941, their number had swollen to 8,182 as against 1,095 of 1931 and 686 of 1921.[163] It is significant that in the C. M. S. Girls School and Srinagar Girls High School, the Muslim girls formed a majority .[164] Towards the last years of the Dogra rule, education had made remarkable progress in Srinagar.[165] This is borne out by the fact that during 1931-41 there was an increase of about 12% in the literate population of the city.[166] Besides, the existence of various government - run and private-managed primary, middle and high schools are sufficient proof of the educational acitivity that was going on in Srinagar.[167]

But in spite of this, post-graduate education remained confined to only a small section of the people. For obvious economic reasons, many a parent could not afford to send their children to the Aligarh or Punjab universities for post-graduate studies. It should also be remembered that the higher education of girls[168] remained a dream owing to the non-existence of a women's college in Srinagar. Many parents were not in favour of co-education.[169] They did not send their daughters to the S.P. College or the Amar Singh College for fear of public opinion.[170]

Regarding practical education, the Dogra Government did not take effective measures for its propagation. True, that there existed the Amar Singh Technical Institute in Srinagar, but it was neither popular nor did it play any effective role in the development of crafts and cottage industries in the city. The products of this institute either hankered after services or suffered from unemployment.[171] It is obvious that the Dogra rulers did not give due attention to a proper scientific and technical education.

NOTES:

1. George Grierson, *Linguistic Survey of India*, Vol. VIII, part 2, p.241
2. Ibid., p.251
3. Ibid., p.241
4. Aba Rafi-ud-din Ahmed, *Nawadir-ul-Akhbar*, B. M. Add. 24029, f.29 b.
5. Brain Holmes, *Educational Policy and the Mission Schools*, p.151
6. J&K/File No. 27-Z-6 of 1967 (*Samvat*)
7. This information was supplied by Mr. Wynne, the then Officer on Special Duty in Kashmir, to the Secretary to Government, Punjab. NAI/Foreign, Pol A, Feb. 1874, Nos. 271-278
8. *Administration Report of J&K (Report-i-Majmui),* 1873, p.114
9. Ibid., p. 63
10. Ibid., p. 64
11. Stein, *Catalogue of the Sanskrit Manuscripts in the Raghu Natha Temple Library of His Highness, the Maharaja of Jammu and Kashmir*, See introduction, I, p. VI.
12. *Report of the Educational Reorganization Committee* (1939), p. 10
13. Quoted in *Beyond the Pir Panjal,* p. 68; See also Robert Clark, *op. cit.*, p. 167.
14. *Kashmir in Sunlight and Shade*, p.260; *Fifty Years Against the Stream,* p.1.
15. Brain Holmes, *op. cit.*, p.160.
16. Ibid.
17. *Fifty Years Against the Stream*, p.1.
18. Brain Holmes, *op. cit.*, p.160.

19. Proceedings of C. M. S. in Africa and East for the year 1884-85 (Lond. 1885), p. 122 (Brain Homeless, *op. cit.*, p.14).
20. Brain Holmes, *op. cit.*,p.161.
21. Ibid.
22. Annual letter extract for years 1889 to 1890 from J. Hinton Knowles, p. 237 (Brain Homeless, *op. cit.*, p.161).
23. *Kashmir in Sunlight and Shade*, p.260.
24. Ibid.
25. Ibid.
26. One of the Brahman carpenters, writes Biscoe, "having arrived at man's estate, wished to take unto himself a wife, but no Brahman could be induced to give his daughter to a man who was engaged in such an ungentlemanly job as that of a carpenter. He put up with his lonely condition for some time, but finally the desire for a spouse proved greater than love of his adze and saw, so he gave up his unholy profession and took up the work of a chaprasi, which was considered to be an honourable profession,whereupon the Brahmans smiled upon him and he became a married man, bless him!" (Ibid.,pp.260-261).
27. Ibid; *Still Carrying on in Kashmir*, P. 5.
28. *Kashmir in Sunlight and Shade*, p. 263.
29. Ibid.
30. Biscoe, *Autobiography*, pp.49-50.
31. *Kashmir in Sunlight and Shade*, p.265.
32. Ibid., p. 268
33. Biscoe, *Autobiography*, pp. 49-50; Brain Holmes, *op. cit.*, p.164.
34. *Fifty years Against the Stream*, p.xv.
35. Ibid; p. 4. *Rock Shifting in Kashmir*, p.11.
36. *Fifty years Against the Stream*, p.7.
37. Ibid.
38. Ibid.
39. Brain Holmes, *op. cit.*, p. 163.
40. Rev. J. Hinton Knowles to Robert Clark dated March 3, 1890 (MS.), No. 151, G2/ 14/06, 1890, p.1. C.M.S. Archives (Brain Holmes, op. cit., p. 163); See also *Kashmir in Sunlight and Shade*, p. 276.
41. Carus-Wilson, *op. cit.*, pp.249-50.
42. *Kashmir in Sunlight and Shade*,p. 276.
43. Ibid., p. 278.
44. Ibid., p. 298.
45. Ibid., p. 281.
46. Ibid.
47. Ibid., p. 300.
48. Ibid., p. 299.
49. *Beyond the Pir Panjal*, p.58; See also *Fifty years Steeple Chase in Kashmir*, p. 8; *Sharp's Report* (1916), p. 23.

50. *Against the Current*, P. 7.
51. *Op. cit.*, p.29.
52. Character-builiding was the key-note of Biscoe's training (Wakefield, *Recollections*, p. 194).
53. *Daughters of Vitasta*, p. 221
54. Ibid.
55. *Kashmir in Sunlight and Shade*, p. 257
56. Ibid., pp. 257-258
57. *Jerry Building in Kashmir*, p. 31
58. *Road Making in Kashmir*, p. 16.
59. *Rock Shifting in Kashmir*, p. 19.
60. Ibid.
61. *A School in Being in Kashmir*, p. 22.
62. See old attendance registers of students.
63. *Inspection Record for May*, 1944.
64. Ibid., June 1947.
65. *Still Carrying on in Kashmir* (Annual Report of C. M. S. School, Srinagar, 1930-40), p. 16.
66. Ibid.
67. See NAI/Foregin, Sec, E. Oct. 1886, Nos. 235-300. p.22
68. Writing in the sixties of the last century Arthur Brinckman remarks about the state of education in Kashmir: "The rajah will not allow eduaction there but to blind us sends a few thousand rupees occasionally to our Punjab schools. The Cashmerees are not allowed to improve any way by the rajah. 'Keep them grinding for our benefit' is the sole thought of their rulers. If Thomas Hood had ever been to Serinaghur the 'Song of the Shawl', would have made him more pathetic than he has in his 'Song of the Shirt'." *op. cit.*, (typed copy), Chapter III, p. 23
69. *The Paisa Akhbar*, Lahore, Nov. 30, 1901 (*Report on Native Newspapers*, 1901, p. 762); *The Rahber-i-Hind*, Lahore, Nov. 16, 1891 (Ibid., 1891, pp. 252-253).
70. J.C.Bose, *Cashmere and its Prince*, p.20. The first school opened in the city in 1874 by the Government was upto the middle standard. The school made provision for the teaching of Sanskrit and Persian. There was also a seperate department for teaching Arabic for Muslim students. The number of students in the school was 450 in 1883, 260 in 1889, 160 in 1890 and 249 in 1891. It was in 1892 that the Srinagar Middle School was converted into the High School. The following statistical information is available in regard to the enrolment of students in the High School:

Year	Number	Year	Number
1892	303	1897	405
1893	343	1898	465
1894	371	——	——
1895	314	1900	427
——	——	1901	440

For more statistical details, see S. L. Seru, *History and Growth of Education in Jammu and Kashmir*, Chapters VIII, and IX.

71. *Report on Native Newspapers*, 1901, p.762
72. *Imperial Gazetteer*, p. 75
73. NAI/Foreign, Feb. 1907, intl., Nos. 163-64; *Imperial Gazetteer*, p. 80; J&K (H. H. P. R.) File No. 2 of 1906).
74. *Beyond the Pir Panjal*, p. 256
75. *Sharps' Report* (1916), pp. 43-44.
76. Ibid., p. 41; See also Education Minister's letter dated Jan. 13, 1913 to the Chief Minister, J & K (G.R), File No. 254/P. 127 of 1912.
77. *Sharp's Report*, p. 41.
78. Ibid.
79. Ibid.
80. Ibid.
81. Ibid., p. 42.
82. Ibid.
83. Ibid.
84. Ibid., p. 3.
85. Ibid.
86. See Education Minister's Note, J & K (G.R.) 101/P. 102, 1907; also *Census*, 1901, I, P. 12
87. Ibid; The *Zamindar*, Sept. 17, 1923 (*Report on Native Newspapers*, Punjab, 1923, p. 514).
88. Majid, *op. cit.*, p. 73; The *Statesman*, June 11, 1946; The *Hindustan Times* June 2, 1946.
89. The *Afghan, Peshawar*, Nov. 1, 1911 (*Report on Native Newspapers*, 1911, p. 1160); The *Zamindar*, Sept 17, 1923 (Ibid., 1923. p. 514); The *Paisa Akhbar*, Nov. 30, 1901 (Ibid., 1901, p. 762); The *Muslim Outlook*, Oct. 31, 1923 (Ibid, 1923, p.599).
90. The *Paisa Akhbar*, Sept. 9, 1911 (*Report on Native Newspapers*, 1911, p. 975).
91. Ibid., The *Afghan*, Peshawar, Nov. 1, 1911 (*Report on Native Newspapers*, 1911, p. 1160).
92. Copy of a letter from representatives of Kashmiri Mussalmans to Sir Louis Dane, Secretary to the Government of India in the Foreign Department, NAI/Foreign, Intl., Feb. 1097, Nos. 163-164; Petition

(without date) from the representatives of the Kashmiri Mussalmans on the subject of employment of the Mussalmans in the Kashmiri State. NAI/Foreign, Jan. 1909, Genl. B., Nos. 15-16.

93. NAI/Foreign, Feb. 1907, Intl., Nos. 163-164; The *Afghan* (Peshawar) dated Ist Nov. 1911 (*Report on Native Newspaper*, 1911, p.1160).
94. Ibid.
95. NAI/Foreign, Jan. 1909, Genl. B, 15-16.
96. Ibid; NAI/Foreign, Feb. 1907, Intl. Nos. 163-64.
97. *Sharp's Report* (1916), p. 40.
98. Ibid.
99. Ibid., pp. 40-41; J&K (O.E.R), File No, 217/P-96, 1913.
100. Sharp's Report, p. 41.
101. See Appendix B.
102. NAI/Foreign, Pol. Establishment, Aug. 1916, Nos. 167-68, Part B.
103. *Sharp's Report*, p. 14.
104. Ibid., p. 32.
105. Ibid., p. 33.
106. Ibid.
107. Ibid., pp. 33-37.
108. Ibid., p. 27.
109. Ibid., p. 42.
110. Ibid., p. 43.
111. Ibid.
112. Ibid.
113. Ibid.
114. Ibid., p. 37.
115. Ibid., p. 38.
116. Ibid.
117. The All India Muslim Kashmiri Conference sought an audience with the Maharaja in this connection, but the interview was not granted. J&K (G.R.), File No. 2/Misc, 14, 1920.
118. "It is a frequent cause of complaint that his (Mr. Sharp's) recommendations have not been given due publicity and have been to a great extent ignored." See *Report of the Commission Appointed under the Orders of His Highness the Maharaja Bahadur dated the 12th Nov. 1931 to enquire into Grievances and Complaints*, 2nd ed. Jammu, 1933, p. 9.
119. The *Kashmiri Magazine*, Lahore, Feb. 28, 1920; J&K (G.R.), F. No. 204/9-C of 1920; See also *The Civil and Military Gazette*, Lahore, Nov. 1, 1923, p. 13.
120. *Census*, 1921, I, p.111
121. The *Pioneer*, Sept. 4, 1931.
122. The *Tribune*, Aug 22, 1931; The *Daily Herald*, Lahore, July 7, 1946;

Ganga Nath Report, p. 198; *Administration Report of the J&K State*, Oct. 16, 1946 to April 12, 1943, p. 46.
123. See *Administration Reports of the J&K State.*
124. Ibid., 1937, p. 47.
125. See Ibid (1925-1946).
126. Ibid., 13 April 1943 to 12 April 1944, p. 114.
127. Ibid.
128. Ibid., 13 April 1944 to 12 April 1945, p. 112.
129. Ibid.
130. The *Ranbir*, 5 December, 1932.
131. Quoted in *Daughters of Vitasta*, p. 222.
132. Ibid.
133. Ibid., p. 223.
134. Ibid., p. 224.
135. Ibid.
136. Ibid., p. 226.
137. Quoted by Iravati Mehta in *Appeal for Funds* dated Aug. 6, 1938, Ibid., p. 227.
138. *Census*, 1941, Part I, p. 37.
139. *Report of the Educational Reorganization Committee*, 1939, p. 3.
140. Ibid., p. 1.
141. Ibid.
142. Ibid., p. 31.
143. Ibid.
144. Ibid.
145. Ibid., p. 20.
146. Ibid.
147. Ibid., p. 51.
148. Ibid., p. 53.
149. Ibid.
150. Ibid.
151. Ibid.
152. Ibid., p. 54.
153. Ibid.
154. Ibid., pp. 54-55.
155. Ibid., p. 55.
156. Ibid., p. 71.
157. Ibid., p. 84.
158. Ibid., p. 85.
159. Ibid., p. 86.
160. Nurullah and Naik, *A History of Education in India*, p. 895.
161. Majid, *op. cit.*, p. 274.
162. *Census*, 1941, p. 279.
163. Ibid.

164. Majid *op. cit.,* pp. 21, 73.
165. The *Ranbir*, June 7, 1943.
166. *Census*, 1941, Table, p. 279.
167. The *Ranbir*, June 7, 1943.
168. See *Ganga Nath Report*, p. 205.
169. For Mr. K.G. Saiyidain's views on women's education in the State, see *Administration Report of the Education, Boy Scouts, Libraries, Archaeological, Research and Museum Departments* (Last 6 months of *Samvat* 1998 and *Samvat* 1999), p. 24.
170. In 1994 the total number of girls studying in the two colleges of the city was 47. (*Administration Report of the J&K State*. April 13, 1944 to April 12, 1945, p. 112).
171. *Report of the Educational Reorganization Committee*, 1939, p. 90.

CHAPTER VII

GROWTH OF PUBLIC OPINION

In the different regions of the British dominion in India groups with new interests and new ways of living were appearing and a new system of education was moulding their mind into modern ways of thinking and feeling; the city of Srinagar was also becoming familiar with Western means and devices which helped to propagate them. In course of time, these new groups came together and, as a result, public opinion in Srinagar began to be shaped.

Some of the administrative and other reforms in Srinagar were introduced on the initiative of the British Residency and these in turn had a direct or an indirect effect on public opinion. And so English ideas and institutions came to be introduced into the city and to influence in turn indigenous ideas and local institutions. Now opinion began to be expressed through petitions which were addressed to the Residents from time to time. In fact, the Resident came to be regarded as a saviour by the people.[1] This is evident from the petition which was sent in 1909 by some thirty representatives of Kashmiri Muslim to the Private Secretary of the Viceroy of India:

"No sooner the Kashmir Residency was established here than the things took a turn for the better. Laws were enforced to protect life and property. Disorder and chaos gradually gave way to order in all the departments of the State ... We feel certain that the Residency is anxious soon to bring justice and safety to the Kashmiri Musalmans and relieve them of the tyranny and *Zulm* which has with the advance of times taken a new form to express itself ... The policy of reform inaugurated on the advent of the British Residency, evidently meant equality, impartiality, fair play and no favour."[2]

In another letter written in 1907 to Sir Louis Dane, Secretary to the Government of India in the Foreign Department, the Muslim petitioners drew the attention of the British Government to the unrepresentation of the Muslims in the State administration.[3] They also implored the Government of India to take effective measures for the propagation of education among the Kashmiri Muslims.[4]

It is remarkable that opinion also began to be expressed through the press outside the State as the press was practically non-existent in Kashmir. The Muslims utilised the Punjab press in order to give vent to their feelings. In an open letter to His Highness the Maharaja and the Resident in Kashmir published in the *Observer* (Lahore) dated 16th September, 1911 some Kashmiri Muslims wrote:

"Our present condition is, in certain respects, no better than that of dumb animals, who instinctively feel pain but cannot give expression to their feeling. Similarly, we too have no representative in the State to reproduce the photo of our condition before our kind and merciful ruler. All those gentlemen who have got access in the Kashmir Darbar may attribute our cries and lamentations to our wickedness and ignorance and show the dark side of our affairs."

"In the first place, there is no influential Muhammadan belonging to the State and intimately knowing our condition to represent our case to our benign ruler. But you are the representative of the benign British administration and protector of mankind. We are proverbial for poverty and degradation."[5]

These petitions clearly mark an important stage in the growth of public opinion in Srinagar. They also show that there was no contact between the Government and the people, no suitable opportunity for representing grievances. The Government's ban on the formation of societies, even social and religious, also points to this fact.[6]

It has been stated that the Kashmiri Pandits were the first who took to modern education in Srinagar. With the growth of modern ideas they began to express their opinion through associations and organizations. Educated young men like Mr. Jia Lal Kilam, Mr. Shankar Lal Koul and Mr. Jia Lal Jalali, after obtaining degrees from various Indian universities, returned to Srinagar, imbued with new ideas. It is they who started an agitation in Srinagar "through the outside press for securing the right of the State subjects."[7] Public meetings were also organized and conferences were held at Srinagar.[8] This struggle was the outcome of the change of the court language from Persian to Urdu in Maharaja Pratap Singh's reign.[9] As a result, the Kashmiri Pandits who were not acquainted with the new language, were thrown out of employment.[10] An influx of jobseekers from the Punjab followed, and the administration had to be manned by them.[11] The resultant bitterness among the Pandits can better be imagined than described.

The Residency also supported the Pandits in their struggle against the outsiders.[12] The result was the appointment of the State Subjects Definition Committee soon after the accession of Maharaja Hari Singh in 1925 A.D. The definition arrived at by the Committee was accepted by the new Maharaja in 1927 and "he declared that none who was not a hereditary State Subject should be appointed to any post in State service, big or small, without his own express permission."[13] A hereditary State Subject "had been narrowly defined as any one descended of any person domiciled in the Jammu and Kashmir State, prior to the death of Maharaja Ranbir Singh, that is to say, in the `eighties of the last century."[14]

The spread of modern education made the Muslims of Srinagar deeply conscious of their backwardness. In 1924, when the Viceroy, Lord Reading, visited Srinagar, some of the leading members of the Muslims community submitted a memorial to him.[15] Among other things they demanded "a larger representation of Muslims in Government service[16] and improvements in the condition of Muhammedan education in the State." The Maharaja took offence at its submission to the Viceroy.[17] There also took place some demonstrations in the State-owned Silk factory at Srinagar and disturbances of a semi-political nature in the city during the summer of 1924.[18] It may also be pointed out that organized demonstrations had already taken place during 1922-23 "pressing the government to solve the food problem."[19] But the movement for social justice was in its rudimentary stage and the Government put down the disturbances with a firm hand.

At this stage of the awakening of social consciousness almost all classes of the people in Srinagar were seething with discontent. The shawl trade which had been subjected to rigorous impositions had declined. This caused a great deal of unemployment among the weavers. Though the carpet industry had absorbed many shawl weavers, there were many who were wandering in search of employment. Equally deplorable was the condition of the *papier maché* artists, most of whom were thrown out of job on account of the non-availability of raw material. Distress and frustration were writ not only on the faces of the silk factory workers and the artisans but also on those of the emerging group of educated Muslims who were unemployed.

A far-sighted observer like Sir Albion Bannerji deplored such a state of affairs. Disgusted with the unimaginative mind of the rulers, he resigned the post of the Foreign and Political Minister which he had held for over two years. On March 15, 1929 he made certain remarks regarding the political, social and economic conditions prevailing in the State in a press interview. He said:

"The Jammu and Kashmir State is labouring under many disadvantages, with a large Mohammadan population absolutely illiterate, labouring under poverty and very low economic conditions of living in the villages and practically governed like dumb driven cattle. There is no touch between the Government and the people, no suitable opportunity for representing grievances and the administrative machinery itself requires overhauling from top to bottom to bring it up to the modern conditions of efficiency. It has at present little or no sympathy with the people's wants and grievances."

"There is hardly any public opinion in the State. As regards the press, it is practically non-existent, with the result that the government is not benefitted to the extent that it should be by the healthy criticism."[20]

The observations of the trained British Civil Servant produced a deep effect on several Muslim young men,[21] fresh from the universities in India, particularly, Aligarh, where they had come in contact with Muslims leaders and propagators of Pan-Islamism. They had organized themselves into a group holding frequent meetings at the Muslim Reading Room in Srinagar. It is the members of this group who started the movement against the Maharaja in July, 1931.

One of the active members of the Reading Room Party was Sheikh Muhammad Abdullah.[22] He was born in 1905 at Sowra in Srinagar. Having passed his intermediate examination from the Sri Pratap College in Srinagar he went to Lahore and took his degree from the Punjab University. In 1930 he received his M. Sc. from the Aligarh Muslim University. On his return home he was appointed a teacher in a State school. But moved, as he was, by the abject servility of the oppressed people of Kashmir, Sheikh Abdullah resigned his post after serving the State Education Department for some time. He organized mass public meetings of Muslims in various mosques of the city and delivered incendiary speeches that roused people to anger. The policy of the Government in keeping the Muslims out of State service, and the issues such as heavy taxation and consequent destruction of the industries, forced labour, and a law severely punishing the Muslims for cow-slaughter, and the open oppression carried on by the Maharaja's officials became the focus among the discontented Abdullah and other educated Muslims in Srinagar. In June 1931 the young Muslims held a meeting at the Jama mosque protesting against the actions of "high state officials ... trampling on the rights of Muslims."[23] Srinagar, which had witnessed the revolt of the working class in 1865, again proved itself to be the storm-centre of a struggle against intolerable conditions on 13th July, 1931.

13 July, 1931 was a historic day in the annals of Srinagar. The 'dumb driven cattle'— the phrase Sir Albion Bannerji used to describe the people of Kashmir — had raised the standard of revolt. The Government did whatever it could do in its power to quell the mass uprising. But the people had risen never to be cowed down again by the punitive police. Even the women had come into the struggle and to them still belongs the honour of facing cavalry charges in Maisuma Bazar of Srinagar.[24]

In the aftermath of the July incident, the Maharaja appointed an official Committee presided over by the Chief Justice of the State, Sir Barjor Dalal to enquire into the firings of the 13 July. But it was boycotted by the Muslims, who, besides questioning its independent character,[25] demanded the setting up of an impartial commission of enquiry.

The impact of public opinion upon the Government policy at this stage of development of social consciousness was considerable. Not only was the Government unable to ignore any opinion publicly expressed, but it was very often obliged to modify its policy in the face of public sentiment. The Resident also played a very important part in influencing the policy of the State Government. The Resident delivered a peremptory note to the Maharaja demanding its acceptance within twenty-four hours. Among other things, the note mentioned the desirability of the Government of India to hold a full enquiry into the grievances and demands of the Muslims under a completely unprejudiced British officer.[26]

The Maharaja had thus to yield to the public opinion. On 12th November, 1931 he announced the appointment of the Commission under the chairmanship of Sir B. J. Glancy of the Foreign and Political Department of the Government of India.

The Glancy Commission's Report was of great importance. It brought to light the grievances of the Muslims and made recommendations for their redress. The main recommendations of the Commission were readily accepted by Maharaja Hari Singh. Among them was "the desirability of extending primary education, an increase in the number of Muslim teachers and appointment of Special officers to supervise Muslim education."[27] As to the crucial question of the distribution of Government posts, it was recommended that the "minimum qualifications should not be pitched unneccessarily high."[28] The Commission also recommended the grant of proprietory rights in respect of all land "of which the ownership is retained by the State and the right of occupancy is enjoyed by private persons."[29] It also recommended the abolition of several vexatious taxes and stressed the need for removing unemployment by promoting industries in the State.[30] Not the least important among Mr. Glancy's recommendations was the grant of freedom to the press on lines similar to those which existed in British India.[31] It goes without saying that the report was in the nature of a 'Magna Carta' of the State of Jammu and Kashmir. It provided a firm foundation on which to build the future.

Growth of Press in Srinagar

As late as 1924 there was not a single newspaper printed or published in the State of Jammu and Kashmir.[32] Only the *Jammu and Kashmir Government Gazette* was the official weekly with a circulation of 900.[33] The newspapers that a limited number of people read came from the neighbouring province of the Punjab.[34] The *Civil and Military Gazette* and the *Tribune* of Lahore, and a number of Urdu weekly magazines circulated in the State. Sometimes the *Statesman* and the *Pioneer* found their way with the European visitors to Srinagar. So whenever a Kashmiri intended to write he had to approach these papers and "it all depended on their goodwill to publish or reject a contribution."[35] The people had thus no paper of their own wherein they could ventilate their feelings regarding various social and political problems.

It should, however, be remembered that the papers published from Lahore which reached the Maharaja's dominions covered a great deal of information with regard to Kashmir affairs.[36] The *Khair-Khawah-i-Kashmir,* an Urdu weekly, published from Lahore and edited by Pandit Hargopal Khasta during 1882-1883, was critical of Maharaja Ranbir Singh's government. The *Kashmir Prakash,* a monthly magazine of Lahore, edited by Pandit Manka Meghar (1898-1901) worked for the social uplift of the Kashmiri Pandits. The *Kashmiri Gazette,* Lahore, an Urdu monthly founded by Chaudri Jan Muhammad Ganai and edited by Munshi Muhammad Din Fauq during 1901-1904 "worked for the social and political awakening of Kashmiri Muslims." The *Kashmiri Makhzan*, Lahore, an Urdu monthly during 1905 was devoted to social uplift of the Kashmiris. The *Kashmiri Magazine*, Lahore, founded by Fauq in 1906 was dedicated to the historical, social and political movement "that agitated the mind of the people of Kashmir in the time of Maharaja Pratap Singh." Among other papers must be metional the *Akhbar-i-Kashmir*, the *Safir*, the *Subh-i-Kashmir*, the *Bahar-i-Kashmir*, the *Hamdard-i-Hind*, the *Kashmir*, the *Kashmiri Musalman*, the *Mazlum-i-Kashmir*, the *Maktub-i-Kashmir etc.*

The influence of these papers on the educated community of Srinagar was great, indeed.[37] The newspapers of the Punjab, as a matter of fact, were organs of local Kashmiri opinion. When the Daily *Inqilab*, Lahore, passed strictures against the administration of Maharaja Hari Singh in about 1929-31, its entry into the State was banned.[38] Subsequently, the *Kashmiri Muslman* took its place. When this paper too was banned in 1931, the *Mazlum-i-Kashmir* was issued.[39] When this paper was also proscribed in the State, the *Maktub-i-Kashmir* took up the work. But this was also banned.[40]

It is apparent that although the circulation of all these papers was small, their appearance in Srinagar was notable for two reasons. In the first place, the newspapers, after a couple of fitful starts, took roots in Srinagar, drawing their strength from the power of the press in the Punjab.[41] In the second place, a more serious note was gradually introducing itself into discussion. The implications of these changes did not escape the Government's notice.

The most important of the Glancy Commission's recommendations provided for the freedom of the press and platform and free association of the people for political activity.

Pandit Prem Nath Bazaz holds the distinction of being the first to start an Urdu weekly namely the *Vitasta* in Srinagar[42] in 1932. This was followed by the *Martand*, the *Sadaqat*, the *Haqiqat*, the *Kashmir-i-Jadid*, the *Albarq*, the *Bekar*, the *Dehqan*, the *Khalid*, the *Hidayat*, the *Kesari*, the *Muslim*, the *Desh*, the *Weekly Hamdard*, the *Daily Hamdard*, the *Daily Khidmat*, the *Paigham*, the *Kashmir Guardian*, the *Qaumi Dard*, the *Islah*, the *Vakil*, the *Hurriyat*, the *Nur*, the *Rahbar*, the *Tawhid*, the *Zulfiqar*, the *Jahangir*, the *Roshhi*, the *Gaash*, the *Shamsher* and the *Khalsa Gazette*.

With the passage of time newspapers in Srinagar grew to be a real power in public life. The strength of the press in Srinagar arose from the organisation of liberal opinion against corruption and misrule. Prem Nath Bazaz's *Vitasta* was begun with the specific intention of instructing the public and encouraging discussion. The paper discussed themes which were to become journalistic commonplaces in the succeeding years: the need for internal reform in Hindu and Muslim society; the position of women in Kashmir society; admiration for modern education; and the question of Hindu and Muslim unity. It was critical of the Maharaja's government for not taking action against those who indulged in 'sins' like early marriage and juvenile smoking.[43]

The weekly *Hamdard* was started by Bazaz in collaboration with Sheikh Muhammad Abdullah on Ist August, 1935 with the purpose of laying of foundation of "progressive nationalism in the State."[44] The inauguration of the first issue of the journal was performed by Dr. Saif-ud-Din Kitchlew in a big public meeting at Hazuri Bagh, Srinagar.[45] From the very begining the *Hamdard* "attempted to blaze a new trail in the affairs of the State. It was a standard-bearer of democracy and unity of all Kashmiris without any considerations of caste or creed they professed."[46] Often in its editorials, the *Hamdard* advocated the cause of secular politics in the State.[47] It was valued for the vigour of its writings. There can be no doubt that it was mainly through the sober, thoughtful and inspiring writings of this weekly that the Muslim Conference was converted into the National Conference in 1939.[48]

The illustrated weekly issues of the *Hamdard* contained a lot of information with regard to the history, sociology and literature of Kashmir. It was equally alert in influencing the social life of the people of Srinagar. The *Hamdard* had sections for women, children, literature, science, cinema, health etc. This indicates the variety of information in which a reader was interested.

The *Hamdard* became a daily when Bazaz broke his partnership with Sheikh Abdullah. As a daily it displayed great courage in discussing political, social and economic problems. Often it tried to pry into official secrets, excoriate the administration and thereby earn the antipathy of the oppressive police and magistracy. The popularity of the *Hamdard* is judged by the fact that when, in August, 1943, Kailas Narian Haksar, the then Prime Minister, demanded a heavy security from the Daily for forcefully and fearlessly criticising the policy of the government, the editor issued an appeal to the people for funds. It is significant that the full amount of the security was subscribed to in small pieces of annas and rupees within the prescribed time.[49] Again, on 25th August, 1945, the *Hamdard* in a vigorous article captioned "Whiter Ram Chandra Kak?" exposed and denounced "the unholy alliance of the despotic Prime Minister with the national fascists of Kashmir."[50] Three days later on 28th August, the Government banned the Daily "ordering the publisher to get every word censored by the District Magistrate before it was printed in the columns of the journal."[51]

The *Martand* belonged to the *Sanatan Dharam Yuvak Sabha*, which represented the minority point of view in Kashmir. The chief function of the paper was to discuss all social, economic and political problems facing the Kashmiri Pandits and educated unemployment among the Kashmiri Pandits was one of its main grievances.[52] Often it attacked the 'Muslim' press of Srinagar for raising the 'bogey' of unrepresentation of the Muslims in Government services.[53] The paper always urged the Government to make merit and efficiency the sole criterion of recruitment to the public services. But apart from pleading the case of the minority community, the *Martand* did devote its columns to themes such as Hindu-Muslim unity,[54] improvement in the industries,[55] labour welfare etc.[56] True, that the paper was deferential in its tone to the Government,[57] but, sometimes its equanimity was disturbed by the steep rise in the price of articles of daily use.[58] It launched a virulent attack on the black-marketeers, profiteers and grain-hoarders (*galladars*).[59] The *Martand* was able to make itself popular by raising counter arguments in the controversies of the day. It was, for instance, vehemently opposed to the abolition of the Food Control Department. When some papers of Srinagar suggested the liquidation of the Food Control Department the *Martand* sought to mobilise public opinion against the proposed measure.[60] The Government's policy in regard to the industries came in for a great deal of criticism. It was alleged by the paper that the decline of the industries in Srinagar and the consequent impoverishment of the artisans were the result of the Government's indifferent attitude towards the industries.[61] Credit can hardly be denied to the *Martand* for focussing the attention of the Government on the miserable condition of the artisans and labourers.[62]

The Srinagar Municipality often became the butt of the readers in the *Martand* for not taking care of the traditional part of the city.[63] This points to the growing awareness of the people of the dangers of insanitary conditions.

In social matters, the *Martand* dwelt on the backwardness of the Pandit community and attacked social evils like child marriage,[64] dowry[65] and the maltreatment of Hindu daughters-in-law at the hand of their mothers-in-law.[66] An unending war was waged by the paper against ostentatious spending on the occasion of *Shivratri* and other social and religious ceremonies and festivals.[67] It is significant that the paper encouraged the Pandits to adopt such professions as were abhorrent to them.[68]

That the *Martand* was not a losing concern is evident from the fact that it had an uninterrupted career during the period under review. Its circulation is said to have reached even 1900, which was much higher than that of any other local paper. Both in typography and contents the *Martand* maintained a fairly good standard. Its coverage of news was certainly good and by representing news and comments from the other local newspapers, it enabled the readers to have some acquaintance with different sections of public opinion.

However, there was a certain timidity in the *Martand* in exposing the shortcomings of those who were in position and authority. There was a tendency to suppress facts which were unfavourable to the interests of some big officials.[69] Also, the paper always doubted the motives of the nationalist leaders and not unoften, the nationalism of Kashmir leaders came in for carping criticism in the *Martand*.[70]

The *Sadaqat*[71] and the *Haqiqat*[72] had a fairly well-defined range of questions to which they gave a regular airing. Most of them were problems which had been calling for solution since the dawn of the twentieth century. One of the most important questions frequently referred to was that of employment of the educated Muslims. It was argued that the Muslim community was not duly represented in the Government services. This 'injustice' was regularly proclaimed not only in the *Sadaqat*[73] and the *Haqiqat*[74] but also in the *Hidayat*,[75] the *Islah*,[76] the *Albarq*,[77] the *Islam*,[78] the *Hurriyat*,[79], the *Khalid*,[80] the *Zulfiqar*[81] and the *Rahbar*. The *Islah* and the *Albarq* made frequent editorial criticism of the Government accusing it of favouritism and injustice. The *Albarq*, in particular, was very vociferous in voicing the demands of the Muslims.

One of the special features of the *Albarq*, [82] the *Hidayat*[83], the *Zulfiqar*,[84] the *Rahbar*,[85] the *Haqiqat*[86] etc. was to publish regular reports of the misdeeds by officials. This brought the wrath of the officials upon the editors who were often summoned by the court and punished.[87] But nothing could daunt their indomitable spirit. In many cases they gave a fine display of courage.

The conversion of the All Jammu and Kashmir Muslim Conference into the All Jammu and Kashmir National Conference[88] in 1939 considerably changed the tone of the press, and brought politics into the forefront of discussion. The more important papers like the *Hamdard*, the *Khidmat*, the *Khalid*, the Kesari, the *Desh* etc. now sought to educate the public in the political ideal of the National Conference. But the papers, such as the *Islah*, the *Albarq*[89] and the *Millat*[90] criticised the political ideal of the National Conference as chimerical and were definitely hostile to it. In this they reflected the Muslim League and the Muslim Conference's attitude which was opposed to all national aspirations. Mutual discord and discussions, arrogance and rivalry clearly manifested itself in their outlook on political questions. Sheikh Abdullah was vigorously opposed by the most powerful section of the Muslim League and the Muslim Conference, but he could carry on easliy because he had mass appeal and had a vast following and was a product of the masses, while the editors of papers like the *Albarq* and the *Islah* represented small segments of opinion.

With the growth of nationalism and political consciousness, the tone of the press became more and more vehement. The valuable services rendered by the *Khidmat*, the *Qaumi Dard,* the *Kesari*, the *Desh*, the *Khalid* and the *Nur* to the cause of nationalism and political progress in Kashmir can hardly be overestimated.

From the very beginning, the *Khidmat*[91] distinguished itself by a scathing exposure of the abuses of administration and a free and frank discussion of the political problems of the day. Guided by a robust spirit of nationalism, the *Khidmat* did not spare any effort in serving the interests of the people. In many editorial comments and articles the paper stressed the eternal conflict between the interests of the rulers and the ruled, and held out Responsible Government in the State as the only solution of the problem. There can hardly be any doubt that the *Khidmat* raised the tone of the Srinagar press and infused a spirit of strength, fearlessness, and nationalism in Srinagar journalism. It was a battle sheet and shared the vicissitudes of the nationalist struggle. During the Quit Kashmir Movement every word of it was censored.[92]

The *Khidmat* began to be edited by Moulana Muhammad Sayyid Masudi on becoming the official organ of the National Conference.[93] The Moulana[94] was an honoured name, both in politics and journalism and he was highly respected by the people for the depth of his views and the sobriety of his judgement. The *Khidmat* under his editorship acquired power, influence and prestige.

The *Kesari* brought out by Pandit Kashyap Bandhu in 1936 wholeheartedly supported the demand for Responsible Government.[65] It counselled both Hindus and Muslims to shun party politics and fight shoulder to shoulder with one another against the despotic Government.[96] Nationalism, the paper stressed, would lead to the common good of Hindus and Muslims in Kashmir.[97] The paper lampooned corrupt officials.[98] The slow progress of education in Kashmir was also debated in the *Kesari*.[99] The Government did not like this spirit of criticism and on some occasions it succeeded in preventing the Broca's press from printing the *Kesari*.[100]

The *Desh* followed the *Kesari*. Kashyap Bandhu was the heart and soul of the paper. He was outspoken in his comments and was a zealous and unflinching advocate of consitutional reform. Under him the *Desh* made its mark by its high ideals of disseminating useful knowledge and information and discussing all problems of public interest with a view to instructing the people. Like the *Kesari*, the *Desh* by its vigorious denunciation of the big *Zamindars* and heroic stand on behalf of the helpless and the oppressed cultivators, occupied a unique position in Srinagar journalism. Often it exposed the terrible miseries inflicted upon the cultivators.[101] It also wrote against communalism and parochialism.[102] Owing to its pro-nationalist attitude, the *Desh* was blacklisted in 1946.[103]

The *Nur* started by Mohi-ud-Din Nur not only championed the cause of the freedom struggle in Kashmir but also wrote a great deal about the distress of the labourers and cultivators.[104] The articles published in the *Nur* advocated socialist ideas. The Dogra oligarchy was boldly pilloried by the paper and on account of his animadversions on the malpractices of the officials, Mohi-ud-Din Nur had to court arrest. Again, during the Quit Kashmir Movement the editor of the *Nur* was jailed for writing against the Government.[105]

The *Bekar*, the *Dehqan* and the *Khalid* were started by Kh. Sadr-ud-din Mujahid. [106] The *Bekar* was short-lived. The Government ordered a ban on the *Dehqan* when its hostile writings caused resentment in Government circles.[107] The activities of the National Conference always filled in most of the columns of the *Khalid*.[108] The scarcity of grains,[109] the steep rise in the price of rice,[110] the fuel problem,[111] the question of Muslims' share in Government jobs[112] etc. were commonplaces in the paper.

The religious organisations of the Muslims had their own papers. The *Jahangir* started in 1932 was the official organ of the *Anjuman-i-Tablig-ul-Islam*. It contained scholarly articles.[113] The *Hidayat* was the spokesman of the *Jamait-i-Hamadani*[114]. It was critical of the Government for ignoring the merit of the educated young Muslims.[115] The *Tauhid* was brought out in 1936 by the *Anjuman-i-Ahl-i-Hadith*.[116] Another paper issued by the *Anjuman* was the *Muslim*. The aim of the *Muslim* was to purge contemporary Islam of ceremonies and beliefs which made it ridiculous in the eyes of Western rationalism, in particular, the extravagant ceremonies associated with funerals. Besides writing against the 'worship' of shrines, the *Muslim* also criticised the custodians of shrines.[117] In an editorial entitled *Kashmiri Musalman ki Gulami*, Mubaraki held the *mullahs* responsible for much of the ills of Muslim society. Since the credulous followers of the *mullahs* were always under the thumb of their so-called spiritual masters, their condition was described as being worse than that the political slaves.[118]

Although the history of the *Muslim* indicates that its aim was to strengthen and not weaken Islam in the eyes of its critics, its writings attacking traditional beliefs and practices, initially outraged the majority of the Muslims in Srinagar.

The *Muslim* was only devoted to religious issues, but occasionally it focussed on social and political problems too. For example, the cause of women's education was advocated.[119] The leaders of the Kashmir political movement were criticised for creating discord and dissension in the Muslim community for their own selfish ends.[120] The paper also wrote against the Ahmediyas.[121]

Among English weeklies, mention may be made of the *Kashmir Times*, the *Kashmir Chronicle* and the *Qaumi Dard*. Pandit Gawasha Lal Kaul was one of the founders of the English weeklies in Srinagar. He edited the *Kashmir Times* in 1934. Later in 1939, he started the *Kashmir Chronicle*.

The *Kashmir Times* was a standard weekly and held independent views. It carried some material of educational value[122] which made it respected and popular among educated people. The Government's attitude towards the paper was favourable and it was allowed to be circulated through the schools of the State.[123] Even Maharaja Hari Singh consulted the *Kashmir Times* in order to feel the trends of public opinion. Reformist and liberal-minded Hindus generally found in this paper a valuable ally because of its strong support in favour of social reform.[124] Its correspondence columns reflected an important section of the Kashmiri opinion of the time:

Though moderate in views, the *Kashmir Times* did not fail to criticise the views and attitude of the Government and also that of the local papers from the minority point of view. While refuting the charges of communalism levelled against it by the *Hamdard*, the *Kashmir Times* in an editorial said:

"The *Kashmir Times* always stands for [the] progress of the country in all spheres and has never preached communalism or adopted offensive or provocative attitude. But we claim that we cannot overlook the just claims of the minorities to placate the majority and if we have defended them sometimes within reasonable limits it cannot be said that this attitude was anti-nationalistic."

"The *Hamdard* should understand that the voice of a Responsible Government at present is raised by a communal body. Our contemporary instead of singing the tune like 'His Masters Voice' should have advised the majority leaders to form a new inter communal body on national lines. But instead of that it is acting as a publicity organ of the Muslim Conference ... We should expect from our 'Nationalist' contemporary to advise Mr. S.M. Abdullah and other Muslim leaders to resign from the Muslim Conference and leave it alone to work for [the] cultural, religious and social uplift of the Muslims. *There is a strong need for an organization on the lines of the Indian National Congress having a common flag, common slogans, common programme and a common goal.* If the Muslim Conference thinks it can safely play a double role and command others to come under its banner it is sadly mistaken. Nor should the *Hamdard* flatter its vanity with such a hypothesis."[125] (*Italics* mine).

Again, on 20.3.1937 the *Kashmir Times* in an editorial heading "Kashmir Should Lead," wrote:

"A large section of the people of Kashmir is already demanding a responsible form of Government in the State. The minorities in the State have never opposed this demand but what they want is safeguards. The cry for responsible government cannot be deferred too long. Thwarting the way of progress of the country and the nation was never conceived by any school of patriotism. This is high time, therefore, that the various communities in the Jammu and Kashmir State should sink their differences and evolve a common formula so that Kashmir may be able to give a lead to the other Indian States."

"Should we hope that the leaders of all communities in the State will take up the problem seriously in the best interests of the country in general?"[126]

The extracts quoted above are sufficient proof of how the leaders of the Muslim Conference responded to the call of public opinion when the prominent among them founded the National Conference so as to win the confidence of the minority community.

The *Kashmir Times* endeavoured to fight against illiteracy and advocated the establishment of a network of primary schools throughout the State.[127] It whole-heartedly supported the demands of the Muslim Conference for the spread of education, the establishment of a university, extension of medical aid and the exploitation of mineral resources of Jammu and Kashmir.[128] The lifting of the ban on the Kashmiris' entry into the army was also pleaded. Wrote the paper:

"We cannot understand why Kashmiris have been declared ineligible for military service when history provides ample evidence that Kashmiris were always a martial nation."[129]

The top heavy administration, due mainly to the high salaries of officials, was strongly criticised by almost all the papers in Srinagar.[130] While describing the speech of the Finance Minister in the *Praja Sabah* as 'a mere eye-wash,' the paper remarked:

"A small beneficiary measure here and a small beneficiary measure there cannot satisfy a whole people whose legitimate demands are repeatedly crushed under the hackneyed slogan 'want of funds.' How can funds be available when the cream of revenue is absorbed by [the] top-services? The growth in number as well as emoluments of gazetted officers has been so great that it requires [an] immediate weeding and pruning so that funds may be spared for beneficent works."[131]

There was a sharp reaction in the *Kashmir Times* when some cases of supersession in services took place in the State. Thus the Government was criticised for "its bankruptcy in the sense of justice."[132] In an editorial captioned "Bankrupt judgement" (Sic) the paper said:

"In spite of our judgement we get so many opportunities when we have only to pity the Government because the step it takes smacks of bankrupt judgement (Sic). It is this which causes resentment and consequently discontent. If the Government sometimes errs (and to err is but human) it ought to feel no hesitation to rectify the wrong at any stage when something is proved to the hilt supported by chapter and verse."[133]

The *Kashmir Times* also agitated for the protection of the rights of the State subjects. It was critical of the Government's policy of giving high posts to non-State subjects. As the paper wrote:

"In this State every new officer imported from outside chalks out his own policy which may not be in conformity with the general policy of the government."[134]

It is then evident that the Srinagar press always tried to bring home to the Government the public point of view on important matters.

The *Qaumi Dard* initiated in 1935 by Pandit Jia Lal Kilam was first published in Urdu and later it began to appear in English. The sole function of the paper was to educate the people on healthy non-communal lines and to inculcate in them a sense of common citizenship.[135] It always fought for the redressal of the genuine grievances of the people.[136] While supporting the popular demand for Responsible Government, the paper wrote:

"The Muslim community is becoming aggressively calamorous (Sic) for the introduction of responsible government. How long can the Government ignore their pressing demands."[137]

And as against the opposition of the Yuvak Sabha to the setting up of the Responsible Government, the *Qaumi Dard* remarked:

"Woe betide the lot of the community that has created such a narrow outlook for itself."[138]

The *Qaumi Dard* always kept itself busy in creating a strong public opinion in favour of the political and social reforms. The *sine-qua-non* for getting political freedom, the paper believed, "was that communalism should be banished from the body politic, and the good will of the minorities should be secured."[139] It was critical of Hindus and Muslims for showing a callous indifference to social reform. In an editorial the paper commented:

"We are of the firm belief that half of our economic misfortunes are due to the defective and obnoxious social customs. Nowadays we hear so much about indebtedness amongst (Sic) the Muslim masses. But we can prove it to anybody who has an open mind that three-fourths of this indebtedness is due to [the] wasteful expenditure which is indulged in by them on the occasion of their marriages or mourning ceremonies..."[140]

The paper, therefore, urged upon the Muslim leaders to pay serious attention to the amelioration of the social condition of their community.

The articles published in the *Qaumi Dard* were often directed against the 'capitalists' and the bureaucrats.[141] And while criticising the bureaucracy, the paper wrote:

"The high officials of the Government are generally engrossed in routine work-transfers, appointments, travelling allowances and pension cases. They have almost no time to look to proper work (Sic) for which they are presumed to be appointed. Even if they have time, they have generally no will to do it. This is the case with all irresponsible

Governments; in Kashmir it is only in a greater degree ..."[142]

A RESUME

From the above, it would be clear that the press in Srinagar had made a big advance during 1932-1947.[143] The free expression of a variety of opinions was all to the good.[144] By 1946 three dailies were published from Srinagar. On a number of occasions, the Government managed to counter public opinion on any given issue by a stream of counter-statements through the columns of the favoured section of newspapers.[145] Actually, the position with regard to the press in Srinagar in 1946 was that in spite of the Government's curbs,[146] the press was emerging as an effective organ of public opinion.[147] The fact that the standard of journalism was improving[148] is evident from various editorial comments. In its column, '*Kashir Kath*', the *Khidmat* ridiculed the *Praja Sabha* (the Legislative Assembly) in the following words:

"The bills presented by the representatives of the people could not be passed, or even if they were passed, no action was taken on them. Whatever the Government likes is passed because the Assembly is full of its own members. The conclusion is that we should forget dreams of constitutional progress and stregthen our organization so that we can again use the natural weapon of struggle in order to win our freedom."[149]

The role of the press in providing a momentum and leadership to political discussion is worthy of note. The editors of the papers of Srinagar could rarely boast of a degree or diploma in Journalism, but they brought a fund of common-sense and a great courage in discussing social, economic and political problems. In their criticism of the despotic rule they were relentless and brought out the ruthless nature of the Government in a number of ways. Their handling of news was calculated to bring about an estrangement between the ruler and the ruled, for these editors laboured under no illusion about the Government's justice or fairplay. The need for consitutional reform, public health, the sanitation of Srinagar, day to day incidents of administration related to cases of official corruption and oppression, educational matters, and the woeful condition of the peasants agitated the press like any other important issue and the resultant resentment was easily directed against the Government.

To a great extent the press did echo the social and religious resilience of the period. Among the Muslims, the '*Ahl-i-Hadith*' and the Ahmediyas were attempting social reforms. Religious discussion formed a part of peoples' life and many papers would not exclude this aspect from their purview. There was, for instance, much more reforming and crusading zeal at work in the *Muslim*, the *Islah* and the *Albarq*. True, the influence of these papers was limited to a few families in Srinagar, yet by throwing light upon the abuses, which like a canker, were eating into the vitals of Muslim society, the Srinagar press did raise the conscience of the people and awakened them to the need and necessity for reform.

Similarly the economic interests of the State were also catered to by the Srinagar press. The *Kesari*, the *Desh* and the *Nur* were inclined to the left. The daily *Hamdard* vigorously championed the cause of the Kisan Movement. The throbbing pulse of the country, therefore, was best reflected in the press of Srinagar.

Though the number of papers published in Srinagar had only a very small circulation,[150] yet, as a disseminator of ideas, the worth of the newspaper was substantially increased considering the fact that in the city as well as in some rural areas it used to be a feature of evening gossip when the school master or the *patwari* would read it aloud to the people. Thus the significance of the period (1932-1947) was the rise of the press in Srinagar which became a powerful medium for creating and reflecting public opinion.

NOTES:

1. Earlier in 1886, some 17 or 18 Kashmiri Muslims who had interest in land sent two signed petitions to the Viceroy and the Resident requesting them earnestly to appoint a 'compassionate, just and courteous Englishman' as Settlement Officer in Kashmir. The petitioners hoped that they would 'be able to explain to him their circumstances without fear.' From the Resident in Kashmir to the Secretary to the Government of India, NAI/Foreign, S.E Oct. 1886, Nos. 235-300, p-20. It is also noteworthy that Plowden, the Resident in Kashmir, suggested that "an English Settlement Officer should be appointed instead of a native", and to add weight to his representation to the Government of India, he sent them the two petitions of the Kashmiri Muslims (Ibid; see also J. C. Bose; *op. cit.*, p. 3). He also approached the Maharaja in this behalf (NAI/Foreign, Pol. Sec, E.Oct. 1886, Cons. 289-291). The result of Plowden's efforts was the appointment of A. Wingate as the Settlement Officer in January, 1887. Wingate started the settlement operations at Jammu in April, 1887, 'and completed within a year, the preliminaries of the settlement work of both Kashmir and Jammu.' When Wingate went to England on furlough in April, 1889, Lawrence, the Under-

Secretary to the Government of India in the Revenue and Agriculture Department was appointed as his successor. Lawrence found the work very difficult. He had to face the opposition of the landed aristocracy of the Maharaja. But despite the opposition of the absentee landlords, Lawrence was successful in his work.

2. NAI/Foreign, Genl B, Jan. 1909, Nos. 15-16.
3. NAI/Foreign, Intl Feb. 1907, Nos. 163-164.
4. Ibid.
5. *Report on Native Newspaper*, Punjab, 1911 p. 975. For the condition of Kashmiri Muslims in the State, see NAI/Foreign and Pol. Deptt. Deposit-Internal, Pros. June 1919, No. 78; *Chaudwin Sadi*, Rawalpindi, July 13, 1895 (*Report on Native Newspapers*, Punjab, 1895, p. 447); The *Hamdard-i-Hind*, Lahore, Sept. 16, 1895 (Ibid., 1895, p. 590); The *Rahbar-i-Hind*, Lahore, Aug. 22, 1895 (Ibid., 1895, p. 517); The *Vakil*, Amritsar, May 17, 1923 (Ibid., p. 279); The *Afghan*, Peshawar, Nov. 1, 1911 (Ibid., 1991; p-1160); The *Rahbar-i-Hind*, Oct. 4, 1894 (Ibid., 1894, p. 475).
6. As late as 1921 the State Government very unwillingly gave permission to the formation of an association whose object was the teaching of the Quran and ordered the police "to watch that the Anjuman does not take part in political matters." J & K (G.R.) File No. 66/102-C of 1921). The Government accorded permission to Sanatan Dharam Sabha to open its branch in Srinagar in 1923 on the "distinct understanding that the Sabha will take no part in politics." The Sabha was "a purely religious institution." J&K(G.R), F. No. 46/G-39 of 1923.
7. Kilam, *op. cit.,* pp-290-91.
8. Ibid.
9. Ibid; The *Tribune*, August 27, 1931; The *Pioneer*, Sept. 27, 1931.
10. Ibid; J&K (G.R) File No. 24 of 1891.
11. Ibid; Col. Henderson's letter dt. Nov.4, 1889 to W.J. Cunningham, NAI/Foreign, See.E. Jan. 1891, Nos. 118-120; Henvy's note on famine, Foreign Sec E. March, 1883. No. 86, p. 40; Confidential note on Kashmir Affairs for 1907-08 by Major Francis Younghusband, Foreign, July 1908, Sec. I, p. 51.
12. Kilam, *op. cit.,* pp. 290-91.
13. Ibid; The *Tribune*, Aug 27. 27, 1931
14. The *Tribune*, Aug. 27, 1931; See also *Inside Kashmir*, pp. 86-87.
15. The *Pioneer*, Sept. 4, 1931; *Inside Kashmir*, p. 84; *Daur-i-jadeed*, July 8, 1955. Kh. Saad-ud-din Shawl, one of the signatories to the memorial, was banished from the State by Pratap Singh. But so great was the pressure of public opinion that Maharaja Hari Singh was obliged to lift ban on the exiled leader's entry into Kashmir. On his return home in 1927, Saad-ud-din Shawl was given a hero's welcome by the people of Srinagar. Rashid Taasir, *Tahreek-i-Hurriyat-i-Kashmir*, I, p. 72. See also

The *Ranbir*, Aug. 23, 1927.

16. It cannot be denied that the proportion of the Muslims in the administrative services was 'infinitely small'. See article on Kashmir situation by G.S. Raghavan, The *Tribune*, Aug. 26, 1931; See also *Rahbar-i-Hind*, Oct, 4, 1894, Lahore (*Report on Native News Papers*, Punjab, 1894, p. 475); G.E.C. Wakefild, Recollections, p. 195.
17. Bazaz, *The History of Struggle for Freedom in Kashmir*, p. 146.
18. *The Amrit Bazar Patrika*, Aug. 25, 1931.
19. Bamzai, *History of Kashmir*, p. 653.
20. Quoted in the *History of Struggle for Freedom in Kashmir*, pp. 140-41.
21. Sir Albion Bannerji's words "produced a stir in the young minds. He may fitly be said to have awakened them from the slumber. The political awakening owes its origin to his pen", wrote the Resident of Kashmir. See *The Eastern Times*, Feb. 18, 1932. See also Jalali's note entitled "Wither Kashmir" (J.L.Jalali's Collections).
22. A brief reference to his contact with the Ahmediyas in the earlier phase of the freedom struggle in Kashmir is necessary. The latter are said to have supported Sheikh Abdullah in his work (See Aziz-ur-Rahman, *Raisul-ul-Ahrar, Maulana Habib-ur-Rahman, Ludhianwi*, P. 155). That Abdullah received support from the Ahmediyas is also evident from a reference by the British Resident in his Report of Oct. 3, 1931 in which he referred to the arrest of S.M. Abdullah, "a Qadiani". NAI/File No. 35p., Foreign and Political Deptt. Report on Kashmir for the period ending October 3, 1931. But it should not be supposed that the Kashmir leader had turned an Ahmadi, for "the record of a conference of All Jammu and Kashmir Muslim Conference held at Sialkot, Feb. 10, 1934, shows that Abdullah staunchly denied being an Ahmadi." Spencer Lavan, *op. cit.*, p-159. See also Sheikh Abdullah's letter (written in 1932) to Moulana Anwar Shah (Sheikh-ul-Hadith) in which he affirms his faith in *Khatam-i-Nabbuwat*.
23. *Crown Papers,* Government of India, Foreign and Political Deptt. File No. 35p. (Secret), 1931, Fortnightly Reports on the Internal Situation in Kashmir, Report for the period ending July 2, 1931.
24. The *Khidmat* (English), April 17, 1946.
25. The Riots Enquiry commission released its report on Oct. 4, 1931. The Commission justified the actions of the Maharaja and showered praise on him for his prompt dispatching of troops to prevent further troubles. The claims of Muslims against the Maharaja's military and police were denied by the report. N.N. Mitra, *The Annual Register: An Annual Digest of Public Affairs in India*, Vol. II, 1931 p. 19 and pp. 394-395.
26. Bamzai, *History of Kashmir*, p. 659.
27. The *Statesman*, June 11, 1946.
28. Ibid; *Glancy Commision's Report*, p. 19.
29. *Glancy Commision's Report*, p. 52; The *Statesman*, June 11, 1946.

30. The *Statesman*, June 11, 1946.
31. Ibid.
32. *Census*, I, 1921, p-118; The *Ranbir*, July 7, 1941; *Kashmir Today*, Vol v, May 1961, p-5. Bazaz, *Inside Kashmir*, p. 353.
33. *Census*, I, 1921, p-118; *Kashmir Today*, Vol v, May 1961, p-5.
34. *Kashmir Today*, Vol. v, May 1961, 15.
35. Ibid.
36. *Kashmir*, p-11.
37. Ibid; Kurshid, *Suhafat Pakistan Wa Hind Maen*, p. 450; *The Amrit Bzaz Patrika*, Aug. 15, 1931; *Inside Kashmir*, 11. 116-117.
38. *Kashir*, I, pp. ixi-ixxi; Khurshid, *op. cit.*, p-450; The *Tribune*, Mar. 1931; *Inside Kashmir*, pp-116-117.
39. *Kashir*, I, pp. ixix-ixxi; Khurshid, *op. cit.*, p-450; *Inside Kashmir*, pp. 116-117.
40. Ibid.
41. Dr. Sufi writes: :The Glancy Commission and the Reforms following it may be said to be due to the powerful writings of these papers coupled with the Ahrar Movement, the advice and assistance of the Kashmir Committee, and the agitation within the Valley of Kashmir under the leadership of Sheikh Muhammad Abdullah, Chaudri Ghulam Abbas and others." *op. cit.*, pp. ixix-ixxi; Also see *The Tribune*, Aug. 25, 1931; *The Amrit Bazaz Patrika*, Aug. 15, 1931.
42. Earlier in 1904, Maharaja Partap Singh did not permit Munshi Muhammad Din Fouq to start even a social magazine from Srinagar. J & K (G.R.) 117/P. 51 of 1904. I was told by the octogenarian Pandit Gawash Lal Koul that he was denied permission for starting a newspaper from Srinagar in 1927.
43. *The Ranbir*, Dec. 5, 1932.
44. *The History of Struggle for Freedom in Kashmir*, p-167.
45. Ibid.
46. Ibid.
47. Ibid; *The Hamdard*, March 19, 1938.
48. Ibid; *Inside Kashmir*, p. 365.
49. *The History of Struggle for Freedom in Kashmir*, p. 204; See also *The Martand.*, Sept. 11, 12, 1943.
50. *The History of Struggle for Freedom in Kashmir*, p. 204.
51. Ibid., p. 247.
52. *The Martand*, Feb, 21 1933; July 4, 1934; March 29, 1933; April 10, 1933; Sept. 21, 1934; Sept. 19, 1934; Feb. 18, 1933.
53. Ibid., June 19, 1936; June 27, 1936; June 30, 1936.
54. Ibid., Feb. 7, 1933; Feb. 17, 1933; March 3, 1933; April 22, 1934; March 30, 1933. In an editorial comment on Febuary 24, 1946 the *Martand* writes that in spite of the political differences both Pandits and Muslims in Kashmir are tolerant and participate in each other's festivals. See

also Ibid., June 27, 1934; Feb. 12, 1936.

55. Ibid., March 20, 1934; Sept. 11, 1943; Sept. 12. 1943; Oct. 12. 1943; Oct 16, 1943; June 1, 1934.
56. Ibid., Aug. 29, 1943; Sept. 12, 1943.
57. *The Martand* was always at pains to prove its loyalty to the Government. See Ibid., March 11, 1936; Oct. 1, 1934; March 29, 1940; July 19, 1946; July 18, 1946; August 17, 1934.
58. Ibid., Aug 28, 1943; Aug. 29, 1943; Sept. 1, 1943; Sept. 4, 1943; Dec. 17, 1938; April 5, 1946; April 3, 1946; Jan. 19, 1946; Jan. 10, 1945; Aug. 24, 1946.
59. Ibid., Dec. 17, 1939; Feb. 17, 1940; April 3, 1946.
60. Ibid., Feb. 13, 1936, See also *The Haqiqat,* June 10, 1937.
61. *The Martand*, June 1, 1934.
62. Ibid., Sept. 12; Aug. 12, 28, 29, 1943.
63. Ibid., May 2, 1934; March 7, Feb. 18, 20, 1936; Mar. 21, 1940; Mar, 19, 1939; Feb. 20, 1942; March 13, 1942; Sept. 19, 1944.
64. Ibid., Feb 17, 1933; March 3, 1933; March 11, 1933; June 30, 1934; July 11, 1934; July 13, 1934; Jan. 3, 1937.
65. Ibid., Feb. 17, 1933; March 3, 1933; March 11, 1933; June 30, 1934; March 22, 1933; Jan. 3, 1937.
66. Ibid., Feb. 17, 18, 22, March 3, 11, 1933; June 30, 1934; Jan. 3, 1937.
67. Ibid., Feb. 17, March 3, 11, 12, 1933; June 30, 1934; Feb 21, 1936; Jan. 3, 1937; Jan. 31, 1942.
68. Ibid., Aug, 24, 1934.
69. See, for example, the July 31, 1937 issue in which the paper pays glowing tributes to a corrupt official. As against this, the *Kesari* and the *Zulfiqar* brought to light his misdeeds. The *Haqiqat*, the *Albarq* and the many other papers were often criticized by the *Martand* for their attack on officials.
70. Ibid., Feb. 25, 1940; Jan. 15, 23, 25, 1942; Dec. 5, 1944.
71. It represented the views of the Muslim Conference and came to an end before the brith of the National Conference.
72. Originally brought out by the Muslim Conference, the *Haqiqat* began to serve the interests of the National Conference from 1939.
73. The *Sadaqat*, March 23, 1933; See also *The Martand,*, June 19, 27, 30, 1936.
74. See, for example, The *Martand* Sep., 29, Dec. 23, 1934.
75. Ibid, March 27, 1940.
76. The *Islah*, August 26, 1938.
77. The *Albarq*, No. 26, 1936, Dec. 23, 1938.
78. It wrote series of 'vicious' articles against the Ahmediyas, see Spencer Lavan *op. cit.*, p-159 and n.
79. The *Hurriyat* followed the *Islam*. Both were started by Moulvi Muhmmad Yusuf Shah.

80. The *Khalid* Aug. 3, 1941; Nov. 14, 1941; Sept. 20, 1941; Aug 11, 1941; Jan. 15, 1942. The *Martand* of Dec. 5 and 6, 1940 quotes the *Khalid* as saying that the Kashmiri Pandits could no longer monopolise Government offices on account of increasing education among the Muslims and other socially backward classes. Ealier in Oct. 1931, Maharaja Hari Singh made it clear to a deputation of the Kashmiri Pandits saying "... ... I am certain you will be the first to recognise that with the steady growth of education in other communities the position of advantage which your community enjoyed in the past in regard to State service cannot continue." The *Tribune,* Oct. 27, 1931.
81. The *Islah*, Aug. 26, 1938. Sometimes the writings of the *Islah* became the subject of debate in the *Praja Sabha.* See the *Martand*, Oct. 8, 1937.
82. See *The Albarq*, July 1, 1938.
83. See *The Martand*, Dec. 21, 1937.
84. Ibid., July 25, 1937; *The Hamdard*, Aug. 31, 1937.
85. See *The Martand*, April, 16, 1935.
86. Ibid., Aug. 20, 1936; Sept. 13, 1936.
87. See *the Hamdard,* Aug. 31, 1937; also *Jammu wa Kashmir maen Urdu Suhafat*, pp. 73-74.
88. Commenting on the conversion of the Muslim Conference into the National Conference, the correspondent of the *Statesman* dated june 11, 1946 remarks:
"The change gave fresh impetus to the movement. The occasion was unique. Never had any other communal organisation in India achieved this amazing conversion. Large-heartedness seemed to have combined with far-sightedness to bring about this consummation." See also *The Hindustan Times*, March 30, 1946.
89. The *Albarq* saw in this conversion the conspiracy of the Kashmiri Pandits against the Muslims. See Ibid.,Jan.24,1942.The strong reaction against this change was also noted in the *Pasban* of Jammu.It was highly critical of Sheikh Abdullah and attributed the Muslim Conference's conversion into the National Conference mainly due to the influence of Gandhi and Nehru on the Kashmir leader. See *The Martand,* March 28, 1939.
90. It started publishing from Srinagar in 1936. Moulvi Yusuf Shah was the proprietor and Moulvi Nur-ud-din the editor of the *Millat*. See *Jammu wa Kashmir maen Urdu Suhafat*, p. 164.
91. It was the most popular paper in Kashmir during 1942-47.See *Jammu wa Kashmir maen Urdu Suhafat*, pp.151-152.
93. Ibid.
94. He was killed by the militants in recent years.
95. See *The Martand,* July 15, 1938.
96. Ibid.
97. Ibid. Aug 3, 1938.
98. See *The Kesari*, july 28, 1937.

99. Quoted in *The Martand*, Oct. 11, 1938.
100. *Jammu wa Kashmir maen Urdu Suhafat*, p. 139.
101. My views on the *Desh* are entirely based on interviews with some prominent journalists of the Dogra period. Attention may, however, be drawn to the August 1, 1943 issue of the *Martand* critising the *Desh* for supporting the *Zamindars* and *Jagirdars*.See also the *Martand*, July 28,1943.
It seems that the *Martand's* criticism is not justified. While writing about the *Desh*, Bazaz remarks: "Every line in the paper is readable and espouses the cause of the poor and the down-trodden." *Inside Kashmir*, p. 364.
102. *Jammu wa Kashmir maen Urdu Suhafat*, p.140.
103. Ibid.
104. Ishaq, "Growth of Press in Srinagar, 1932-1947 (*The Research Biannual,* Vol. I, 1976, p. 42.)
105. *Jammu wa Kashmir maen Urdu Suhafat*, pp. 145-146.
106. Ibid., pp. 147-148.
107. Ibid.
108. Ibid.,p. 148; See also The *Khalid*, sept. 20, 1941;Aug.11 1941; May8,1942.
109. The *Khalid,* June 13, 1952; March 12, 1942.
110. Ibid., March 12, 1942; Dec. 27, 1941; Dec. 10, 1941.
111. Ibid., Feb. 16, 1942; Feb. 24, 1942.
112. Ibid., Nov. 14, 1941; Sept. 20, 1941; Aug. 11, 1941; Jan. 15, 1942; Aug. 3, 1941.
113. *Jammu wa Kashmir maen Urdu Suhafat*, P. 141.
114. Ibid., p. 143.
115. See The *Martand*, March 27, 1940.
116. *Jammu wa Kashmir maen Urdu Suhafat*, p. 143.
117. *The Muslim,* Oct. 2, 1941; March 2, 1942; Safar 1360 H; Moharram 1360 H.
118. Ibid., Safar, 1360 H.
119. Ibid., April 16, 1942; May, 1942.
120. Ibid., June 16, 1942.
121. Ibid., Nov. 16, 1942; Sept. 2, 1944.
122. *The Kashmir Times,* Dec. 18, 1937; July 20, 1937; May 25, 1937.
123. Ibid., Feb. 4, 1939.
124. In an editorial dated May 26, 1936, *The Kashmir Times* wrote against juvenile smoking.
125. Ibid.. Aug. 7, 1937.
126. See also Ibid., April 3, 1937.
127. Ibid., July 20, 1937.
128. Ibid., May 25, 1937.
129. Ibid.

130. Ibid., April 27, 1937; Nov. 27, 1937.
131. Ibid., Oct. 20, 1936.
132. Ibid., Oct. 30, 1937.
133. Ibid., June 22, 1937.
134. Ibid., Oct. 30, 1937; The *Khidmat* looked at the question of favouring the State subjects in the matter of government service from purely economic point of view.
135. *The Qaumi Dard*, July 20, 1937.
136. Ibid., June 29, 1937.
137. Ibid., July 27, 1937.
138. But the *Martand* (August 5, 1937) severely criticised the views of The *Qaumi Dard.*
139. *The Qaumi Dard*, July 20, 1937.
140. Ibid.
141. An article in the May 11, 1937 issue of the *Qaumi Dard* gave a clarion call to the workers to unite against the 'capitalists' and the bureaucracy.
142. Ibid., July 13, 1937.
143. *Census,* 1941, p. 39; *The United India and the Indian States*, June 26, 1937.
144. Ibid., Majid, *op. cit.,* p. 75; *The United India and the Indian States,* June 26, 1937.
145. *The Khidmat*, April 17, 1946.
146. Ibid.
147. Majid, *op. cit.,* p. 75.
148. *Census,* 1941, p. 39
149. *The Khidmat*, April 17, 1946.
150. *Inside Kashmir*, p. 367; *Census, 1941, p. 39.*

CHAPTER VIII

LITERARY AND SOME OTHER CULTURAL ACTIVITIES

Literature portrays the life of a society and records its yearnings, aspirations and doubts. It is, therefore, an invaluable record of the changes through which society passes."[1] The literature of the Dogra period may be divided into five parts: (1) Persian (2) Sanskrit (3) Urdu (4) Kashmiri and (5) English.

PERSIAN

Persian, which continued to be the official language for more than 400 years in Kashmir, acquired the status of the language of culture and influenced and enlarged Kashmiri vocabulary to a great extent.[2] New forms like the *ghazal*, the *masnvi*, the *naat*, the *marsiya* and the *naama*—all Persian in form, metre and language were imported. The Kashmiri writers also borrowed Persian epithets, figures of speech and themes. The typical Persian themes to which the Kashmiri poet turned were—the story of Laila and Majnun, of Shirin and Khusrau and of Soharab and Rustum.

Among some Persian poets of the Dogra period may be mentioned Mirza Mehdi Mujrim, Mulla Ubaid Ullah, Kh. Hasan Koul, Hasan Shah Zirak, Shams-ud-din Hariat Kamili, Kh. Muhammad Shah Asad, Mirza Saad-ud-din and Hashyar.[3]

Mirza Mehdi Mujrim was a well-known poet. He has been compared by several critics to Ghani for his forceful expression. Another poet,

Mehdi Shah Dika was very popular among the masses. He was subject to paroxysms of insanity and "composed couplets which at once convey praise and blame, eulogy and censure." Kh. Hasan Shah Zirak was a teacher in the Islamia High School, Srinagar. At the begining of the present century, when the price of food grains rose in Srinagar, Zirak wrote against the Government's economic policy.[4] As a result, food riots took place in the city in which Zirak had a prominent role.[5] The poet was arrested, but subsequently the Government reduced the prices of *shali,* wrote Zirak:

Zirak az ziraki ba jail raseed
Nirakh-i-shali ba asal khiseesh raseed

Another notable poet of the Dogra period was Mirza Saad-ud-din. He was a friend of Shibli Noumani, an eminent Urdu Scholar who 'held enlightened and to a moderate degree, Westernized views. Saad has mourned the intellectual degeneration of the Muslim community of Kashmir. He points to the differences of his co-religionists over trivial matters and lampoons the reactionary *mullahs* of his time.[6]

The Persian prose writers of this period are very few. Among them Ghulam Nabi Shah Khanyari and Haji Mohi-ud-din Miskin deserve special mention. Khanyari wrote *Wajeez-ut-Tawarikh.*[7] It contains useful matter pertaining to the social, economic and political history of the Sikh and earlier part of the Dogra rule in Kashmir. Miskin lived at Sara-i-bala in Srinagar. He wrote his *Tarikh-i-Kabir-i-Kashmir*[8] in 1892. Miskin's work is a running summary in one handy volume of the political, religious and literary history of Kashmir.

SANSKRIT

Maharaja Ranbir Singh is said to have taken several measures for the rivival of Sanskrit. He founded Sanskrit *Patshalas* and employed proficient Pandits to teach Sanskrit. He established a translation bureau where Sanskrit texts were edited and sometimes translated into Persian, Hindi and Dogri. Sahib Ram, a well-known Sanskrit scholar, wrote his *Tirtha Sangraha* describing the legends and geography of the famous places of pilgrimage in Kashmir. Another notable writer of this period was Pandit Madhusudhan Koul who edited with critical annotations and comments Abhinavagupta's *Tantralok* and some ancient Sanskrit classics.

KASHMIRI

But from the beginning of the twentieth century, a new order begins to emerge and a fresh era is inagurated in the literature of Kashmir. While Persian had almost exclusively occupied the field till now, it henceforth falls into the background and continues to lose its significance and inspiration. Kashmiri Poetry which was so far dominated by Persian themes found itself stagnant. Within a few decades it became a powerful and supple instrument of expression. This new development marks the end of the medieval ways of thinking and the beginning of the modernisation of the Kashmiri mind. Various historical and political forces brought about this change. The improved means of communications and transport, linking the Valley with the rest of India made it possible for tourists to come here and young Kashmiris to go outside for higher studies. Contact with outside forces and the powerful impact of the freedom struggle in India created a new ferment in the minds of the intelligensia and an awakening in the souls of men. At the same time the sudden introduction of Urdu in place Persian as the court language in the beginning of this century led to the decline of Persian and made the middle classes develop a keen interest in Urdu and English.

The Christian missionaries were another agency in the evolution of modern Kashmiri literature. Their main contribution was the preparation of grammers, dictionaries, and translations from English. T. R. Wade compiled a Kashmiri grammer and translated the New Testament into Kashmiri. J. Hinton Knowles collected a number of Kashmiri proverbs and riddles and published them along with English translation and notes and comments. He also published a collection of Kashmiri folk-tales in English. Another collection of folk-tales was published under the title *Hatim's Tales* by Sir Aurel Stein and Sir George Grierson. The latter also translated from Sanskrit the Kashmiri grammer by Pandit Ishwar Koul. A Kashmiri-Sanskrit Dictionary of Ishwar Koul was also utilized by Grierson for the preparation of his Kashmiri-English Dictionary which was published in 1932 by the Royal Asiatic Society under the title of 'A Dictionary of the Kashmiri Language'. Another publication of Grierson was *Lalla Vaakh* (Lalleshwari's sayings).

With the new sense of identity and a changed environment, some educated young men felt that Kashmiri poetry needed radical reform.

The pioneer of the new age was Ghulam Ahamd Mahjoor.[9] He may be considered the father of modern Kashmiri literature. The preoccupation of his predecessors was either romance or religious thems. They ignored the hard realities of life and accepted the existing social order with all its inequalities and inequities.

Born at Metragam, Pulwama, in 1888, Mahjoor was educated in Persian and Arabic. After passing the middle school examination from the *Nusrat-ul-Islam* School, Srinagar he went to the Punjab where he came in contact with Urdu poets like Bismil Amritsari and Moulana Shibli Noumani.[10] On his return to Srinagar in 1908 he started writing in Persian and then in Urdu. As he was not satisfied with these media, he began writing in Kashmiri.

Mahjoor's greatest contribution was in popularising Kashmiri. "There are thousands who write in Persian", said he, "only Kashmiri remains a helpless, neglected language." And indeed it was owing to the efforts of Mahjoor that all the renowned poets of the modern era, namely, Abdul Ahad Azad, Abdul Sataar Aasee, Zinda Koul and Nadim gave up their early devotion to Udru.[11]

Though love is predominant in his poetry, Mahjoor touched new thems such as *The Country Lass, My Youth, Arise O Gardener* and *Our Country is a Garden.* "In his songs he can catch the melody of the earlier *Lol-Lyric*[12] of the sixteenth and seventeenth centuries; but there is a singing quality and a rhythmic lilt in him which was akin to, and perhaps inspired by the popular Hindustani *geet* and song of the early decads of this century as they came to Kashmir through the Punjab."[13] After July 1931, Kashmir began to stir with patriotic fervour, and Mahjoor proved equal to the occasion. In his *Arise O Gardner*, the poet urged his countrymen to attain freedom through "earthquakes, gales, thunder and storm." Mahjoor had to suffer at the hands of the authorities for composing the poem "but finally he escaped unmolested." The song gained such a popularity that it was adopted by the National Conference as a national song.[14]

Mahjoor was a poet of profound intellectual convictions. His compositions are full of ideas about human freedom, the brotherhood of man, religious tolerance and respect for manual labour. He had a deep sense of history. To him religious humanism was one of the chief characteristics of Kashmiri culture.

> "Hindus will keep the helm and Muslims ply the oars;
> Let us together row ashore the boat of this country."

Another great poet of the modern era is Abdul Ahad Azad. Born in 1903 at Ranger, about 13 miles from Srinagar, Azad remained a poor teacher in a primary school till his death in 1948. He met Mahjoor in 1935, when he was undergoing training at the Normal Training School, Srinagar. Under his influence he started writing Kashmiri but, as Prof. Raina observes, "there is no evidence in Azad's poetry of any abiding thematic influence of Mahjoor."[15] His literary influences were Sir Muhammad Iqbal and "the progressive writers as far as spirit, forcefulness and technique are concerned."[16] Mahjoor was a nationalist, but Azad yearned for a socialistic pattern of society. He calls nationalism "jugglery" and a "cause of enmity" between man and man."He brackets nationalism and communalism together. In his opinion neither the one nor the other can liberate mankind."[117]

Azad definitely "struck the note of modernity in Kashmiri poetry. For, if modernity can be defined as an insight into social change and intellectual awareness of the new values of life, Azad surely possessed that insight and had that consciousness within him."[18] This is clear from the following verse which nowhere shows him in a mood of nostalgic sympathy with the past.

> "To become free, to end tyranny and to abolish superstition
> This is my cherished dream, this my desire and this slogan."

Azad was a fiery genius of remarkable vitality and dynamism. In content, his verses covered a wide range, protesting against social injustices and inequalities, generating a revolutionary impulse and struggling against conservative conformities.

In his *Inqalab* Azad advocated change. The poet exhorted:

> "What is life but the book of change?
> Change—more—change and yet more change;
> Flux is the living reality,
> And the change meaning of flux.
> It is change that brought forth religion,
> Banished doubt, revealed true faith.
> Now reason has banished prophecy
> Only poetry and trade remain.
> Advance; open the gates of garden of love;
> Your own sight is veiling your eyes.
> Ask flowers how cruel is spring,
> Breaking frost with a shower of hail,

To the sheep and the goat, the butcher and the wolf
Are alike—one slays, the other drains blood.
The law has sanctioned human slaughter;
Mean jackals are feasting on lions' blood.
O compulsion; slavery; subjection;
O restless, helpless heart: O Shame;
Rend the veil; uncover the seething, bubbling heart;
Change: Change: Bring a new change."

But Azad's brillant composition is the 'Song of the River.' It was his message to the Urdu edition of the weekly *Vitasta* which Prem Nath Bazaz started during the summer of 1945. In it lies the essence of the philosophy of life that Azad taught. It cannot be denied that in its imagery, profundity of thought, vigour of language and clarity of ideas, the 'Song of the River' stands 'unrivalled' in Kashmiri literature. "The rhythmic movement of the waters," writes Bazaz, "is [a] symbolic call for action and revolt against the iniquitous social order."[19]

The River sings:
"When I witness ups and downs, banks and demarcations,
I lose my temper
I seek oneness and equality, for that
I run and foam and fret;
Hence is it that, water though I am,
I have fallen on the burning coals of the mulberry-woods."

Pir Abdul Qadir Aasim (1897-1946) is an unknown figure in modern Kashmiri literature. But he too seems to have been increasingly drawn into the vortex of the social and political changes of his time. In one of his poems[20] Aasim expresses the tensions felt by his innermost soul urging people to unite under the banner of freedom.

Abdul Sataar Aasee started his career as a coolie. At the beginning he wrote Persian *ghazals*, but influenced by the freedom struggle and Mahjoor, he truned towards Kashmiri. His poetical songs express the urge of the people for liberation. Among his popular poems may be mentioned *Siyasi Qaidi* (political prisoner), *Mazoor* (labourer) and *Naujawanun Se Khitab* (Address to Youth). Aasee was popularly known as *Mazoor Shair* or the labourer's poet. In 1942 he was arrtested for his outspokenness and radical views.

Mirza Ghulam Hasan Beg Arif (b. 1910) has been associated with various literary and cultural activities. He has been one of the prominent figures in the field of Kashmiri literature for the last 77 years. He founded the *Bazme Adab* in 1940 and organized a number of *mushairas* in Srinagar. His object was to give Kashmiri and its literature the status it had been denied. His literary influences were Iqbal, Ghalib, Chakbast, Hasrat Mohani, Josh, Faiz and Munshi Prem Chand. But he has never shown any liking for romantic poetry, for he does not regard romance a subject fit for poetry. He has composed a good many of quatrains in which he shows the various aspects of social and political life in Kashmir.

Arif believes that national freedom can assume its full significance only if it acquires a social revoultionary content. He has found his themes in the life of the labourers, artisans and beggars. He portrays the profound agonies and small joys of the peasantry and the army of men trekking long and weary miles in search of a livelihood. Arif has become a conscious 'proletarian' and has used the sonorous cadences of poetry in his *Mouzreni* (woman labourer) to breathe forth fire of a revolutionary idealism.

Arif has written his poems with messianic zeal, and in this trend of writing his aim has been not simply to delineate the sufferings of the working class but principally to denounce the existing social order and rouse the weak against the exploitation of the strong. The unburnt brick which grows firmer and finer after burning in an oven, has been made a subject of verse. Arif's confidence in the greatness of man is obvious here. His main purpose in writing this poem is to impress upon his readers the fact that every man can grow more perfect by burning in the fire of hardship.

Master Zinda Koul's first poetical attempts were in Persian and Hindi. He started writing in Kashmiri in 1942 at the age of 58. One of his poems entitled *Majbooriah* (compulsion) is worthly of praise. In it we find the finest expression of his belief in the supremacy of faith over reason. Besides Zinda Koul, there were two other traditionalists in mystical poetry namely Shams Faqir and Samad Mir.

Daya Ram Ganju is didactic. He instructs women on household affairs, cleanliness and good manners.

Pitmabar Nath Dhar Faahi is a materialist. He stands for the destruction of the existing social, political and enconomic order. He denies the existence of any super-natural force. Like Azad he hates communalism and nationalism.

Dina Nath Nadim's career as a poet is most intimately linked with the political developments in Srinagar during the period under review. He was arrested in 1938 for participating in the national struggle, and all his poems were seized by the police and destroyed. He sang the dawn of freedom when the Quit Kashmir Movement started in 1946 in his *Wouthee Baagich Kukilee*.

KASHMIRI PROSE

Kashmiri literature of the Dogra period is not rich in prose. It was in 1936 that Prof. J. L. Kaul, for the first time, introduced a Kashmiri section in the *Pratap Magazine* of S. P. College, "adapting Perso-Arabic alphabet with suitable modification."[21] *Satach Kahwat* (The Touchstone of Truth), *Ramun Raj* (the reign of Sri Rama), and *Paz Pativaratae* (Savitri) were adaptations and translations from Hindustani plays reproduced in the magazine. But an attempt at writing original Kashmiri prose was made by Ibn-i-Mahjoor when in 1940 he started the first weekly magazine in Kashmiri. It was called *Gaash* (light), and covered not only current news but also published the poems of Mahjoor. The magazine's column entitled *asun ta gindun* (Laugh a while) was full of interest. Unfortunately, the *Gaash* was very short-lived.

The need for writing prose was also felt in 1945 when a branch of the Indian People's Theatre (IPTA) was set up in Srinagar under "the impetus of the Quit Kashmir Movement."[22] Prem Nath Pardesi wrote a Kashmiri play entitled *Bata har* (The Food Fight) on the exploitation of the peasantry. But the play could not be staged since it was not passed by the Censor, and the manuscript was confiscated and lost.[23]

URDU

Under the stress of the new factors, Urdu began to develop and a spirit of dissatisfaction with Persian began to show itself. Among Urdu poets and story writers of this period may be mentioned Khushi Mohammad Nazir, Master Zinda Koul, Nand Lal Talib and Ghulam Rasool Nazki.

Nazir is the author of *Nagmai Firdous* and Talib the author of *Rushat-ul-Takhayyal*. Nazki published his collection of poems, *Nazaakat*, in 1932-33.

The prose writers in Urdu were Abdul Ahad Azad, Prem Nath Pardesi and Pitambar Dhar Faani. Azad was also a literary critic. He devoted many years to the collection of the published and unpublished material of all well known poets of Kashmiri for his monumental work entitled

Kashmiri Zuban Aur Shairi. This book decribes the history of Kashmiri literature. Pardesi is a talented writer. His short stories graphically depict the social evils of Kashmiri society.

The freedom of the press which followed the Glancy Commission's report resulted in the publication of a number of newspapers and weeklies. Among the prominent Urdu journalists of this period must be mentioned Mir Abdul Aziz, Moulvi Mohammad Sayyid Masudi, Janki Nath Zutshi, Ghulam Ahmad Kashfi, Sabir, Nand Lal Watal, Kashyap Bandhu, Jagan Nath Sathu and Prem Nath Bazaz.

ENGLISH

The spread of english education created both a taste for western literature and a receptiveness to modern ways of thinking. The dawn of the modern era also witnessed the emergence of Kashmiri authors who wrote in English. The pride of place goes to Pandit Anand Koul, a product of the mission school, who wrote *The Kashmiri Pandit, Geography of the Jammu and Kashmir State* and *Archaelogical Remains in Kashmir*. He also contributed articles to journals in India and abroad on the history of Kashmir, folk-lore and literature. Among other writers may be mentioned R. C. Kak, Prem Nath Bazaz, Jia Lal Koul, Jia Lal Koul Jalali, Gawash Lal Koul and Som Nath Dhar. *Bazaz's Inside Kashmir* is very useful for understanding the various social, economic and political factors leading to the growth of freedom. Prof. Jia Lal Koul selected and translated old and new lyrics in Kashmiri into English in a book entitled *Kashmiri Lyrics*. Dhar's *Kashmir, Eden of the East* gives us clues in understanding the social evils.

DRAMA

The impact of modern ideas also found its effective and direct expression in drama. In the changed situation the stage also became vehicle of propaganda for social justice. It was no longer regarded as a place for providing mere entertainment. While political plays had no chance of being approved for the stage by the State-Censor, plays embodying themes from mythology or folk-lore and social plays were staged by several dramatic clubs like the S. P. College Dramatic Club and the *Natak Vibhag* of the *Samaj Sudhar Samiti*, Srinagar.[24] One of these plays, *Vidwah* (The Window), songs for which were written by the coolie poet, Abdul Sataar

Aasee' became very popular.[25] Reference has been made to *Batahar* (The Food Quarrel) of Prem Nath Pardesi which depicted the exploitation of the peasants.

PAINTING

Maharaja Pratap Singh established a Technical Institute at Srinagar in which training was imparted to students in various arts such as painting, engineering, smithy, wicker-work, sculpture and carpentry. It should, however, be borne in mind that Sir Walter Lawrence[26] had earlier drawn the attention of the Kashmir Government towards the establishment of a technical school. For many years the Amar Singh Institute, as it was called, produced some artists, though not of a high standard. But subsequently for want of financial assistance, the school registered a decrease in the number of its students. It was only after 1931 that a few painters shot into prominence. Dina Nath Wali, Triloki Koul, Sat Lal Kharoo and Ghulam Rasool Santosh are some notable examples. Dina Nath Wali incurred the wrath of the Government for having contributed two sketches to the Special Responsible Government Number of the *Hamdard* in August 1938. One of his paintings "depicted a horrible scene in which the hideous looking alien despotic Government was trampling upon the teeming, toiling millions of Kashmir."[27]

This brief review of the cultural achievements shows that the Kashmiri mind was ready to absorb the modern ideas and to adopt the modern attitudes and modes of expression. We have seen that the Kashmiri poets of this period were greatly influenced by new ideas. Indeed the necessity of literature as a living force was ushered in by the political, social and enonomic conditions mainly under the yoke of Dogra rule. The new school of poets appeared with its mind alive to the changing social order. But it should be remembered that excepting Azad all others respected tradition and did not make a serious departure. The new school of poets was prepared to modify, even to reject, much of the old, but it was not prepared to repudiate totally the inheritance of the past. Its endeavour was to preserve what may be considered of permanent and abiding value in its own culture and to assimilate from the outside forces what was necessary for building up a new society. Its principal achievement lies in creating a common outlook and a fund of ideas and sentiments, which are the precondition for the emergence of national consciousness.

NOTES:

1. Tara Chand, *History of the Freedom Movement in India*, Vol, II p. 582.
2. Ishaq, "Persian influence in Kashmir, 1320-1586" (*Islamic Culture* Vol, LI, No.I Jan. 1977, pp. 5-6).
3. For greater details on the Persian poets of the Dogra period, see Mohi-ud-din Miskin, *Tarikh-Kabir-i-Kashmir*, pp. 350-252; Pir Hasan, *Tarikh-i-Hasan*, Iv, pp. 53-55; Abdul Qadir Sarwari, *Kashmir Maen Farsi Adab ki Tarikh.*
4. Miskin, *op. cit.,* p. 352.
5. Ibid.
6. Abdul Qadir Sarwari, *op. cit.,* pp. 301-303.
7. It is in manuscript form and has not been published yet.
8. It was published in 1894 by Suraj Prakash Press, Amritsar.
9. Most of the poets who used their art as a vehicle of propaganda for social and political justice in Srinagar, came from rural background. This reciprocal pull between the city and the villages was made possible by the fact because the urban literati, the artisans, the working class and above all the public leaders found the trenchant expression of their yearnings and aspirations in the works of the poets like Mahjoor, Azad and Arif.
10. Azad, *Kashmiri Zuban Aur Shairi,* Vol. III, pp. 192 and 197.
11. Trilokinath Raina, *An Anthology of Modern Kashmiri Verse,* p. 5.
12. Human love is expressed by the typical Kashmiri *lol-lyric*. *Lol* is a Kashmiri word signifying an untranslatable "complex of love longing and a tugging at the heart." The *Lol-lyric* is "very musical, very brief, rarely more than ten lines including the repeated refrains, abounding in rhymes and assonances, put in the mouth of a woman lover, a cry from her heart, expressing in a flexible pattern more a mood than a thought." In its early phase from the fourteenth to the seventeenth century it was mystical, spiritual or didactic. it is no longer so now. (Jai Lal Kaul, *Kashmiri Lyrics,* Introduction, page xvii).
13. *Kashmir*, Oct. 1956, p. 231.
14. While writing about the popularity of Mahjoor, Mr. Balraj Sahani remarks: "His songs and his poems are the cherished property of every man, woman and child living between Baramulla and Pir Panchal. If Mahjoor writes a poem today it will be on the lips of the populace within a fortnight. Children on their way to school, girls thrashing rice, boatmen plying the paddle, labourers bending in their ceaseless toil, all will be singing it." *(The Vishwa-Bharati* Quarterly, November 1938, Vol. iv, part III, new series, pp. 213-221).
15. *op. cit.,* p. 7.
16. *Ibid.*
17. *The History of Struggle for Freedom in Kashmir*, p. 301.

18. *Kashmir Today*, Volume VI, August 1962, p. 23.
19. Ibid., p. 302.
20. See Mohi-ud-din Hajini, *Koe: Shir Shoe: Yiree*, p. 162.
21. Kaul, *Studies in Kashmiri Literature*, p. 99.
22. Ibid., p. 102.
23. Ibid.
24. Ibid., p. 291.
25. Ibid.
26. *The Valley of Kashmir*, pp. 7, 230.
27. *The History of Struggle for Freedom in Kashmir*, p. 312.

CHAPTER IX

CONCLUSION

In this work we have studied the changing pattern of the society of Srinagar, analysing its various angles related to different social activities. A summary of these changing trends provides a running commentary upon the process of social change in Srinagar from 1846 to 1947.

If we look at the history of Srinagar, we find that it has mainly grown as a nucleus of political, administrative and economic activities during the period under review. It should, however, be remembered that the changes in the economic activities form a complex web woven round different coordinated interests of life. They bring to focus the stresses and strains resulting from the adjustment and adaptations in various spheres of life's activities.

The opening of the Jhelum Valley Road was an event of far-reaching significance. The city of Srinagar was now exposed to various types of pulls and pressures from outside. The new line of transport and communication helped, not a little, to accelerate the process of urbanization. Consequently from 1901 to 1941 the city expanded. Trade and industry, which, in the meantime, marked a rapid growth also provided the stimuli for the speedier development of the city. The extention in the area of the city as a centre of politico-economic activities, all interdependent phenomena, cannot be taken in exclusiveness. We have, therefore, examined their operation in an integrated sense and their impact has been determined in totality. The increase in population might, by and large, be proportionate to the increasing opportunities of employment. Srinagar was passing through such a stage that it had to expand its limits to cope with the influx from the suburbs. There was a perceptible increase in the population between 1891 and 1941. The rural-urban drift gave rise to a number of human problems. However, improvements in the conditions of sanitation, lighting, water works, medical aid and general administration facilitated the process of accommodation of increasing population.

Besides, the rapid growth of population was generated by the inauguration of an era of industrial development. There was a remarkable growth of silk, woollen and tourist industries. Fresh avenues of employment to labour were provided also by such gainful activities as electric installations, hotels and restaurants. The neighbouring quarries were exploited for construction of roads and private and public buildings. These pursuits along with the general industrial development widened the embrace of the city and enabled it to take within its lap the sizeable addition to the population.

The rapid growth and extension of the urban character of Srinagar during the period review is nothing short of a silent revolution in Kashmir society. Apart from providing increasing employment opportunities to the villagers, the wind of change blowing from the centre of urban development did not fail to affect and change the mode of life of the rural population in the hinterland. Growth of the tourist industry was a new phenomenon. Increased tourist traffic raised the dcmand for dairy and poultry products. In close proximity to the city rose a suburb humming with activity. This obviously pushed further and further out the hinterland. Villages, viz., Lassagan, Pampore and Shalteng took to dairying, poultry-farming and market gardening to cater to the requirements of the main urban centre of the Valley. The villagers coming for business to the city began taking advantages of the medical, educational and recreational facilities available to the city dwellers. The inference is that the city acted as a catalyst in the whole process of socio-cultural transformation.

The growth of city life with its migratory population gave rise to hotels and restaurants. The exigencies of office work affected the orthodoxy of many. Even in the so-called Muslim hotels people belonging to different creeds and groups had often to take their meals together, as the hotel keeper could not afford to make separate arrangements for members of different religious communities.

In the old economy almost every occupation was hereditary. But the period under review saw a radical change in the occupational pattern of many of the trading and artisan classes. This was necessitated by the decline of industries like those of shawl and paper-making and above all by the expansion of silk, carpet, woollen, hotel and tourist industries. We have seen how the decline of shawl industry forced the shawl weavers to take to carpet-making and sawing. Even the Kashmiri Pandits overcame their prejudices against manual labour. By 1901 some of them were found working side by side with the so-called 'low-born' Muslims in the silk factory. They were also found gradually giving up their ideal of Government service and turning to trade in increasing numbers.[1]

The emergence of rudiments of capitalist relations involving the hiring of wage labour for the production of surplus value seems to have been present in the economy of Srinagar during the period under discussion. As feudal exploitation grew, so did the forms of struggle by the emerging groups of the proletariat against the exploiters become more diverse and acute. In course of time did also grow class consciousness of the workers and their class solidarity as is evidenced by their protests from the very start of the Dogra rule against the practice of employing them in bondage, arbitrary acts by officials and heavy taxation. Their struggle took such forms as creating hullabaloo, stopping business activity, refusal to fulfil orders and pay taxes, migration to the Punjab and last but not the least their historic revolt of 29th April, 1865 against the extreme forms of exploitation. Since the shawl weavers were weak and immature, they could not shake the power of the strong exploiting class. But there can be no blinking the fact that the ruthless suppression of the shawl weavers rebellion heralded a new sense of awareness among the oppressed people of Srinagar.

The close of the first quarter of the twentieth century marked significant economic and political developments. In 1924 the workers in the State-owned silk factory resorted to strike. It was an important event in the socio-economic life of Srinagar. The strike did not last long, as it perhaps could not in those early days. Nonetheless, it showed itself as a harbinger of a new age—an age of socialism and trade unionism. These new developments projected the social tensions inherent in the emerging industrial system.

With the advent of Christian educators in Srinagar, the indigenous educational institutions known as *maktabs and patshalas* gradually began to go into oblivion. The Hindu and Muslim education both was in the hands of the *Pandits* and the *Ulama*. Therefore educational reform did not keep pace with the changing social conditions. The traditional social and religious matrix was loosened only after English education initiated by the Church Missionary Society began to make itself felt.

There seems to be little doubt that Srinagar continuously improved in point of literacy during 1901 and 1941. It would be noticed that the decline in illiteracy was more pronounced between 1931 and 1941. The literate population was only 2% percent at the beginning of this century. In 1941 it formed nearly a quarter of the population of the city. Though the Pandits were educationally advanced, the Census figures, however, reveal that education was slowly percolating among the Muslims too. As literacy and learning spread new avenues of employment began to open before the Hindus and the Muslims.

It is also important to note that the different reactions of the Hindus and the Muslims to English education profoundly moulded the development of the two communities. While modern education increasingly spread among the Kashmir Pandits, this naturally meant that they dominated the liberal professions and higher posts in the Government. Thus concessions and privileges in education and appointment to government jobs were demanded for the Muslims from the Government by various Muslim organizations. There was an attempt to argue that the Muslim community was backward and that concessions were necessary to enable it to catch up with the advanced community. But it should be remembered that backwardness was claimed in a secular context. The modes of expressing public opinion were distinctly western, or rather modern—newspapers, associations and organizations, public meetings and petitions.

Western education brought in its wake a number of cultural changes. Even purely personal matters like wedding customs could not escape the new influence. At least the educated among the city-dwellers, and sometimes other sections of the urban population, in partial imitation of their westernized brethren, hired jeeps and motor-cars for the bridal procession. Not unoften were the bridegrooms clad in western style suits and shoes. It was here that the cultural impact of the British on the neo-literati was felt. That such an influence was mostly displayed at weddings, which, otherwise, were solemnized in the traditional manner, suggests an assimilation of new types of behaviour rather than a displacement of the old by the new patterns of behaviour.

Modern education with an occidental bias together with the influence of European teachers led inevitably to change in taste and fashion of the youth. The change in fashion was evident in the dress of the educated, who now put on trousers, jackets and waist-coats in preference to the traditional *pheran* and *pochh*. The out-door games that the students were required to play in the C. M. S. School conspired to rule out the use of old and out-of-date Kashmiri dress. The use of nose-rings, heavy earrings and wooden clogs was given up too in the process. Thus Biscoe, the pioneer of English education in Kashmir, used games as a powerful instrument of change and reform.

Hitherto people had been indulging in leisure time activities which were age-old and traditional. Because of poverty, Kashmiris took part in games and sports which were least expensive. However, the innovations like radio and cinema revolutionized the whole concept of pastime. Apart from serving as useful media of enterainment and instruction, radio and cinema both began to occupy a prominent place in the changing social order. No doubt, with the spread of vulgar tastes owing to the advent of the cinema as also with the increasing popularity of film dance and Hindustani film music, the *hafiza* dancers lost their hold on the people. With the recession of *hafiza* dance and music, *Sufiana Kalam*, —vocal—cum instrumental music, essentially mystic, had only the surival value. It may appear paradoxical to observe that *sufiana kalam* which was once sung by the trained dancers is now sung by men.

The increase in the population of Srinagar made it exceedingly necessary for the Government to relieve pressure on the old city. The readily available land at Sheikh Bagh and around Amira Kadal was acquired for constructing buildings for offical and public purposes. Amira Kadal and the area above Sheikh Bagh are today the sites of the former Kashmir Residency, new courts, schools, colleges, hotels and restaurants. For the first time was a British urban pattern of architecture imposed on the new part of the city,[2] which came up in seeming contrast to that of the old part of Srinagar. Main features of the new part of the city were broad and straight roads, impressive mansions, parks and playgrounds.

Nature abounding in scenic beauty has kept Kashmiris ever sensitive. It was for the Christian Missionaries in Srinagar to make the sensitive people critical of their own social organisation and some, if not many, of its institutions. A number of organisation—the *sabhas* and *anjumans*—came up to the counter the religious propaganda of the missionaries. These organisations held meetings in an orderly manner; passed resolutions and made their views known to the people and the authorities. The matters dicussed at these meetings and covered by several resolutions passed pertained to the age of marriage of girls, girls education, rich dowry, widow remarriage, high cost of wedding, funeral ceremonies and similar other issues of vital importance to society. In consequence, the Government also evinced a keen interest in social reform. It is significant that Maharaja Hari Singh placed on the statute book of the state some measures vital to the advancement of the people, such as the prevention of Infant Marriage Regulation, raising the age of consent to 14 for girls and 18 for boys and prohibition of juvenile smoking.

By 1947 the press in Srinagar had developed as the most effective organ of public opinion. Not only did the press reflect the news and aspirations of the various classes of people; it actually helped in moulding opinion itself. *In fact, the ideas which constituted public opinion in Srinagar during 1932-1947 laid the ideological foundation of the 'New Kashmir.'*

The national movement started in 1931 led to a new awareness, a new awakening and a new urge to question the accepted, "orthodox" and traditional values in all fields of social activity. There was a desire to have a just society. It is against this background that the literature of this era has been studied. The new poets breathed a fresh life into the literature of the land bringing forth the importance of new themes such as poverty, social inequality and peace.

With the contact of a foreign culture, mainly English, there was a great shifting of values in the older and new modes of thinking and behaviour. Although there is no evidence whatever of the joint family system having broken up under the impact of western, mainly English education, it is more than likely that small tensions and conflicts must have generated in families which, in our day, have, manifestly cracked, if not disintegrated.

The pattern of culture receiving the traits, acts, reacts and operates like a sieve in the process of assimilation. Social change was not merely cumulative but integrative and synthetic. Srinagar, which for a long time stood as a separate culture area, grew sensitive to change, and was drawn into the vortex of an integrative system, which one may conclude is very much in evidence even today.

NOTES:

1. *Census,* 1931, part I, p-102.
2. The construction of new buildings in the English style with many glass windows marked the decline of famous *pinjara* work of Srinagar.

APPENDIX A: FORCED LABOUR

It is important to note that occasionally *begar* was also conducted in Srinagar, though its burden always fell on the poor villagers. On one occasion, about three to four hundred Muslims offering prayers in a mosque of the city were seized by Gulab Singh's officials and they were forced to carry ammunitions (Mirza Saif-ud-din, *op.cit.*,vol.iv, f. 62a).In the earlier part of Gulab Singh's reign it was a common practice to impress men and women of the city for work at the time of saffron collection. No remuneration was given to them. Instead, they were beaten by the officials. (Mir Saif Ullah, *op.cit.*, pp.60, 81). This evil custom came to an end owing to the efforts of Raj Kak Dhar *(ibid,* pp.87-88). Sometimes artisans and traders were also seized for *begar.* See *Cashmere Misgovernment* (*Kashmir Papers*, p.74); also *Where three Empires Meet*, pp.69-70. For greater details ,see Ishaq Khan, "Some Aspects of Corvee in Kashmir," *Research Biannual* , Vol. I, No.II 1976 pp. 58-71

APPENDIX B: GROWING AWARENESS OF THE MUSLIMS TO THE BENEFITS OF GIRLS EDUCATION

Earlier in 1909, some Muslims of Amira Kadal submitted a petition to Maharaja Pratap Singh's Foreign Minister. Wrote the petitioners:

"There is no Girls School for Mohammedan Girls in the vicinity of Ameera Kadal and the want for such a school has been keenly felt by your petitioners for a long time. Proper school mistresses are not available by private and individual efforts and moreover the benefits derived from systematic public institutions of this kind are much more in number and value as compared to private tuition arranged for girls at their own houses."

"We are alive to the fact that the State is graciously lending proper impetus to the spread of female education among the subjects of H.H. the Maharaja under your guidance and confidently hope that you will kindly see your way to recommending the establishment of a Girls School for Mohammedan Girls at Ameera Kadal. A similar institution already exists for our Hindu brethren in this part of the city and it is our earnest request that the favour may be extended to the other section of His Highness the Maharaja Sahib Bahadur's subjects and others in His Highness's territory." See J&k (G. R.), F. No. 30/P-94,1909.

GLOSSARY

Alwand	plain pashmine
anharish	virgin
Asthan	shrine
Babzada	custodians at the shrine of Hazrat Makhdoom Sahib
Bachha	male dancer
Badamwari	almond garden
Bahi	account ledger
Bania	money-lender
Begar	forced labour
Bahands	actors
Bohar	Hindu grocer
Bund	embankment
Burka	veil worn by Muslim women in Kashmir
Butadar	embroidered
Charkha	spinning wheel
Charkgar	cleaner
Chhan	carpenter
Daesh	a piece of string tied by the devotees to the inner entrance of shrines in Kashmir.
Dal-guldar	applique
Darogah	superintendent
Darvesh	a saint
Dastar	turban
Degchi	cauldron
Doonga	boat
Dumbael	a kind of folk dance
Dusa	shawl
Futwa	decree
Gad Hanz	fisherman

Gaash	light
Ghazal	elegy, song of love
Gair	water chest-nut
Gogij	turnip
Hadith	sayings of Prophet Muhammad (SAW)
Hafiza	dancing girl
Hakim	a physician
Hamam	warm bath
Hanji	boatman
Hashia Bafi	fringe weaving
Herat	shivratri
Hokh phal	dried fruit
Jalakdozi	embroidery
Jamawar	a flowered shawl of typical style
Kadal	bridge
Karkhana	workshop
Karkhanadar	owner of the work shop
Kar-i-Kalamdani	art of making pens cases, trays, books, etc. of papier mache.
Kangar	a portable brazier
Khar	blacksmith
Kharavas	wooden clogs
Kharwar or khar	ass' load. It weighs two maunds corre-sponding to 177 lbs. The *kharwar is* divided into 16 *tracks*, the *track* again into 6 *seers*.
Khatam-i-nabuat	finality of the Prophethood
Khusnavis	men of beautiful penmanship
Kori-i-Moul	father of daughters
Lagenchir	marriage contract deed (among Kashmiri Pandits)
Leig	an earthen vessel also used for preparing vegetables
Lois	woollen blankets
Manan	an earthen vessel also used as a portable brazier
Marsiya	a poem of mourning
Masnavi	narrative poem composed of distichs corresponding in measure
Mela	fair
Mufti	a specialist in Muslim law who gives an authoritative opinion.
Munda kath	progeny of widows

Murid	disciple
Nadru	leaf-steam of nilum-bium specicosum
Naghma	song
Nangar	a landless labour or village artisan
Naqash	engraver
Nautch	dance
Nazrana	gift
Pardah	a veil
Pattu	coarse woollen rug
Pheran	a long loose wrapper
Pinjara	lattice-work
Pir	a spiritual guide
Pirzadas	descendants of Sayyids
Pochh	inner garment of cotton
Qalamadan	pen boxes
Qanz	mortar for thrashing rice
Qasaba	headgear of Muslim women
Qazi	the Islamic judge
Rabab	guitar
Rufugar	darner
Roshanghar	polisher
Sahi	account ledger
Samavar	kettle
Shagird	pupil
Shali	grain
Shalwar	trousers
Sharbat	a drink or a sip
Shikara	small boat for passengers
Shootilbud	gini of smallpox
Sufiana Kalam	classical music of Kashmir
Tahar	cooked rice; rice coloured with turmeric
Talim	paper on which design of carpets or shawl is written
Tapan tsini	charcoal
Taranga	Pandit women's headgear
Tawiz	amulet
Tur	adze
Ustad	master workman
Vidwah	the widow
Waba	cholera

Wagu	mat
Waza	a professional cook
Wani	a trader in salt, oil, spices, snuff, sugar, tea, cotton piece goods etc.
Watal	scavenger
Wazwan	feast
Yander	cotton spinning wheel
Yarmadozi	embroidery
Zhep Zhep	hide and seek

BIBLIOGRAPHY

I. PERSIAN MANUSCRIPT SOURCES

Aba Rafi-ud-din Ahmed, *Nawadir-ul-Akhbar*, B. M Add. 24029, Research Library, Srinagar.

Baharistan-i- Shahi (Anonymous), Research Library, Srinagar.

Khanyari, Ghulam Nabi Shah, *Wajeez-ut-Tawarikh*, Research Library, Srinagar.

Mirjanpuri, Mulla Mohammad Shah Khalil, *Tarikh-i-Kashmir*, Vol. II, No. 800, Research Library, Srinagar.

Mishkati, Daud, *Asrar-ul-Abrar*, Research Library, Srinagar.

Saif-ud-din, Mirza, *Akhbarat-i-Darbar-i-Maharaja Gulab Singh*, 13 Vols. Research Library, Srinagar.

Saif-Ullah, Mir, *Tarikh-nama Kashmir*, Ibn-i-Mahjoor's transcript.

Sayyid Ali, *Tarikh-i-Sayyid Ali*, Research Library, Srinagar.

II. PERSIAN PRINTED SOURCES WITH TRANSLATIONS

Abul Fazl i) *Ain-i-Akbari*, Calcutta (Bib. Ind.) 1872-73, English Tr., Vol. I by Blochmann, Calcutta, 1927, Vols. II and III by H. S. Jarret, Calcutta, 1868-94. ii) *Akbar-nama* (3 vols.), English Tr., by Henry Beveridge, Calcutta, 1897-1939.

Badauni, Abdul Qadir, *Muntakhab-ut-Tawarikh*, Calcutta (Bib. Ind.), 1865-69 English Tr., 3 Vols. by Ranking, Lowe and Haig, Calcutta, 1884-1925.

Diddamari, Mohammad Azam, *Tarikh-i-Azami,* Muhammadi Press, Lahore, A. H. 1303, Urdu Tr. under *Tarikh-i-Kashmir Azami* by Munshi Ashraf Ali, Delhi Madrassa, Delhi, 1846.

Ganesh Lal, Munshi, *Siyahat-i-Kashmir*, March-June 1846, English Tr., by Vidya Sagar Suri (The Punjab Government Record Office Publication), Simla, 1955.

Hassan Shah, Moulvi, *Tarikh-i-Hassan*, 4 Vols. Research Library, Srinagar. Urdu translation of Vol. III (Political) by Moulvi Mohammad Ibrahim, Srinagar.

Jahangir, Empror, *Tuzuk-i-Jahangiri*, 2 Vols., English Tr., by A. Rogers and H. Beveridge, London, 1909-14.

Kripa Ram, Dewan i) *Gulzar-i-Kashmir*, Lahaore, 1870. ii) *Gulab-nama* Jammu, 1875.

Mirza Haidar Daughlat, *Tarikh-i-Rashidi*, English Tr., by E. Denison Ross with introduction by E. N. Elias, London 1895.

Miskin, Haji Mohi-ud-din, *Tarikh-i-Kabir-i-Kashmir*, Amritsar, A. H. 1322.

Nizam-ud-din Ahmad, *Tabqat-i-Akbari*, 3 Vols. Calcutta (Bib. Ind.), 1927-36; Lucknow Edition, 1920.

III. TRANSLATIONS OF SANSKRIT SOURCES

Jonaraja Pandit, *Rajatarangini*, Calcutta and Bombay Editions, 1835 and 1875; English Tr., by J. C. Dutt under the title *Kings of Kashmira*, vol. III, Calcutta, 1879-98, pp. 1-98

Kalhana, Pandit, *Rajatarangini*, English Tr., with introduction and notes by Sir Aurel Stein, 2 vols. London, Westminster, 1900; Indian edition, Moti Lal Banarsi Das, Delhi-1961.

Khemendra, Pandit, *Lokaprakasa*, English Tr., of some extracts by Dr. A. Weber, *Indische Studien*, XVIII, 1898.

Srivara, Pandit, *Jaina-Rajatarangini*, English Tr., by J. C. Dutt as *Kings of Kashmira*, vol. III, pp. 98-336, Calcutta, 1935.

Suka and Prajabhata, *Rajavalipatika*, English Tr., by J.C Dutt under the title *Kings of Kashmira*, vol. III, pp. 337-427, Calcutta, 1935.

IV. OFFICIAL RECORDS

A) The National Archives of India, New Delhi.

Proceedings, Foreign and Political Department, 1846-1924.

B) The Jammu and Kashmir Sate Archives, Jammu Repository.

Persian Records of the Jammu and Kashmir Government, 1846-1867.

General Records of the Jammu and Kashmir Government, 1868-1924.

V. UNPUBLISHED OFFICIAL REPORTS

Ganga Nath Report, Srinagar, 1944.

IV. PRIVATE PAPERS

J. L Jalali's Collections, The J & K State Archives, Srinagar.

VII. PUBLISHED SOURCES

A) **Parlimentry Papers**
Papers relating to Kashmir, London, 1890.

B) **Official Reports**
Census of India, Reports on the Jammu and Kashmir State, 1891. 1911, 1921, 1931, 1941, 1961.
Census of Srinagar District, 1961.
Adminstration Reports of the Jammu and Kashmir State, 1873-1945.
Report on the Municipal Administration of Srinagar, 1920-1921 by P. A Koul Bamzai, Srinagar, 1921.
Report on the Municipal Adminsitration of Srinagar (1923-1924) by P. A. Koul Bamzai, Srinagar 1924.
Annual Administration Reports of The Jammu and Srinagar Municipalities, Town Areas and Visitors Bureau, Jammu, 1940-1942.
Annual Adminstration Reports of the Jammu and Srinagar Municipalities, Town Planning and Public Health Departments, Jammu, 1944-1945.
Report on the Sanitation of Srinagar city by Sardar Mohammad Hayat Khan, 1893 (Printed at the Ranbir Prakash Press).
Report on Cholera Epidemic in Kashmir by Rai Bahadur Asutos Mitra, Calcutta, 1982.
Annual Adminstration Reports of the Education Department, J & K State (1911-1924).
The adminstration Report of the Education, Boys Scouts, Libraries, Archaeological, Reserch and Musuem Deparments (last 6 months of Samvat 1998 and Samvat 1999), Jammu, 1945.
Report on the Economic Survey of Gubba Manufacture in Kashmir by R.K Bhan, Srinagar, 1938.
Report on the Economic Survey of Wood Carving Industry and Trade in Kashmir by R.K Bhan, Srinagar, 1938.
Report on the Economic Survey of Silverware Industry in Kashmir

by R.K Bhan, Lahore, 1938.

Report on the Economic Survey of Carpet Industry in Kashmir by R.K Bhan, Srinagar, 1938.

Report on the Economic Survey of Embroidery Industry in Kashmir by P. N. Chaku, Lahore (n. d).

Report on the Cottage Textile Industries in Kashmir and their Prospective Development by Alfred F. Barker, Leeds, England, 1933.

Sharp's Report, Calcutta, 1916.

Report on the Educational Reorganisation Committee, Srinagar, 1939.

Report on the Commission Appointed under the order of His Highness the Maharaja Bahadur dated 12th November, 1931 to enquire into Grevances and Complaints, 2nd, ed. Jammu, 1933 (Referred to in the text under the title Glancy Commission's Report).

Note on the High Prices of Shali in Srinagar by Khan Bahadur Ahmed Khan, Jammu, 1903.

Report with regard to the Floods in Jammu and Kashmir, Srinagar. 1928.

Report on State Granaries Srinagar (1927-1928) by Capt. R. G. Wreford, Srinagar, 1929.

Techno-Economic Survey of the Jammu and Kashmir State, 1969, New Delhi.

(C) Selections from the Punjab Government Records.

Lahore Political Diaries, 1846-1849, Vol. III to VI.

(D) Punjab Adminstration Reports

Select volumes.

(E) Report on Native Newspapers, Punjab

Years: 1888, 1890-95, 1901, 1907, 1911, 1923, 1926.

(F) Annual Report of the C. M. S. School, Srinagar.

Jerry Building in Kashmir, 1913.

Men in the Making, 1914.

Road Making in Kashmir, 1915.

Rock Shifting in Kashmir, 1916.

Forging up Stream in Kashmir, 1917.

A School in Being, 1918.

Harnessing the Waters in Kashmir, 1917.

Still Pegging Away in Kashmir, 1920.

Straighter Streeing in Kashmir, 1921.

A School in Action, 1922.

Amphibious Scouts in Kashmir, 1927.

Crusading in Kashmir, 1928.
Grinding Grit in Kashmir, 1929.
Steeple-Chasing in Kashmir, 1930-31.
Pile Driving in Kashmir, 1931-32.
Riding the Storms in Kashmir, 1932-33.
Hewing Timber in Kashmir, 1933-34.
Victory After Defeat, 1934-35.
Digging Foundations in Kashmir, 1935-36.
Driving the Djinns out of Kashmir, 1936-37.
Against the Current in Kashmir, 1937-38.
With pick and shovel in Kashmir, 1938-39.
Still Carrying on in Kashmir, 1939-40.
Fifty Years Steeple Chase in Kashmir, 1940-41.

(G) **Reports and Pamphlets of the Christian Missionaries**
An Account of Kashmir Medical Mission, Lahore, 1891.
Cashmere (Pamphlets India collected by E. Bickersteth), Calcutta, n.d.

(H) **The Indian Annual Register:**
An Annual Digest of Public Affairs in India, edited by N. N. Mitra, Annual Register Office, Calcutta, July-Dec., 1931 and January-July, 1932 issues.

(I) **Travellers Accounts**

Adams, W. L — *Wanderings of a Naturalist in India etc.* Edinburgh, 1867.
Arbuthnot, James. — *A Trip to Kashmir*, Calcutta, 1900.
Arora, R. C. — *Kashmir: Land of Celestial Charms* Agra, 1940.
Bellew, H. G. — *Kashmir and Kashghar*, London, 1875.
Bernier, Dr. Francois. — *Travels in the Mogul Emprior*, London, 1891.
Bourbel, Major General de. — *Routes in Jammu and Kashmir*, Calcutta, 1897.
Boys, H. S. — *Seven Hundred Miles in Kashmmir*, Lucknow, 1886.
Brinckman, Arthur — *Wrongs of Kashmir*, London, 1868.
Burrows, R. A — *Cashmir En Famille,* Calcutta, 1895.
Bruce, C. G. — *Kashmir*, London, 1915.
Clark, H — *Summer Scenes in Kashmir*, London, 1858.
Darrah, H. Z — *Sport in the Highlands of Kashmir*,

London, 1898.

Denys, F. Ward — *Our Summer in the Vale of Kashmir*, Washington, 1915.

Doughlas, Willian — *Beyond the Himalayas*, London, 1953.

Doughty, Marion — *A foot through the Kashmir Valleys*, London, 1901.

Du Jarric — *An Account of the Jusuit Missiion to the Court of Akbar* Eng. Tr. by C. H Payne under title *Akbar and the Jesuits*, Broadway Series, London. 1926.

Dugsal — *Letters from India and Kashmir*, London, 1874.

Dunmore, — *The Earl of* *The Pamirs*, Vol, I London, 1893.

Eckenstein, Oscar — *The Karakoroms and Kashmir*, London, 1896.

Etherton, P. T. — *Across the Roof of the World*, London, 1911.

Forster, George — *A Journey from Bangal to England , through the Northern Part of India, Kashmir, Afganistan, and Persia, and into Russia by the Caspian Sea*, 2 vols. London, 1808.

Gilbert. C. F — *Hints to Travellers in Kashmir*, Calcutta, 1887.

Gordon J. D. — *Work and Play in India and Kashmir*, London, 1893.

Harvey, Mrs. — *Advantures of a Lady in Tartary,Tibet, China and Kashmir*, London, 1854.

Honiberger, — *Thirty - five years in the East*, London, 1852,

John Martin — Second edition, Calcutta, 1905.

Hugel, Baron Charles — *Travels in Kashnir and the Punjab*, London, 1845.

Knight, John — *Diary of a Pedestrian in Cashmere and Tibet*, London, 1863.

Lal, Munshi Ganesh — *Siyahat-i-Kashmir*, March-June, 1846, Eng. Tr. by Vida Sagar Suri (The Punjab Government Record Office Publication), Simla, 1955.

Lam bert, Cowley — *A Trip to Kashmir and Ladakh*, London, 1877.

Majid, Moulvi Abdul — *Sair-i-Kashmmir* (Urdu), Lucknow, 1935.

Mar, Walter Dal — *The Romanitic East*, London, 1906.

Milne, James — *The Road to Kashmir*, London, 1929.

Moorcroft, William and George Trebeck — *Travels in the Himalayan Provinces of Hindustan and the Punjab, in Ladakh and Kashmir*, 2 Vol, London, 1841.

Montogomerie, T. G. — *Routes in the Western Himalayas*, Dera Dun, 1909.

Morison, Margaret C — *A Lonely Summer in Kashmir*, London, 1904.

Murray, Aynsley — *Our Visit to Kashmir, Hindustan and Ladakh*, London, 1879.

Murray, John — *Hand-book of the Punjab*, Kashmir,etc. London, 1883

Nazaroff, P. S. — *Moved on from Kashghar to Kashmir*, London, 1935.

Norris, Dermot — *Kashmir: The Switzerland of India* Calcutta 1932.

Oconnor,V.C. Scoff — *The Charm of Kashmir,* London,1920

Parbway, Plorence — *The Emerald Set with Pearls,* London, 1909.

Pelsaert, Francisco — *The Remonstrantie*: Translated from the Dutch by W.H.Moreland and P. Geyl, Cambridge,1925.

Petrocokino,A — *Cashmere*: *Three weeks in a Houseboat*, Bombay,1920.

Pirie, P. — *Kashmir, The Land of Streams and Solitudents*, London,1908

Prinsep, val.c — *Imperial India and Kashmir*,2 vols. London,1853.

Schonberg, Baron — *Travels in India and Kashmir*, 2 vols. London, 1853.

Swinburne,T.R. — *Holoday in the Happy Valley*: *with pen and pencil*, London, 1907.

Taylor, Bayard — *Travels in Cashmere etc.*, New York, 1893.

Temple,Sir Richard — *Journals Kept in Hyderabad, Kashmir, Sikkim, and Nepal*, 2 vols. 1859-71, London, 1887.

Thorp, Robert — *Cashmere Misgovernment*, London, 1870. (Typed copy in the State Archives, and Srinagar).

Torrens,L.T col.Henry — *Travels in Ladhak, Tartary and Kashmir*, London,1863

Vigne, G.T — *Travels in Kashmir, Ladhak, Iskardo, countries adjoining the mountain courses of the Indus and the Himalaya, north of the Punjab*, 2 vols. London, 1842

Wadia, A.S. — *In the Land of Lalla Rookh*, London, 1921.

Wakefield,W. — *The Happy Valley*, London, 1879.

Wilson, Andrew — *The Abode of Snow*, London, 1875.

(J) Other Published Sources

(a) ENGLISH

Aitchison, C.U. — *A Collection of Treaties, Engagements and Sanads relating to India and Neighbouring countries*, Fifth Edition, Calcutta, 1929-33.

Bamzai, Anand Koul, — *The Kashmiri Pandit*, Calcutta, 1924.

Barton, W — *The Princes of India*, London,1934

Bazaz, Prem Nath — *Inside Kashmir*, Srinagar, 1941.

271

Bascoe, Tyndale — *Kashmir in Sunlight and Shade*, London, 1922.

Fifty Years Against the Stream, Mysore, 1930.

Autobiography, London, 1951.

Bose J.C — *Cashmere and its Prince*, Calcutta, 1889.

Buhler, George — *Detailed Report of a Tour in Search of Sanskrit Manuscripts made in Kashmir, Rajputana and Central Asia*, Bombay, 1877.

Carus-Wilson, Mrs. Ashley — *Irene Petrie, Missionary to Kashmir*, London, 1900.

Calrk, Henry Martyn — *Robert Clark of the Punjab*, London, 1907.

Clark, Robert — *The Mission s of the C. M. S. and C. E. Z. M. S. in the Punjab and Sindh*, London,1904 (Edited and revised by Robert Maconachie). Collet, John *A Guide for Vistrors to Kashmir*, Calcutta, 1898

Dhar, M.A. *Kashmir: Eden of the East*, Allahabad, 1945.

Digby, William *Condemned Unheard*, London, 1890.

Drew, Frederic *The Jummoo and Kashmir Territories*, London, 1875.

The northern barier of india, London, 1877.

Duke, J. *Kashmir Handbook*, Calcutta, 1903.

Elmsile,w.j.and thompson, *Seed Time in Kashmir*, London, 1875.

Gadru, S.N. *Kashmir Papers*, Srinagar,1973(ed.)

Galwan, Ghulam Rasool. *Servant of Sahibs*, Cambridge,1923.

Ince, Dr. John *The Kashmir Handbook*, calcutta, 1888.

Jalali, Jia lal *Economics of Foodgrains in Kashmir*, Lahore,1931.

Kashmeer and its Shawls (Anonymous), London, !875.

Knight, E.F. *Where Three Empires Meet*, London, 1905.

Koul, Saligram *Bioghrapy of Maharaja Gulab Singh*, Srinagar,1923.

Lawrence, Sir Walter *The Valley of Kashmir*, London, 1895.

The India We Served , London, 1928.

Molony *History of Kashmir Christian Society for India*, Madras, 1920.

Neve, Ernest *Beyond the Pir Panjal*, London, 1915.

A Crusader in Kashmir, London, 1928.

Things Seen in Kashmir, London , 1913.

Neve, Arthur *Picturesque Kashmir*, London, 1900.

Thirty Years in Kashmir, London, 1913.

The Tourist Guide to Kashmir, Ladhak, Skardo etc., Lahore, 1896.

Sedgwick, W. *India for Sale : Kashmir Sold*, Calcutta, 1886.

Shephered, A.P. *Arthur neve of Kashmir of Asia*, Allahabad, 1943.

Stock, Eugene *The History of the Church Missionary Society , its Enivorment, its Men and its work,*
4 vols. London , 1889, 1916.

Wakefield, G. E. C — *Recollecions — Fifty Years in the Service of India*, Lahore, 1943.

Ward,Colonel A.E. — *Sportsman's Guide to Kashmir and Ladhak,* Calcutta, 1887.

Wardle, T. — *Kashmir* : its New Silk Industry, London, 1904.

White, Charles — *The Cashmere Shawl*, London, 1840.

Younghusband, Francis — *Kashmir*, Edinburgh, 1909.

(b) URDU

Azad, Abdul Ahad — *Kashmir Zuban Aur Shairi*, 3 vols. Srinagar, 1959.

Fouq, Mohammad din — *Mashahir - i - Kashmir*, Lahore, 1930.

Khasta, Hargopal Koul — *Guldasta - i - Kashmir*, Lahore, 1883.

Majid, Moulvi Abdul — *Sair - i - Kashmir*, Lucknow, 1936.

(c) KASHMIRI

Arif Beg, Ghulam Hasan — *Rubaiyat*, Srinagar.1954.
Aagar Wonie, Srinagar, n. d.

Hajini, Mohi-ud-din — *Koe : Shir Shoe : Yiree* (Intikhab), New Delhi, 1960.

Koul, Zinda — *Sumran*, Srinagar, 1955

Mahjoor, Ghulam Ahamad — *Kalam -i- Mahjoor*, Srinagar, 1949.
Payaam -i- Mahjoor, Srinagar, 1946.

VIII. NEWSPAPERS
(a) URDU

The Akhbar -i- Kashmir, Lahore.
The Albarq, Srinagar.
The Daur -i- Jadeed, Delhi.
The Hamdard, Srinagar.
The Haqiqat, Srinagar.
The Islah, Srinagar
The Kashmiri Magazine, Lahore
The Kesari, Srinagar
The Khalid, Srinagar
The Khidmat, Srinagar

The Martand, Srinagar.
The Muslim, Srinaga.
The Ranbir, Jammu.
The Sadaqat, Sringar.

(b) ENGLISH

The Khidmat, Srinagar.
The Kashmir Times, Srinagar.
The Qaumi Dard, Srinagar
The Hindustan Times, New Delhi
The Statesman, Calcutta.
The Pioneer, Allahabad.
The Civil and Military Gazette.
The Indian Express, New Delhi.
The Consumer Gazette, New Delhi
The Eastern Times, Lahore.
The Satesman, Delhi.
The United India And Indian States.
The Service of India.
The Sunrise.
Friend of India.
The Times.

IX. GAZETTEERS

Bates,Major Charles Ellison, *A gazetteer of Kashmir and the Adjoining districts of Kishtwar, Badarwah, Jammu, Naoshera, Punch and the Valley of Kishanganga*, Calcutta, 1873.
Imperial Gazetteer of India, Provincial series of Jammu and *Kashmir*, Calcutta, 1909.

X. JOURNALS AND MAGAZINES

Indian Antiquary.
Journal of Asiatic Society of Bengal.
Vaishwa Bharti Journal.
East and West.
Islamic Culture.
Research Biannual.

The Church Missionary Intelligencer.
C.M. Review.
The Struggle.
Kashmir.
Kashmir Today.
Marg.
Cultural forum.

XI. SELECTED SECONDARY WORKS

a) ENGLISH

Bamzai, Anand Koul — *Geography of Jammu and Kashmir State*, Calcutta, 1913
Archaeological Remains in Kashmir, Lahore, 1935.

Bamzai, P.N.K. — A History of *Kashmir*: Political, Social and Cultural from the Earliest Times to the Presernt Day, Delhi, 1962.

Bazaz, Prem Nath — *The History of Struggle For Freedom in Kashmir, Cultural and Political From The Earliset Times*, New Delhi, 1954.
Kashmir in Crucible, New Delhi, 1967.
Daughters of Vitasta, New Delhi, 1959.

Cole, H.H. — *Illustration of Ancient Buildings in Kashmir*, London, 1869.

Cunningham, Major — *The Ancient Geography of India*, London, 1871.

Elmslie, Dr. — *Kashmiri English Dictionary*, 1876.

Faruquhar, J.N. — *Modern Religious Movements in India*, London 1929.

Fergusson, James P. — *Kashmir — An Historical Introduction*, London,1961.

Francke, A.H. — *Antiquities of India Tibet*, Parts I & II, Calcutta, 1914,1926.

Ganjoo, N.K. — *A Digest of Customary Law of Kashmir*, Srinagar, 1959.

Ghose, D.K. — *Kashmir in Transition*, Calcutta, 1974.

Grierson, Sir George — *Linguistic Survey of India*, Vol. , Part 2, Calcutta, 1911.
Dictionary of The Kashmiri Language,4

Volumes,Calcutta 1932.

Holmes, Brain — *Educational Policy and the Mission Schools*, London, 1967.

Husnain, Fidda Mohammad — *British Policy Towards Kashmir*, Delhi.

Irwin, John — *Shawls*, London, 1955.

Kak, R.C. — *Ancient Monuments of Kashmir*, London, 1933.

Kaul, Gwasha Lal — *A Short History of Kashmir*, Lahore, 1933.

Kaul, S. N. — *Kashmir Economics,* Srinagar, 1954.

Kaul, J. L. — *Studies in Kashmiri, Srinagar, 1968.*
Kashmiri Lyrics, Srinagar, 1945.

Kapur, M. L. — *Kashmir Sold and Snatched,* Jammu, 1968.

Kaumudi, Dr. — *Kashmir, its Cultural Heritage,* Bombay, 1952.

Kilam, Jia Lal — *A history of Kashmiri Pandits,* Srinagar, 1955.

Knowles, Hinton — *A Dictionary of Kashmiri Proverbs*, London, 1888
Folk Tales of Kashmir, London, 1983.

Lavan, Spencer — *The Ahmadiyah Movement: A History and Perspective*, New Delhi, 1974.

Madan, T.N. — *Family and Kinship*, Bombay, 1965.

Mohibbul Hasan — *Kashmir Under the Sultans*, Calcutta, 1959.

Nove, Ernest — *English-Kashmiri: A Vocabulary of the Kashmiri language*, Jammu, 1973 (New Ed.).

Nicholls, W.H. — *Muhammedun Architecture of Kashmir* (Archaelogical Survey Report, 1906-07), Calcutta, 1909.

Nurullah and Naik — *A History of Education in India during the British Period*, Madras, 1951.

Pannikar, K.M. — *The Founding of the Kashmir State-A Biography of Maharaja Gulab Singh*, London, 1930.

Parimu R.K. — *A History of Muslim Rule in Kashmir*, New Delhi, 1969.

Pithawalla, Maneck — *Introduction of Kashmir: its Geology and Geography*, Pakistan, 1953.

Raina, Trilokinath — *An Anthology of Modern Kashmiri Verse*, Poona, 1972.

Ray, Sunil Chandra — *The Early History and Culture of Kashmir*, calcutta, 1957.

Saraf, Mulk Raj — *Fifty Years as a Journalist*, Jammu, 1967.

Stein, Sir Aurel — *Memoir on the Map Illustrating the Ancient Geography of Kashmir*, Calcutta, 1899.

Catalogue of the Sanskrit Manuscripts in the Raghunatha Temple Library of His Highness the Maharaja of Jammu and Kashmir, London, 1894.

Stein and Grierson — *Hatim's Tales*, London, 1919.

Strart, Mrs. C.M.V — *The Gardens of the Great Moguls*, London, 1913.

Sufi, G.M.D. — *Kashir, Being a History of Kashmir from the Earliest Times to Our Own*, 2 Vols. Lahore 1948-49.

Tara Chand — *History of Freedom Movement in India*, Vol.1 II, Delhi, 1967.

Wade, T.R. — *Grammar of the Kashmiri Language*, London, 1988

(b) URDU

Aziz-ur-Rehman — *Raisul-ul-Ahrar, Naulana Habib-ur Rehman, Ludhianwi*, Talimi Samaj Markaz, Delhi, 1961.

Bazaz, Prem Nath — *Shair-i-Insaniat: Abdul Ahad Azad Kashmiri*, Delhi, 1952.

Das, Narsingh — *Tarikh-i-Dogra Desh*, Jammu, 1967.

Fani, Pitamber Nath Dhar — *Hubab*, Delhi, 1954.

Fouq, Munshi Mohammad Din — *Mukamal Tarikh-i-Kashmir*, Lahore, 1910.

Tarikh-i-Aqwam-i-Kashmir, Lahore, 1934.

Hamdani, Hakim Ghulam Safdar — *Shian-i-Kashmir*, Srinagar, 1970.

Khurshid, Abdus Salam — *Suhafat, Pakistan Wa Hind Maen*, Lahore, 1963.

Sufi, Mohi-ud-din — *Jammu Wa Kashmir Maen Urdu Suhafat*, Srinagar, 1973.

Taasir, Rashid — *Tahreek-i-Hurriyat-i-Kashmir*, (1931 -

39)., Vol. I, Srinagar, 1968.

(c) KASHMIRI

Rahbar, Autar Kishan *Koe: Shir Adabuch Tarikh*, vol. I, Srinagar, 1965.

INDEX

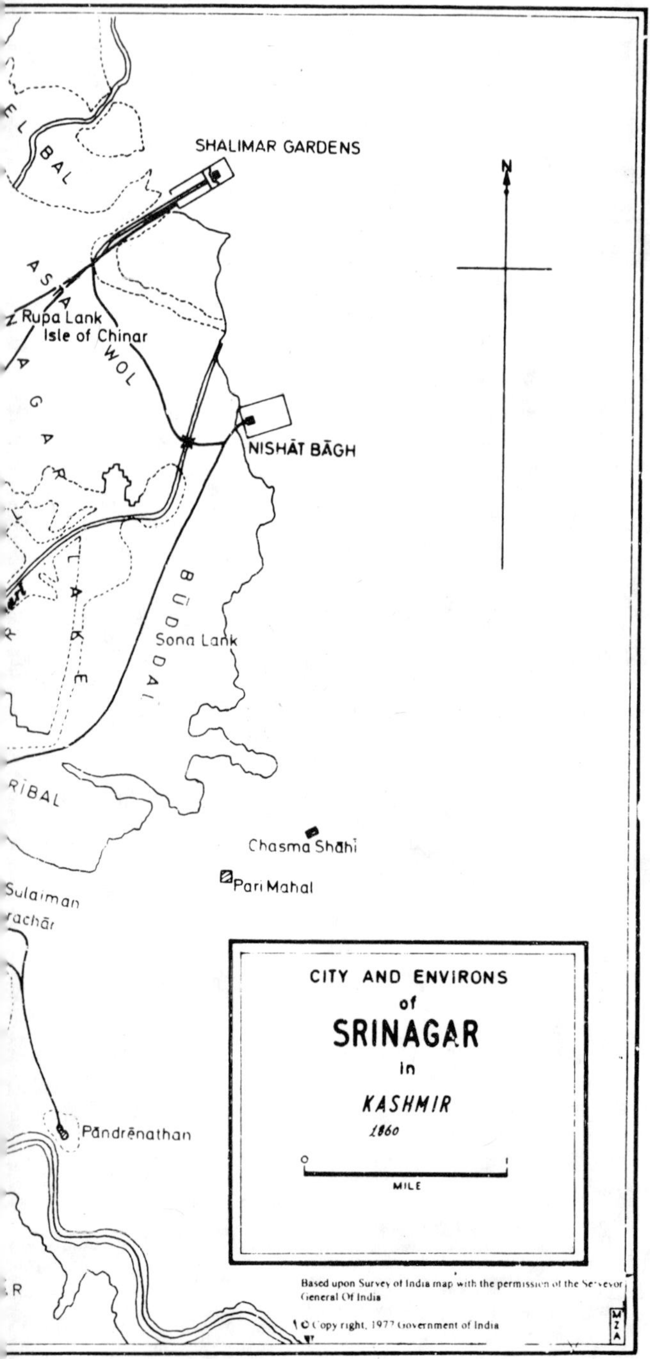
SHALIMAR GARDENS
N
Rupa Lank
Isle of Chinar
WOL
NISHĀT BĀGH
BŪDDAI
Sona Lank
Chasma Shāhi
Pari Mahal
Sulaiman
Pāndrēnathan
CITY AND ENVIRONS
of
SRINAGAR
in
KASHMIR
1860
0
1
MILE
Based upon Survey of India map with the permission of the Surveyor General Of India
© Copy right, 1977 Government of India

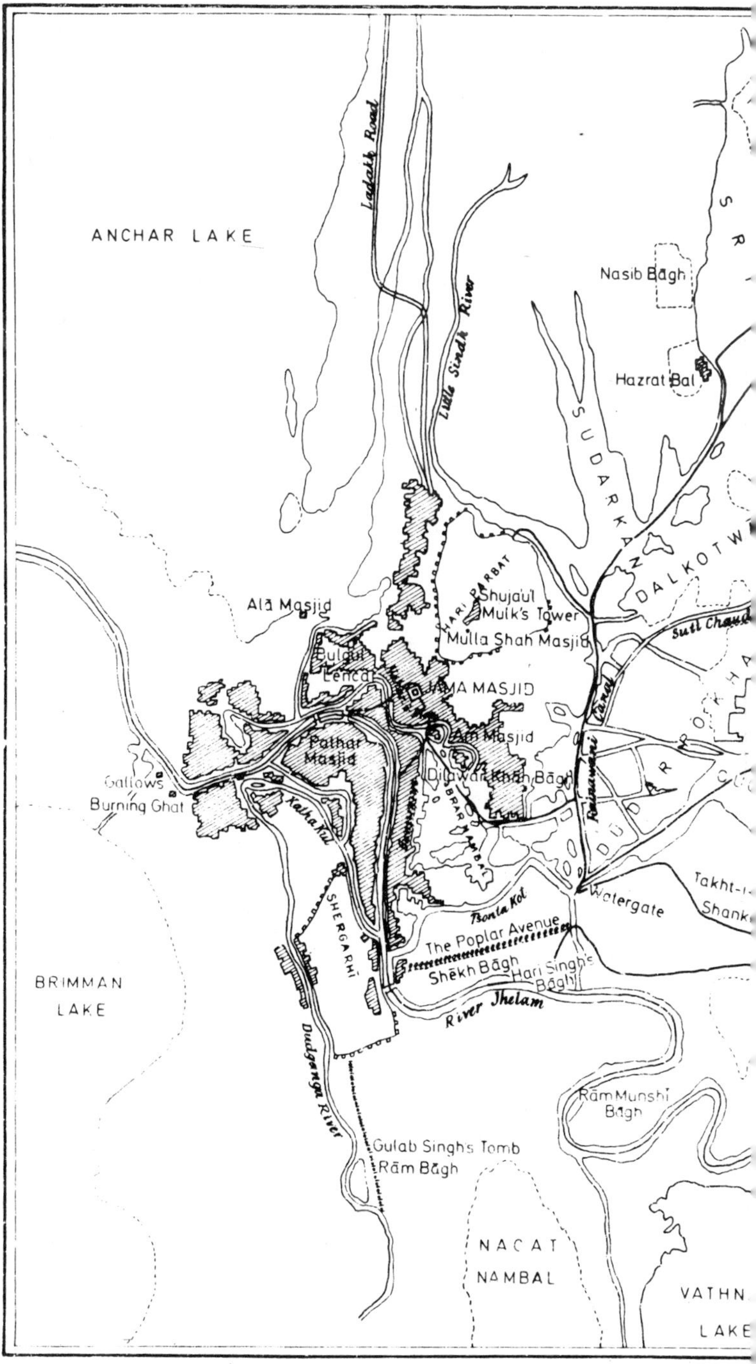

ANCHAR LAKE
Ladakh Road
Little Sindh River
Nasib Bāgh
Hazrat Bal
SUDARKAN
DALKOTW
Alā Masjid
HARI PARBAT
Shujaul Mulk's Tower
Mulla Shah Masjid
Bulbul Lencar
JAMA MASJID
Am Masjid
Pathar Masjid
Dilawar Khan Bāgh
BRAR NAMBAL
Gallows
Burning Ghat
Katha Kul
Sutl Chaud
Raināwari Canal
Watergate
Takht-i-
Shank
Bonta Kol
The Poplar Avenue
Shēkh Bāgh
Hari Singh's Bāgh
River Jhelam
SHERGARHI
BRIMMAN LAKE
Dudganga River
Rām Munshi Bāgh
Gulab Singh's Tomb
Rām Bāgh
NACAT NAMBAL
VATHN
LAKE

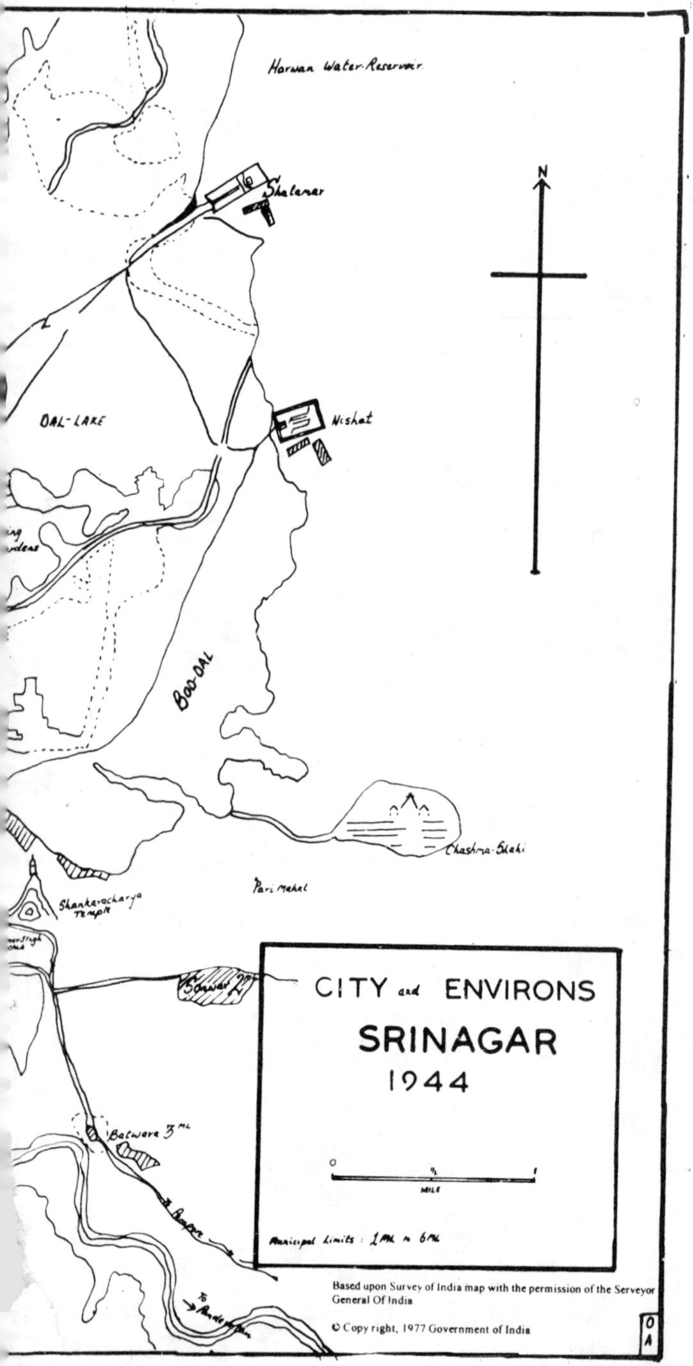

Based upon Survey of India map with the permission of the Serveyor General Of India

Anchar Lake
SOURA
To Ganderbal
Naseem Bagh
Hazrat Bal
Khusal Sar
Nagin Lake
Almond Gardens
Hari Parbat
Ala masjid
IDGAH
To Baramulla
Jama masjid
Gurdwara
Makhdoom Sahib
Boulevard
Khan Kah maula
Golf Ground
Chattabal 6 ml
GOVT HOSPITAL
Polo Ground
S.P. College
Park
Dal Gate
Residency
Palladium
Maisuma
Regal
Bank
Shergarhi
BRIMMAN-LAKE
State Exhibition
Church
River Jhelam
Convent
Amira Kadal
Maharaja Bazar
Hazuri Bagh
Batmaloo 5 ml
Ram Munshi Bagh
Dood Ganga
A.S. College
Government Technical School
Ranibagh 4 ml
SILK FACTORY
FLOOD SPILL CHANNEL
Nagat Nambal